THE OLD GERMAN
BAPTIST BRETHREN

CHARLES D. THOMPSON JR.

The Old German
Baptist Brethren

FAITH, FARMING, AND CHANGE
IN THE VIRGINIA BLUE RIDGE

UNIVERSITY OF ILLINOIS PRESS

URBANA AND CHICAGO

Library of Congress Cataloging-in-Publication Data

Thompson, Charles Dillard.
    The Old German Baptist Brethren : faith, farming,
and change in the Virginia Blue Ridge / Charles D.
Thompson, Jr.
        p. cm.
    Includes bibliographical references and index.
    ISBN-13: 978-0-252-03103-8 (cloth : alk. paper)
    ISBN-10: 0-252-03103-2 (cloth : alk. paper)
    ISBN-13: 978-0-252-07343-4 (pbk. : alk. paper)
    ISBN-10: 0-252-07343-6 (pbk. : alk. paper)
    1. German Americans—Virginia—Franklin County—
History. 2. Old German Baptist Brethren—Virginia—
Franklin County—History. 3. Brethren (Church of the
Brethren)—Virginia—Franklin County—Social life and
customs. 4. German Americans—Virginia—Franklin
County—Social life and customs. 5. Old German Baptist
Brethren—Virginia—Franklin County—Interviews.
6. German Americans—Virginia—Franklin County—
Interviews. 7. Farm life—Virginia—Franklin County.
8. Franklin County (Va.)—History. 9. Franklin County
(Va.)—Social life and customs. 10. Franklin County
(Va.)—Religious life and customs.   I. Title.
    F232.F7T49   2006
    975.5'6800431—dc22   2005035180

For Hope

Contents

Prologue: Of Soil and Stories   ix

Acknowledgments   xiii

Note on Photographs   xv

Introduction: Nonresistance and Change   xvii

PART I. SAINTS IN THE WILDERNESS

1. The Ancient Order   3

2. The Carolina Road   18

PART II. WILDERNESS NO MORE

3. Raising Citizens   43

4. Community-Based Agriculture   72

5. Adversity and Perseverance   101

6. Membership   143

7. Hope   174

Epilogue: They Go Quietly   197

Notes   205

Index   213

Prologue:
Of Soil and Stories

Despite romantic notions of "the land" often associated with agriculture, small farms are not natural places that exist apart from human communities. Rather, farms are the work of people interacting with nature over time, in often unromantic and hardscrabble ways. What people do, believe, and say about their work on farms, in turn, becomes inextricably tied to places, so that in addition to holding crops, the soil of a farm becomes a repository for words. Through narratives, natural history combines with human history and a piece of ground fills not only with layers of work but also with human stories and memories. Through words and deliberation, places take on the characteristics of a people and their identities. These attachments, perhaps as much as economics, cause farms to last. At least this has been true up to now.

Today farms are barraged by forces eroding away the very foundation of rural communities. The stories people tell about farming have become equally dire. Many farmers say the money in traditional farming cannot pay the bills, and that even if they survive, it will be impossible for their children to farm. Corporate farms, aided by powerful market and even governmental forces, undercut smaller-scale producers, forcing many to sell out. Farmers say development threatens to overtake their land and pressures them to sell their land for purposes other than agriculture. In these ways much of the human spirit has begun to drain out of farming. Though farmers have perhaps always

Old German Baptist Brethren woman herding cows into the barn for their evening milking. The farm is located in Franklin County, Virginia, near where the German Baptists first settled in 1765. Photograph by Rob Amberg.

complained about the weather and farm prices, words they use today ring with an ominous finality.

If it is only through constant renewal of both work and stories that farms survive, then the outlook for many farming communities across the United States is bleak indeed. But there are exceptions. And in the broader historical narratives of humanity, the exceptions give us hope.

This book explores one exceptional narrative of faith and farming as it has played out on the eastern slope of the Blue Ridge in Virginia. It is the story of the Old German Baptist Brethren, who came to Franklin County, Virginia in 1765. Since that time, they have lived a rural life, linking their religious beliefs and the story of their lives with agriculture. German Baptists have never believed that farming is essential to their faith and they shun any romantic attachments to land, but the lifestyle of small farming fits closely with their view of the world and their emphasis on hard work, close-knit families, and simplicity. Living these values has been a key to the Brethren's tenure in this Virginia mountain location, and the greater agricultural community has benefited from their presence.

Even as the Brethren have remained committed to their faith, however, their location in Virginia has changed rapidly around them. Today

Franklin County is a fast-growing retirement destination due to the area's natural beauty. It also grows because of its proximity to Roanoke, Virginia, Blue Ridge Virginia's most prominent city, its relatively inexpensive land, and large recreational developments surrounding Smith Mountain Lake, Virginia's second largest impoundment, with five hundred miles of shoreline. In 2001, the Virginia Department of Transportation (VDOT) proposed to cut through the middle of a predominantly German Baptist community in the northern half of the county with Interstate 73. While the Old German Baptist Brethren have been farming in the community for nearly two-and-a-half centuries, their farms are threatened. Indeed, many have left farming altogether, choosing instead to work on carpentry crews building houses for the many newcomers or to leave for other states, such as Wisconsin or Kansas, where farmland is cheaper.

At this writing, individual farms all over Franklin County are going under the bulldozer blade, including the farm once settled in the 1790s by my great-great-grandparents, the Ikenberrys, also members of the Brethren faith. In 2001, the Ikenberry farm—a place where generations of my ancestors lived and were buried, and which we returned to upon occasion to retell its story, an act of grounding ourselves literally— became a subdivision. That farm lineage and narrative came to an abrupt end. Yet, at the same time, many on surrounding farms who could easily profit from development have not sold out. Drawing on their community's strength, some who remain on farms in Franklin County tell hopeful stories of present and future farming possibilities.

The Franklin County Brethren story, built on a foundation of faith, persists despite dramatic changes. Though outside forces work actively against the small farm and local in general, their farm community remains. Franklin County is second in dairy production in the state while all the counties surrounding it have almost no dairies. Seventy-three dairies were still in operation in Franklin County in 2001. Yet this persistence is not due to any particular land characteristic, proximity to markets or roads, or any special abilities of the farmers. Rather, Franklin County farm communities remain intact largely because of the faith of the Old German Baptist Brethren and how they have lived as a result of their faith. Today German Baptist farmers comprise thirty of those seventy-three dairy farm owners. Members of their modern sister church, the Church of the Brethren, own many of the others. Over 550 Old German Baptist Brethren members in three different church districts live in Franklin County. How long their community remains a vital part of the county's agriculture depends on many forces beyond

German Baptist farmer bales hay in a field just before it is developed into a housing subdivision. Several houses had been completed already. Photograph by the author.

local control. This is particularly true of the Old German Baptist Brethren who, for religious reasons, choose not to vote or to speak out politically and thus have deliberately given up their right to influence policy. What can be done to preserve farms? Along with some important work of community planning, I believe the German Baptists' tenancy there also has a lot to do with whether and how their people persevere in word and deed, in both living and telling of farming and community. This book is one such telling, theirs and mine together, a combination of oral histories, ethnography, and historical research; a story of faith, farming, and change in the Virginia Blue Ridge.

Acknowledgments

I dedicate this work to the farmers in Franklin County, and also to those who once possessed and lost farms there, including members of my family. I especially appreciate the participation of those who maintain the Ancient Order today. I also express my gratitude for help and support on this project to Rob Amberg, Benjamin Grob-Fitzgibbon, Erin Avots, Jacky Woolsey, Frances Copeland, Laura Altizer, Naomi Lee, David Bass, Maryam Ali, Diane Hayes, Tal Stanley, Steve Fisher, Randall Kenan, David Cecelski, Roddy Moore, Vaughan Webb, and the staff of the Blue Ridge Institute; Tom Rankin, Iris Tillman Hill, Malinda, Louise, and Waltz Maynor, Richard Scoville, Mark, Mary, and Lois Bowman, Joe Mosnier, Allan Gurganus, John Cohen, Cece Conway, Faran Krentcil, Joe Mann, Allen Creech, Joel Elliott, David Bearringer, Lissa Gotwals, Bonnie Campbell, Carol Crumley, Bea Naff, Jim Peacock, Ruel Tyson, Daniel Patterson, William Peck, Chris Potter, Courtney Reid-Eaton, Nancy Kalow, Melinda Wiggins, Jacquelyn Hall, Betty Bailey, Lu Ann Jones, Keith Megginson, Joe Mosnier, John Chasteen, Department of Religious Studies at UNC-Chapel Hill; Lee Smith, George Thompson and the staff of the Center for American Places; Fred Kellogg, Dale Angle, American Folklore Society; Melissa Walker, Appalachian Studies Association, Oral History Association; Hope Shand, Marshall Thompson, Ethel Naff, Diane and Walter Kingery and family; Ella Jamison and family; Clifford and Cloey Thompson and family; my parents, Claudette and Dillard Thompson; Carl Bowman, Sue Puffenbarger, Henry Jamison and family; and all of the other interviewees and their families whose names appear in this book; and, of course, to the Ikenberrys and their descendants. Many thanks to the Center for Documentary Studies at Duke University's faculty, staff, and students, and the Virginia Foundation for the Humanities and the American Academy of Religion for their financial support of this work. My sincerest appreciation goes to Judy McCollough and the editorial staff of the University of Illinois Press for believing in and improving this work.

Note on Photographs

Most of the Old German Baptist Brethren members interviewed for this book told me they did not wish to have their faces appear in photographs as portraits. Appearing to seek "publicity," as some put it, would be anathema to their belief regarding living plain lives. For this reason, many of the photographs in this volume focus on people at work, in many cases from the back, or sometimes on animals rather than on the people who are just out of the frame. Though photographs of the German Baptists certainly appear in other publications, sometimes to their displeasure, the photographs herein reflect my understanding and acknowledgment of their wishes to remain faithful to the Ancient Order. My hope is that these images and words accurately reflect the requests I heard from the German Baptists who cooperated with this project and who continue to labor to remain in but "not of" this world.

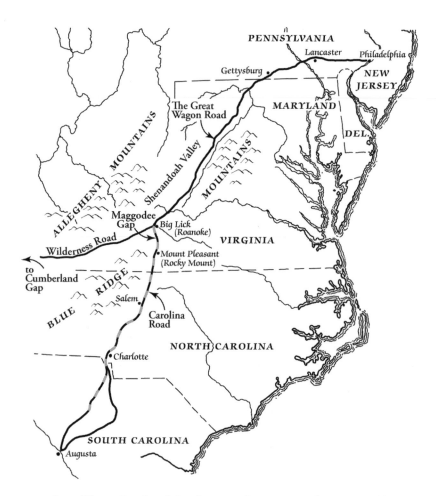

Great Wagon Road and Carolina Road. Major travel routes used by Germans and others during the eighteenth century.

Introduction:
Nonresistance and Change

They offered no resistance to assaults against them as they made their way down the narrow trading path to Virginia. If under attack by displaced Iroquois or by outlaw highwaymen, they prayed that God's will be done and turned the other cheek. Some died in the process. Dressed in conservative black clothing, German Brethren traveled at first with Moravians venturing southward from Pennsylvania in search of places to settle in Virginia and North Carolina. On this journey, by way of the Carolina Road, they were among the first Europeans to pass through the southern Blue Ridge Mountains to present-day Franklin County, Virginia, where they created temporary settlements as early as the late 1730s. In 1765, Jacob Miller established the first permanent German Brethren settlement in the county.[1]

For decades, the Brethren remained separate from other Europeans in the area, living in enclaves reflecting their earlier life in Germany or Pennsylvania. They built bank barns and log houses and made cabinets and furniture, pottery, clothing, and crafts, all with a Germanic flair.[2] For generations, they spoke German or its Pennsylvania Dutch variant.[3] They maintained a strong commitment to simplicity, nonviolence, and nonconformity to the world. They intentionally separated from state-supported churches, the courts, and politics, and did not swear oaths. For these reasons, relatively isolated places suited them, especially where the soil was good.[4]

Brethren faith, cooperation, hard work, and efficiency, along with their commitment to family, made their communities thrive. Eventually they built large farmhouses made for families with as many as ten children or more. They cleared and cultivated the rolling fields, turning forests into a pastoral landscape set against the striking backdrop of the Blue Ridge. Through their deep knowledge of farming and log construction combined with their commitment to community, Brethren helped build a healthy agriculture that was beautiful to look at. They were family farmers in the truest sense: people who farmed together with their families in tightly knit memberships, all working for the common good. In theology and livelihood the Brethren resembled the Amish and Mennonites who settled in some of the same areas of Pennsylvania and farther south.

Over time, the Brethren began picking up English by interaction with their neighbors of Scots-Irish or English descent. Always private but never exclusionary, the German Baptists welcomed others who were drawn to their faith.[5] An Englishman named William Smith, who had first come to the colonies as a soldier during the Revolution, converted to the brotherhood. Eventually he was elected to the Brethren ministry and began preaching, in English, to his counterparts in Franklin and Floyd counties.[6] Many in Franklin County believe Smith traveled and preached with Jacob Miller, both men expounding upon

Restored 1800 Franklin County German homestead at the Blue Ridge Institute at Ferrum College, Ferrum, Virginia. Photograph by the author.

the scriptures in his own language. Today, due to English conversions, many English names mix with those of German origin in the German Baptist community. By the late nineteenth century all of the Germans spoke English, and the German dialect had died out altogether in Franklin County by the turn of the twentieth century.[7]

Growing pressures of modernization in the latter half of the 1800s took their toll on the Brethren denomination. As the Industrial Revolution of the late nineteenth century and the economic and educational opportunities associated with it began to shape modern America, some members of the Brethren faith reasoned that they too should change. Some opted to alter their dress to a more modern style. They began Sunday Schools and seminaries where they educated their ministers. They changed their mode of baptism. Those who clung to what they called the "Ancient Order," however, chafed at these modernizations and held their ground, leading some members to become even more conservative in the process. This led to a church split in 1881, one new denomination eventually called the Old German Baptist Brethren and the other, the Church of the Brethren. Joel Jamison, a German Baptist elder, explains why the former clung to the name.

> The name German had two reasons: One, because the church actually originated in Germany. Another is the word German means a family. It means children of the same parent or cousins. So it really means "brethren," when you get it all summed up. We appreciate that, and by adding the name Brethren to it, it just only substantiates the fact that we are a family. We are the children of God, we believe, and so we're brethren, but we're not the Church of the Brethren. We're just the Old German Baptist Brethren.
>
> There's a lot of folks that get us mixed up a little bit. When we say Old German Baptist, they say, "Well, we're Baptist, too. What's the difference?" So that's where we thought it might be good if we could just add Brethren to it and it would help explain to people a little better.

Over the next several decades following the 1881 Divide, the Old German Baptist Brethren worked hard to delineate their distinctiveness, sometimes with minute detail concerning appropriate dress, conduct, and technology. After lengthy discussions at their Annual Meetings, they gradually adopted some conveniences, including the automobile and the tractor, electricity, and many appliances, but continued to shun radio and television and many forms of secular entertainment. Joel Jamison points out that new inventions were never accepted without much discussion, and as with the automobile, an exact resolution was sometimes elusive.

The automobile question was worked with for several years before they finally allowed members to use it. They never did say it was okay exactly, but they said you could use it on your own responsibility. . . . We were supposed to get one as cheap as we could and the best use for our utility. It's got to where we've got about everything, every color of car, but anyway that's the way it was passed.

Above all, the German Baptists chose to remain faithful to their original theology and their distinctive clothing. The Brethren have remained visibly different from mainstream society, as German Baptist Elder Loyd Jamison explains:

We feel we need to be separate from the world. We're separate in worldly pleasures, feelings, and activities and we try to live a plain, simple life. The scripture says, "Love not the world, neither the things in the world." In these things we feel like we need to come out of and be separate because the scripture says that we are a chosen generation, a royal priesthood of peculiar people. And not that we put ourself above anyone else; we don't want anyone to think that we're better than anybody else, but we're trying to live a type of life that will meet God's standard, God's will.

As the German Baptists describe it today, they want people to know at some distance that they are Christians. The German Baptists dress differently from the Church of the Brethren members and others in Franklin County today. Though the Old German Baptist Brethren have lost some of their distinctiveness, they remain purposefully removed from politics and from public speaking. Many have also tried to remain committed to living a life apart from mainstream society and to make their living while working with family and community. For this reason they strive to keep their farms, even as some of their non–German Baptist neighbors sell out.

Franklin County Agriculture

The German Baptist emphasis on difference and separation, along with their traditional link to farming, has influenced the county's character. Not only have the Brethren represented a significant part of the county's farm population, but they have also helped build agricultural industries there. For example, at the end of the nineteenth century, many of the German Brethren participated in the county's development of apple and peach orchards, and transported fruit by wagon and eventually by rail to Roanoke and Winston-Salem, North Carolina, for sale.[8] As the county's agricultural economy grew to emphasize dairy farming,

A farmer's daughter checks on the cows on an Old German Baptist Brethren farm near Ferrum, Virginia. Photograph by the author.

both the German Baptists and the Church of the Brethren members joined in that industry. Today, a number of German Baptists, somewhat in contrast to the more conservative Amish, are agricultural entrepreneurs who use advanced equipment and farming techniques.

Franklin County has both mountain and Piedmont land. Thus it was a land of two different types of farms in the nineteenth century. The Piedmont possessed larger farms or plantations often worked by slaves, many of whose descendants rented or sharecropped following Abolition. Small owner-operated farms were located mostly in the mountain land where large fields were impossible. The Brethren settled in the western half. Of course, there were exceptions to this characterization on both sides of the county. For example, some farmers, though by no means all of them, on the western side of the county, held slaves, too.

Thirty-five years after the Civil War and the end of slavery, the 1900 Virginia Agricultural Census shows that there were a total of 3,732 farms in the county with an average size of 106 acres. There were 3,066 white farmers, approximately two-thirds of whom were owners and one-third sharecroppers and tenants. There were 666 black farmers, over 250 of whom had struggled against the odds to become landowners.[9] Tobacco remained the main cash crop, but primarily in the eastern part of the county. Those who did not raise tobacco—and this included many Brethren families—subsisted on small-scale sales of livestock, or bartered with their neighbors.[10] Most families fed only themselves and perhaps a few others.

Nationally by 1900, agricultural specialization was accelerating. Grain production, for example, was in process of shifting from broad-based diversified farms all over the country to mainly large Midwestern bonanza farms that specialized in grain.[11] Florida, New Jersey, and the eastern coastal plains had become large-scale vegetable-producing centers, particularly as displaced sharecroppers entered the migrant farm-worker stream stretching up and down the eastern seaboard.[12] California agriculture was also beginning to grow rapidly, with the import of Chinese and Mexican farmworkers. For the first half of the twentieth century, though, Blue Ridge agriculture, including in Franklin County farms, was left out of this movement toward monocultures, and remained diversified and mostly subsistence, with little specialized production.

Three main cash generating alternatives remained for mountain people who did not grow tobacco: selling livestock, butter and eggs, and fruit and vegetable "truck" farming, with many specializing in apples and peaches. Small-scale mountain farms, however, could scarcely compete, particularly as shipping over larger distances became available from some major farming areas such as the coastal Carolinas to places such as New York, Philadelphia, Baltimore, Richmond, and Atlanta by ship, by rail, and eventually by road. There is one exception: as is well-known in the county and beyond, some also engaged in small-scale manufacture of liquor for sale, particularly during and after Prohibition began in 1929, though the Brethren forbade this.[13] The average Franklin County farm in the early twentieth century included a variety of crops and livestock raised for home consumption with supplements from sales in Roanoke twenty miles away. Over time, as the butter market began to improve in Roanoke, dairying became a viable means of improving income.[14] The railroad's arrival, which began its first stops in 1878, aided the marketing process.[15]

Rise of the Dairy Industry

The first dairy farms to ship whole milk to Roanoke were some of these diversified operations. From lots of hard work and some new innovations a few farms began to produce surpluses around 1920, as Church of the Brethren member Frank Layman explains regarding his parents' farm: "It was one of the three oldest dairy farms in the county. Three people up in that community where we lived had to take their milk by horse and wagon to Boones Mill and put it on the train to send to Roanoke. One person of those three would take it for a time, and another person would do it another time."

Mary Layman, Frank's wife, describes how her parents, also from the Boones Mill area, entered the dairy business to begin to earn a regular income from farming. "My dad said you needed to have money coming in every day and the dairy was something that was making money every day that you were going to get paid for." Even during the summer months, long before electricity came to the western Franklin communities, farmers such as Mary Layman's father invented ways to keep their milk cold before it reached the market. She says,

> The winters apparently were colder than they are now, they just had to have been. Papa had a pond, and in this pond we'd get ice thick enough you could skate on it. Thick enough men could go out there with axes and cut out the ice on the pond, put it in a wagon and haul it out to an icehouse. Had an icehouse down in the ground, and they could put ice down in there and cover it with leaves. Then in the summertime they had ice for milk. They had a cement pit, and they put the milk cans down in there and ice in there to keep it cold.

The use of ten-gallon cans to store milk continued well into the 1950s. Church of the Brethren member Galen Brubaker grew up on a dairy farm that began in 1939. In 1950, when he went into the dairy business on his own, little had modernized. "We milked by hand," he says, "and sold C Grade milk that first year and shipped our milk in those ten-gallon milk cans. Milked it, poured the milk into a can, put the cans in a cooler that had an ice bank all the way around, and the water agitated around those cans and cooled the milk. I guess we shipped milk like that for probably ten years."

Farmers began shipping their cooled milk in cans without refrigeration, eventually known as Grade C milk, when the Mandy Brothers Transfer Company started a regular milk route on Franklin's unimproved roads in 1923. By 1926, Highway 220 connected the county to Roanoke.[16] In 1939 two dairy agents working for the Franklin County Extension Service helped secure a Sealtest receiving station in Rocky Mount, the county seat. These two agents, according to Galen Brubaker, "put on a real drive during World War II to get farmers to produce more milk and upgrade their dairies to Grade A." By the 1940s, more than twenty farmers had converted their dairies to Grade A, meaning they were using all stainless steel equipment and constant refrigeration. They had also imported Holstein cattle from Ohio to upgrade their herds.[17]

Grade A milk was more sanitized than Grade C from milking to market. The former is always kept cold and never allowed to sit in conditions where bacteria might grow while Grade C milk was shipped in cans often set out at the end of farm lanes. Eventually, milk companies sold only Grade A milk for fresh consumption. Grade C milk was used in cheese and other dairy products.

By 1955, a total of 119 Franklin County farmers were shipping Grade A milk to the rapidly growing city of Roanoke. Five were even shipping milk to Washington, D.C. Hundreds of others continued producing Grade C milk.[18] This emphasis on dairy farming put Franklin County on the agricultural map as the number two dairy-producing county in the state by the 1950s. Outstripping those in all the surrounding counties, Franklin producers built a thriving dairy infrastructure in their county that eventually included milk wholesalers, veterinarians, feed mills, bull semen sellers, and farm equipment dealers. Gradually farmers gained marketing outlets and good dairy agents working on their behalf. By 1959 there were 208 full-time dairy farmers, all selling milk through wholesalers rather than by offering fresh milk and butter on a truck route through town.[19]

A majority of the full-time dairy farmers came from the side of the county first settled by the Brethren. Callaway, Wirtz, and Boones Mill, all centers of Brethren population, became thriving dairy areas. Today the tall, white silos these farmers built during those years still dot the countryside in the western half of the county, though most are no longer used because of changing technology. As specialization increased, the number of small and part-time farmers decreased. Farm children from these small farms left and entered school or went to work in factories. Also, many who left for World War II or for the Korean War never returned to their family farms. Tenancy decreased as well. By 1959, only fifty sharecroppers remained in the county, down from nearly 1,500 in the early part of the twentieth century.[20] The trend was to go into dairy farming with everything you had or to get out completely.

By the mid-1960s dairy farming had become a full-time job, and, particularly with Grade A production, required a major cash investment to get started. As agricultural schools continued to breed high-priced purebred cattle and to develop new technology, including upright silos, electric milk cooling tanks, and eventually automatic milkers and stainless steel pipes, only a fraction of the farms could afford the improvements necessary to stay in business. Those who had few cows or who had continued to run Grade C dairies were forced to find jobs outside of agriculture, often holding on to their land and turning to part-time beef production. Even as the number of full-time farmers declined, the total number of cows and the number of pounds of milk they produced continued to increase. This was because each farm left in business increased the numbers of cows milked.

Milk, unlike other farm products produced on a small scale, paid a fair wage in the 1960s, so many farmers cut down their marginally profitable orchards to make room for more cropland for cattle feed. From 1964 to 1969 the number of Franklin County dairy cattle increased from 4,077 to 7,883 head.[21] By 1978 there were 9,442 cows in Franklin County.[22] In contrast, from 1954 to 1970, the number of apple and peach tree farms dropped from 339 to just 34.[23] These statistics show that western Franklin County farmers had found their niche in dairy and were forgoing all other types of farming in their push to increase their milk production.

Though through much of the twentieth century dairy farming seemed the best business alternative for a western Franklin County farmer, a worrisome trend had begun by 1978. Overproduction in the dairy business nationally and increased competition from other regions resulted in even the owners of full-time, heavily invested dairy farms feeling an economic squeeze. This was due not just to the invisible hand of the market economy pushing toward ever greater concentration, but also because of federal laws favoring large industrialized farms over family-sized operations. These included unlimited grain subsidies that allowed Midwestern farms to increase in size exponentially and to grow huge acreages on taxpayer support; subsidized water access in the West; low-interest government loans for even the largest of farms; increased domestic transportation systems favoring those who had a lot of a product to sell; and eventually international trade agreements that discouraged small producers in the United States and abroad.[24] During these years of dramatic farm loss, the streets of Washington, D.C. were jammed with long lines of tractors driven by protesting farmers.[25]

On the local level in Franklin County, dairy farmers trying to stay in business were under increasing pressure to enlarge their farms, and even to rent or buy their neighbors' land. Non–German Baptist dairy farmers began to tell their children not to farm, or if they insisted on farming, to first obtain a four-year degree at Virginia Tech in dairy science. Dairy extension agents ran seminars that foretold of new mega-farms in the West and Southwest that would milk thousands of cows each and flood the eastern market. By the early 1980s agents were even suggesting in seminars that farmers sell out while they could. These agents preached efficiency rather than lifestyle, business rather than community. Change was inevitable one way or another, they said. "Get big or get out," the phrase coined by President Nixon's Secretary of Agriculture Earl Butz, was a familiar slogan at the time. Specialization, even on a large scale, had begun to backfire for the family farmer because, having "put all their eggs in one basket," farmers more than ever were at the mercy of a single commodity price dictated by powers they could not control.[26]

German Baptist Dairy Farmers

The Old German Baptist Brethren farmers were, and still are, some of the county's best dairy farmers. Over time most have increased their herds, upgraded their dairies to Grade A, and boosted their efficiency alongside their non–German Baptist neighbors. Brethren too bought new silos, upgraded their barns, and purchased tractors when necessary, though often not as quickly. Despite these upgrades, however, they continued to emphasize working with neighbors. When the German Baptists built their barns or homes, they worked together, and continued to preach community as a primary goal of farming. To help their young people keep farms, the membership worked out creative leasing options that allowed the young to buy after they began earning a profit rather than to become too heavily indebted before even starting. Emphasizing simplicity and community, they tried to keep their farms sized to suit one family, with the clearly stated purpose of being present at mealtimes with their children. Brethren members believed farming could best be taught by example and partnerships rather than through formal education. Though many German Baptists graduated from high school, none considered dairy science at the university level. They preferred teaching and learning in the farm family. Like other farmers, the Old Order Brethren must earn a living at farming, but they also seek to avoid some of the pressures of keeping up with American standards of consumption.

Despite their efforts to remain separate, even the German Baptists have not held on to all that they once had. Their numbers in farming are also declining even with community support and clinging to the Old Order. Like their non-Brethren neighbors, they face not only the age-old challenges of raising animals and crops, but now also managing tighter farm credit and elusive profits. No matter how hard some have worked to remain conservative in spending, to rely on neighbors, and to be efficient, prices paid to farmers have continued to decline, even as the prices of all that farmers must buy goes up in price.[27] Add to this mounting development pressures on farmland and rising farmland prices—an acre of land now sells for $5,000 to $10,000 or more if located near Smith Mountain Lake, while $300 profit per acre on crops would be an excellent year.[28] Because of the potential benefits in the short term, and the good opportunities to find jobs on carpentry crews making houses on the same acreages once farmed, the temptation to sell out is enormous. Yet many German Baptists in Franklin County have not sold out, at least not so far. The reason is not attachment to land, but rather the Brethren's desire to remain a community where their children can grow up well-nurtured in their faith.

Tragically, however, many in rural farming communities who want to remain in farming, including the German Baptists in Franklin County, have had to relinquish their holds on agriculture. Although small-scale farming works in a place socially and environmentally, it also has to make money. This is where the story of American agriculture and of small communities breaks down—one farm at a time. In the case of the German Baptists, there are no protests, no lobbying. There is just a family decision and they are gone. Regardless of a farm's longevity or the talents of its owners, they seek a living elsewhere and the story of that place ends.

A Story of One Franklin County Farm

The Franklin County dairy owned by my Uncle Walter and Aunt Diane is one of the places where I learned about farming. As a child I traveled with my family often to visit there. I knew we had nearly arrived when we passed the big white sign with the picture of a Holstein, a black and white perfectly framed milk cow standing regally on green grass, and the words "Kinvale Farm." Passing the sign we wound along in our car for a couple of miles over the gravel public road lined in the summer with corn and alfalfa planted in strips on the contours of gently rolling slopes. Mountains loomed in the distance. Smells of manure and silage were always in the air long before we could see the house and barn, a pungent but somehow reassuring scent, at least to those who have family members making a living in dairy farming. Over the hill and nestled among old maple trees was their two-story brick house where Walter was raised and he and Diane still live; just across the lane from their house were their white barns and silos.

The family raised blue-ribbon Holsteins. My cousins, four girls, grew up caring for the prize heifers and showing them at the State Fair in Richmond and other dairy shows. My mother is Diane's sister and thus it was not, strictly speaking, *our* family farm. Nonetheless, this farm is where I learned to drive cattle, to scrape manure, to put milkers on cows' teats, to steer a big John Deere tricycle tractor, and to put

A Franklin County dairy farm on a back road near Callaway, Virginia.
Photograph by the author.

silage in the silos. I was awed by the enormity of the daily tasks and by
the ribbons that hung next to photographs of cattle in their kitchen. I
loved pouring milk from jars cooled in the refrigerator with its cream
having risen to the top and knowing exactly where it came from. In
those ways, Kinvale Farm gave me a connection to farming that many
of my friends in our small town in Virginia simply did not have. I
remember arguing with friends in my eighth grade shop class that cows,
as well as bulls, could have horns!

When I was a boy, Walter and his brother William, who lived next
door to him, owned the dairy together in partnership. They inherited
the farm from their father. They trace their ancestry to the German
Brethren, though they are not members. As I grew older, William retired
and William's son Billy bought into the business and worked as Walter's
partner until Walter also retired in the 1990s. By that time I had a son of
my own. When Walter retired, Billy left farming too. Still in his forties,
Billy started selling real estate and became immediately successful,
though when he did, Kinvale Farm, its bloodline of cattle, and its
human lineage ended. It was not a personal tragedy for either of the families involved, as both said they were ready to leave the daily responsibilities of milking cows. They both agreed that one person should never
attempt it alone. In his retirement, Walter took up golf and has managed

part-time some apartment buildings in the county seat of Rocky Mount. Unlike some who got out of farming because they had to, their family did not have to sell their farm.

With the dairy cattle gone, the milking parlor and barns sat empty. The silage and the manure smells were no more. No longer could one hear the buzz of activity of the milking machines from the house, the lowing of cattle and calves, the running of machinery in the fields. Gone also was the possibility of dairy farming remaining in the family. In the last days of the farm's operation, I took my eight-year-old son into the milking parlor for what I feared would be his last chance to see where milk actually comes from.

In conversations after his retirement Walter and I lamented the loss of farms and the fact that family-sized operations like his were under continuous siege from large corporate mega-dairies out West. We mourned the finality of farm retirements. No one could afford to take over a farm, even at the modest scale of the eighty milking head he had maintained. He said, "There's just no way to pay for the land and equipment you would need by farming it. It would take at least a half-million-dollar investment." We wondered aloud whether Franklin County, this hilly place of small fields and herds, could remain competitive in the dairy business, or any kind of family farming at all.

Billy, meanwhile, began selling real estate, including some of his neighbors' farms, sometimes for housing developments, and, because of his personality and work ethic, became the area's most successful rural land salesman. That a good farmer now was making a living selling others' farms to homeowners or hobby farmers struck me as sadly ironic. But Billy did not see it that way. Where I saw endings, he saw financial opportunities for the entire community. His oral history appears later in this book.

While the decision to leave farming was right for Walter and Billy, I wondered pessimistically if every farm in the county would suffer a quiet death, with endings like these so typical that they would not even make the newspapers. Would all the working farms become development sites where investors reap profits as outsiders flocked to the county, all of them happy to get to this area, paradoxically because of its rural character, beauty, and tranquility? After that, would people in Franklin County remember how to farm? Would they ever again raise a new farmer?

A year after Walter and Billy's retirement from farming in 1999 I was heartened to learn that a young couple had come to live in William's house and had rented their farm. The young woman had been raised in the Old German Baptist Brethren Church, so at first we heard they were both "Dunkards," as many non–German Baptists refer to those of the faith. This seemed a good choice of tenants because of the vital community support the young couple would receive. In fact, however, only she had been raised in the faith, not her husband, and she had not continued in the faith after their marriage. The young man had come from a dairy outside the county. Though Walter and Diane lived nearby, the couple attempted to run the farm mostly alone.

Unfortunately, soon after the young couple began to operate the farm, things started to go awry. Milk prices dropped. Feed and equipment bills were left unpaid. The place began to look ragged. Fences broke down. I never met the family and never learned of their hopes for the place, their dreams of raising a family there or of having a prize herd of their own. But most farmers want to be owners and to raise children along with their crops. Most want to build equity and to pass something along to their progeny. These have been some of the long-term rewards of farming. If these were this young couple's dreams, all of them came to nothing. One night the young farmer left the farm without telling anyone, even his wife, and drove his pickup back up the road by the crops and past the Kinvale sign, heading northward out of Franklin County, out of Virginia, and beyond.

Walter and Diane began to notice the cattle had not been milked the next morning. The cattle came to the fence and began to bawl from the pressure in their udders and still no one came to the cattle's aid. Then phone calls alerted the young woman's extended family, and soon they and their community of German Baptists arrived, knowing exactly what needed to be done. Some of them were dairy farmers themselves. Most had worked for one another building barns and homes throughout their lives. They began doing chores as if the farm were their own.

The Brethren milked and fed the cattle for as long as was needed. They also did what they could to help remedy the overdue payments, as well as to care for the family left behind. They repaired fences and barns for Walter and Diane, leaving their place as it had been before the young family moved in. They even repaired the farmhouse. But the young family would never return.

Several days after his disappearance, a passerby noticed the young farmer in Central Park in New York City sitting on a park bench, sobbing. Someone took down the pickup's license plate number and notified the police who, in turn, pieced the story together and alerted his family in Franklin County. Before then, there would have been people racing by him in their running shoes or rollerblades, never imagining that dairy farming of all things was his undoing, or that a farm went under as he sat there. This loss would not lessen the supply of milk any-where, or perhaps even show up in farm statistics. Nevertheless, the farmer's demise left a tear in the fabric of one farm community faraway.

Walter and Diane now rent the farm to a part-time beef cattle farmer. A dairy farmer rents the cropland. Though the land remains pro-ductive, the milking barns and silos again sit idle. Recently a developer approached my aunt and uncle about selling the farm for a golf course. They pursued the idea, because, as many others like them reasoned, the farm is close to the well-known retirement and tourist destination of Smith Mountain Lake and it would make money. Then, in 2001, a new Interstate highway, I-73, was mapped right through Billy's house on the knoll on the upper part of the farm, where the alfalfa and cornfields have always been. Now they must wait on the road, if it comes, know-ing it will certainly change the farm dramatically and possibly end it altogether. Meanwhile, the golf course proposal has been withdrawn.

Franklin County Farming Today

Over the last ten years, farms all over Franklin County have succumbed to bankruptcy and foreclosure. Some were unable to make payments,

This German Baptist dairy farm sits idle after the family decided to leave farming. The land remains in the family and they have resisted selling the land for development. Photograph by the author.

some sold to developers, and others were pushed out by new regulations too difficult to satisfy. And then there were those who left farming through retirement with no one to take over. In the mid-1980s there were 125 dairies in the county. In 2001 there were only 73, meaning a loss of approximately 3 dairies a year for the last 20 years.[29] Even many of the 73 farms left in Franklin County are on uncertain footing. Some farmers predict half of those will be gone in 10 more years.

Even with these recent losses Franklin is still by far the largest dairy producer in southwest Virginia, outpacing all of the adjacent counties. To look only at the soil and the terrain, it is not immediately clear why. Some southwest Virginia counties have no dairies at all.[30] Only a closer look at people makes it apparent: dairy farming thrives because of Franklin County's large Old German Baptist Brethren community. They operate nearly half of the seventy-three remaining dairies. Many other German Baptists work jobs that support dairy farmers. Only lately have their percentages of the total number in agriculture grown this large. This shows their community has weathered the losses of farms slightly better than the rest of the farmers in the county. The Brethren too have lost farmers, but more slowly. Interestingly, the two other Virginia counties producing as much milk as Franklin have similar strongholds of Mennonite farmers in the Shenandoah Valley.

While one Franklin farm, Barny Bay, is among the largest in Virginia, with over seven hundred milking cattle, the majority of farms there, including all of the German Baptist farms, remain at a size one family can manage with a helper or two. These small family dairies stay in business despite Virginia Tech's Dairy Science Professor Jerry Jones's best estimates. In fact, it seems he has given up trying to predict farm loss at all. When I asked him in an e-mail about the future of consolidation and whether small dairies might continue, he replied, "I don't really know. I stopped guessing years ago. We're seeing larger farms, but probably not as many as some would have guessed."[31] It seems there is something at work in farm communities that some experts find mystifying.

The field of agricultural economics and rural sociology measures total output of milk or farm population.[32] But numbers cannot measure how community members help one another stay in business or how a parent teaches by example a child who decides to stay in the dairy business even when other more lucrative opportunities beckon. Numbers alone cannot tell us why someone holds onto land even though developers offer much more money than a farm could ever pay, or the value of neighbors joining together to help make repairs on a fence. Statisticians and economists might call these intangibles, but in Franklin County they certainly have something to do with a community and its stories. I am not referring to romanticism here but to a level of commitment, faith, and work deeper than numbers can measure.

The German Baptist community reliance has not only provided a network of support for their farmers, but also added strength of community for non–German Baptist farmers as well. Because of the number of farm families clustered in one area, they have created a critical mass of farmers that has continued to support feed dealers, equipment dealers, milking machine salespeople, veterinarians, extension agents, and others focused on dairy farming. These businesses are within easy reach simply because there are enough farmers with enough livestock to keep them there. When farmers suffer, so do these businesses.

It is nearly impossible to run a dairy in an isolated place where there are no neighboring farms, so instead of being competitors, dairy farmers need one another to survive. Even when they do not see each other regularly, they help one another just by being around. The Old German Baptist Brethren add another layer to this interdependent work as their faith dictates. German Baptist dairyman Henry Jamison explains.

> The point I want to make is that we try to work together. Anybody can call and we'll try to go help out. If somebody's building a new house, we'll go. I like to go help anybody and everybody. I think it gives us a sense of community to be able to work together like that, and it saves a tremendous amount of labor. It might not be as perfect as a carpenter would do it, but a lot of us have done enough that it's kind of second nature to us.

Dairy farming requires helping hands more than some other types of farming because year-round the cows must be milked twice daily. Large and extended families like those of the Brethren have worked well with dairy because this allows each member to take a few days off now and then. In addition, German Baptists say relying on brothers and sisters is a means of staying faithful to God. Independence from others in the community leads to pride, they believe, and ultimately could result in a fall from grace.

No matter how great is the faith of farmers or how much their neighbors help, however, farms succumb to real economic fatality. At the end of the farm season, farmers must pay their bills. If they cannot do so, their farms go under. On top of weather and other typical farm challenges for farmers, competition from afar has made bills harder to pay than ever. With the American government's help, huge dairies in

Arizona, California, and elsewhere are now pumping milk into stores on the East Coast in increasingly greater quantities.[33] This is only possible because mega-dairies receive government payments for artificially low grain prices brought about by federal farm programs that reward the largest producers and subsidize access to scarce water, and by interstate transportation systems that allow milk to travel at greater distances from the West to stores in Virginia. Farmers also speak of environmental regulations that seem to put undue pressure on them to change their traditional farming practices without providing the cash required to make these changes. People cannot compete against their own government's policies. So as the U.S. food system provides milk in huge quantities transported over great distances, small rural communities like Franklin County suffer. As farms go under we lose our knowledge of where and how our food is produced.

The U.S. food system conceals facts about government subsidies to farmers who are forced to produce food at prices below the cost of production, the effects of food on the environment and animals, and the damage it wreaks on communities, and it hopes you will not ask. This detachment does not happen only in urban places like Atlanta, Washington, D.C., or New York City. At Wal-Mart in Rocky Mount, for example, the milk sitting in the coolers in plastic jugs is more likely to be from somewhere west of the Mississippi, such as California or Arizona, or from Florida, than it is to be from local farms in Virginia. The milk is produced thousands of miles from where people consume it, but the label says nothing about its place of origin. It connects no consumer to a farm or to dairy cattle or to a group of people who have their welfare in mind. This is agriculture without a community base.

Within the last two decades, many Brethren have left farming, turning instead to carpentry and cabinetry. The building trades have been financially rewarding for many, but perhaps troublesome for the group's traditional lifestyle. While carpentry work allows men to work together in crews, it largely leaves women and children out of the business. Families are together fewer hours each day. The building business also adds to the development pressures on rural areas. In some cases, the Brethren are building houses in subdivisions and retirement communities that directly impact the land values where they live. New housing subdivisions and other developments not only inflate land prices, they also increase taxes as well. Just by living in Franklin County the German Baptists experience rising land prices and development pressures from people seeking to live nearby in what they deem a peaceful rural setting.

Andrew Bowman, a young German Baptist farmer, used the metaphor of a harbor to describe their community in the larger world or "ocean": "When the ocean rises and falls," he said, "it affects the harbor, but not as much." Today, as many farms go under, waves of global agricultural change also pound the Brethren in their harbor. The German Baptists are perhaps less susceptible to the world's storms, but still they must weather them.

To understand more about the Old German Baptist Brethren and the agricultural community they have fostered, along with their nonconformity to the world, it is essential to first know about the earliest German farmers and millers to arrive in this county named for Benjamin Franklin. To do so, we must travel back in time nearly three centuries to find a group of eight religious dissenters wading into the Eder River, a tributary of the Rhine in Germany, breaking with tradition and breaking the law, and by their dissent becoming forever bound together as Brethren. And we must also become acquainted with some of the weary travelers walking together down a path known as the Great Wilderness Road, all their worldly possessions on their backs or in a few

German Baptist Brethren farmer Allen Layman guiding his cattle into the milking barn at sunrise in Wirtz in Franklin County, Virginia. Photograph by Rob Amberg.

PART I

Saints in the Wilderness

1 The Ancient Order

German Origins

The first German Baptists were eight exiles who gathered clandestinely three centuries ago in Alexander Mack's millhouse to read the Bible and pray. It was 1708 and Germany was then but a hodgepodge of provinces, all of them war-torn and struggling to redefine and rebuild themselves, and vying for tribute and allegiance, following the Thirty Years' War.[1] Hundreds of thousands of people had died on the Continent from seemingly endless war and persecution or from the famine and disease that followed. Worse, most of the fighting had been couched in religious dogma, often Catholicism battling against various forms of Protestantism.[2] As a result of the agreements that followed, each of the emerging German provinces was permitted by the Holy Roman Emperor to choose one of the three officially recognized Christian denominations—Catholic, Lutheran, or Reformed. All inhabitants of a province had to adhere to the faith chosen by its prince; other religious practices outside the selected one were against the law.[3]

The eight who first gathered in Mack's Schwarzenau home risked all they had in order to seek an alternative faith. Disillusioned with war and the state religions that supported it, the Brethren sought a peaceful spirituality beyond the reach of the state, a version of Christianity unaffiliated with any military or hierarchical support. With soldiers fighting in the name of particular Christian churches, this group took no name but the biblical term "Brethren" and sought no institutional walls, no steeple, no paid clergy. They sought a simple, childlike faith free of

German Baptist farmer Dena Layman feeds dairy heifers being raised as future milk cows. Photograph by Rob Amberg.

hierarchy, Christian unity, obedience to Christ, separation from the world based on a mystical Pietistic union with Christ, adherence to the New Testament, and a restoration of the primitive (apostolic) church.[4] They and others such as the Anabaptists, who deeply influenced them, turned to scriptures regarding the first church of the New Testament Christians. By studying these passages, the dissenters sought to resurrect what they termed the "Ancient Order." Scriptures told the Brethren that the first disciples had gathered in an upper room of an Antioch home far from any church or synagogue, and there they had waited for revelation from God. They had lived communally and shared all they had with other believers. They refused allegiance to Caesar or to institutional religion. Though Rome considered them enemies and imprisoned, crucified, and fed many to lions, they did not capitulate or resort to violence. This history inspired the Brethren also living under religious oppression some 1,600 years later.[5]

These religious dissenters chose to depend solely upon God and vowed to avoid war and killing at all costs, even to the point of martyrdom. They agreed never to swear oaths of allegiance to any principality or power, and avoided participation in either official religion or government. And they turned solely to the New Testament to seek its simple faith, all in the privacy of homes and barns. The Brethren chose to put on the simple and somber clothes of the Protestant pilgrims, to join the Anabaptist tradition of *Die Stillen in Lande,* the quiet ones in the land, and to live in close communion with other believers without trying to draw attention to themselves. They avoided evangelizing and chose instead a simple life of example.[6]

It was a faith of sacrifice and offered little comfort, as Alexander Mack, considered the leader of the original eight, would later write:

> Count well the cost,
> When you lay the foundation.
> Are you resolved, though all seem lost
> To risk your reputation
> Yourself, your wealth, for Christ the Lord
> As you now give your solemn word?[7]

Those counting the cost knew their baptism would mean hardship.

No priest presided and no church sanctioned their first baptism. They entered the river and baptized one another, symbolizing with immersion in water their death to the world. Joel Jamison, a German Baptist minister in Franklin County, explains:

> There were five brethren and three sisters. These three sisters were wives of three of the brethren and they decided to go out and be baptized and start this church. And so they did. They went out early one morning and baptized one another in the river Eder over there in Schwarzenau Germany. The brother that was to baptize them didn't feel he could baptize the others until he had been baptized. So they chose one of the brethren to baptize him and then he baptized the rest and they kept that a secret. Alexander Mack was one of the main leaders and as to who baptized Alexander Mack we don't know and it doesn't really matter. And then Alexander Mack was chosen to baptize the rest of the group and they formed the nucleus of a church there.

Then the eight walked back to Mack's home, their temporary refuge, having just plunged into cold water and feeling renewed.[8]

Their form of baptism, immersing the convert face forward three times, was unique in Christendom. The practice distanced the eight somewhat from the Mennonites, the group of Anabaptists who only

This headstone links the life of Daniel Lehman (with spelling correction retrofitted onto the marble) in the Rhine Valley of Germany and Franklin County, Virginia. German Baptists trace their beginnings to the year 1708 in the province of Wittgenstein, Germany. Photograph by the author.

sprinkled their believers. That they organized themselves without a defined hierarchy also distanced them from the Amish, who retained the bishop figure. Their method of baptism soon gained the Brethren the nickname of *Die Tunken,* meaning those who dunk, which later became in English the Dunkards.[9]

The Brethren combined two strains of religious thought from their spiritual predecessors. Their communal lifestyle and their simplicity came from the Anabaptists and their stress on individual spirituality from the Pietists. They emphasized the Pietist zeal for personal salvation, but retained Anabaptist discipline and strictness regarding banning those who erred and refused to repent. Thus they avoided radical individualism and retained a strong sense of accountability to each other while allowing for direct revelation from God. They settled on tenets shared by other Anabaptists, including a belief that Christians should seek the mind of Christ in conflicts and a refusal to ever take others to court.[10] They called one another sister or brother, without intending to establish a new denomination. No ordinance, law, or structure bound them, only the scriptures and their fellow believers.[11]

By seeking a nonhierarchical path to God outside of official religion, the German Brethren knew they were in danger of arrest and persecution. Merely praying together outside of the established churches challenged the authority of princes and priests. Adult baptism was worse. Earlier in most provinces, the princes and the churches had imprisoned Anabaptists, confiscated their possessions, and even tortured them. Thousands of them were killed. The Brethren expected nothing different for their dissent. Yet two of the dozens of Germanic territories—Berleberg and Wittgenstein—began to tolerate some religious diversity. Thus, unlike the many Anabaptists who had given their lives for their faith during the previous 150 years, the Brethren had found a place to avoid martyrdom.

Count Heinrich Albrecht (ruler, 1698–1723) in the province of Wittgenstein, a tiny Rhineland principality, gave refugees from other provinces temporary sanctuary.[12] As the Brethren made their way to Wittgenstein, the count gained skilled workers and farmers to help rebuild his war-torn province, making his tolerance far from altruistic.[13] Wittgenstein was a rural province with poor soil, few available acres of open farmland, and no population centers. There were neither farms nor cottage industries likely to generate much income. In addition, war had destroyed much of the principality's infrastructure.[14] There was little reason for the Brethren to go there, except safety. As the Brethren had fully expected martyrdom in exchange for their baptisms, they welcomed finding a place to start again.[15]

Wittgenstein became widely known as a safe haven for religious dissidents. Alexander Mack Jr. later wrote of the opportunity: "The Lord showed those persecuted exiles a place of refuge . . . in the country of Wittgenstein."[16] Despite the relative safety of Wittgenstein, suspicion and resentment from neighbors were still common. At least these believers were no longer outlaws there.

The early Brethren were experienced farmers and craftspeople. Their membership included shoemakers, tailors, cap-makers, sack-makers, and button-makers.[17] Barn builders, coopers, wagon-makers, and even a printer later joined their numbers. They were able to make articles to trade and sell, which allowed them to recoup some of their earlier losses, but their reprieve was short-lived.

In 1723, fifteen years after their first baptisms and hundreds had joined the Brethren, Count Albrecht died, and his successor, Count August, began a new wave of persecutions in Wittgenstein. Even before Albrecht's death, the Brethren, sensing change in the air, had begun to migrate elsewhere. They found little solace in their new locations. One group had gone to Solingen, a steel-making town in the Lower Rhine area where they were persecuted and, in 1717, imprisoned, remaining behind bars until 1720. Many of their number died from illness in captivity. A second group of Brethren left for Krefeld, arriving in 1715. These Brethren fared better than those who tried Solingen, but in 1719, a dispute arose among them over whether a member of the Brethren could marry outside of the congregation. As a result of this disagreement, Peter Becker, who wished to marry a Mennonite, left for America with twenty other families in tow. On arrival in the New World, Becker established the first Brethren settlement in the colony, at a small place called Germantown just north of Philadelphia.[18]

The remaining Brethren in Schwarzenau, including the original eight, left Wittgenstein for West Friesland, the Netherlands, in 1720.[19] They remained in Friesland for nine years, farming wetland drained earlier by the Mennonites who preceded them. However, hearing reports from the Krefeld Brethren in Pennsylvania of a religious revival that was "daily increasing," the Wittgenstein/Friesland Brethren decided to head to William Penn's experiment in America to join those from Krefeld. Sailing from Rotterdam to England, they finally left onboard the *Allen* on July 7, 1729.[20] Eleven years had passed since their first baptisms in the Eder River. After exile, imprisonment, and even martyrdom, finally the Brethren were heading to what they hoped would be a peaceful place where they could begin a settled life without fear of persecution for their faith.

Journey to America

Beginning in 1681, when Alexander Mack was only two years old, Quaker convert William Penn along with his followers visited Germany to recruit Quakers and other religious separatists for his colony in the New World. By the early 1700s the migration from the Palatinate to Philadelphia had begun in earnest. Penn called his colony, which he had received from King Charles II because of a large debt the king owed to his father, the "holy experiment."[21] He specifically welcomed dissenters from Germany, decreeing, "We may live together as neighbors and friends."[22]

Germans arrived in Pennsylvania in 1682, only a year after Penn's invitation. They purchased 18,000 acres of farmland and laid the foundations for what would become Germantown. Over the next decades thousands more people came. In 1717, the largest migration of Germans took place, when twenty thousand people, mostly from the Rhineland, settled in Pennsylvania. Along with farming, they opened shops for shoemaking, cabinetry, woodcarving, and pottery.[23] Stepping off the boat the Brethren found much to make them feel at home: language, food, dress, names of towns, and a countryside that had begun to take on characteristics of German agriculture and architecture.

Exuberant descriptions from eyewitnesses in America made it back to the Brethren of both Germany and Holland. Christopher Sauer I, a printer who often worked with the Brethren and was newly settled in Germantown, Pennsylvania, wrote the following in the 1720s: "The country had abundance and was fruitful in all necessary things. There was complete freedom. One could live there as a good Christian in solitude, as one pleased, and if one wanted to work a little, especially craftsmen . . . then one could earn his livelihood in abundance."[24]

Upon reading such accounts dozens of German Brethren families sold all they had to buy passage or became indentured servants known as "redemptioners." Of course, most of the hyperbole proved false, prompting one brother to write from Pennsylvania back to Germany to warn his Brethren considering migration that if they possessed "secondary motives such as escaping pressure and suffering and accumulating wealth or wanting an easier life, then [they] will certainly not succeed."[25]

He was right. The trip itself was expensive, particularly for those who had suffered through war and exile. Traveling by sea was also a huge risk. John Naas wrote of some of these difficulties in a letter composed in 1735, two years after he and over a hundred of his German compatriots had sailed the Rotterdam to Philadelphia route. The first plight befell them before they weighed anchor. Kidnappers in Rotterdam tried to take some of the Brethren away to sell them, Naas reported. After the ship set sail, the journey took fifteen weeks under "horrendous" conditions. They faced storms, delays from lack of wind, sickness from lack of sanitation, numerous deaths, constant fighting between some of the passengers, meager and rancid rations, filthy water, lack of ship sanitation, overcrowding, and lice. Even under terrible conditions, the German families still had to pay dearly for the trip. Despite these hardships, Naas describes a joyous arrival on the Delaware River at Philadelphia: "The Brethren and Sisters came to meet us in small boats with delicious bread, apples, peaches, and other refreshments for the body, for which we praised the great God on the ship, with much singing and resounding prayers."[26]

By Naas's Rotterdam ship's arrival in 1733, nearly all of the Brethren were in America, most in Pennsylvania. The first Brethren settled in the rural areas near Germantown, then only a few miles inland from Philadelphia. Alexander and Anna Mack arrived in late 1729. By then, earlier settlers had long occupied the twenty-seven-and-a-half Germantown lots originally drawn by its designers in 1689, and the Brethren found land prices there prohibitive, even if they had cash. When they were finally able to gain a foothold in property, some bought parcels of land from likeminded Germans who had purchased large tracts earlier when land was much cheaper. Some worked for their neighbors as tenants while saving money for their own land. Most of the Brethren moved outside of population centers where land was less expensive, heading toward the western edge of the European settlements in Pennsylvania and beyond.[27] The new settlers began clearing land to farm.

Brethren theology taught that it was best to live apart from seats of power where there were few worldly amusements. Being among fellow believers in their homes was quite enough. They built no church structures, but met in homes for worship. This insulated the group from outsiders.[28] Thus, most spoke only German for several generations after arrival. As redemptioners worked off their debts and began realizing freedom of religion and even nonviolence where loamy farmland was abundant, the Brethren's yearnings seemed fulfilled.[29] As it turned out, eastern and central Pennsylvania was ideal for small-scale agriculture, as the Amish and Mennonite farms in the area today demonstrate. The Germans were industrious and committed to raising families and laboring together in community. Their farms and population grew rapidly.

On Christmas Day in 1723, the Krefeld Brethren—meeting formerly only in small house groups—held their first collective love feast and communion in America. This meeting brought all Brethren who could travel to one barn near Germantown. The congregation ate the Lord's Supper together, a hearty meal of bread and meat. Then they washed one another's feet as a sign of humility and community before holding communion with wine and bread.[30] This gathering gave the group a renewed sense of identity in this new place, and inspired the congregation to preach more openly in church-like settings. Following this communion, the Brethren began holding organized meetings regularly in Germantown. In the fall of 1724, the Germantown congregation sent out their entire male membership to spread the word among other Germans in Pennsylvania, baptizing as they went.[31] Despite their rejection of evangelicalism, this period of their growth seems to have been a gathering of lost or straying sheep, perhaps many of whom were already inclined to join the Brethren in the old country. By 1735, the year

Alexander Mack died, the original group of eight Brethren from Schwarzenau had joined the Krefeld Brethren in Pennsylvania, and, along with other German converts in the American colony, they now numbered several hundred adult members. Following Mack's arrival in 1729, the leader of the Krefeld Brethren, Peter Becker, stepped aside and from that time until his death in 1735, Mack led the newly united Pennsylvania Brethren.[32]

During these first years of growth in America, the lack of organization and increasing distance between members allowed both a proliferation of new congregations and a freedom of biblical interpretation, which led to some members of the Brethren seeking a radical Pietist expression that nearly broke apart the group.[33] By 1728, a group led by Conrad Biessel pulled away in Lancaster County into a community known as the Ephrata Cloister. In this settlement with married, single, and celibate people whom they referred to as "spiritual virgins," they pledged themselves to living monastically and to holding possessions in common. Following Alexander Mack's death in 1735, a large contingent of Brethren joined the Ephrata Cloister, including Alexander Mack Jr., although he did rejoin the Brethren a decade later.[34] By 1750, the Brethren also had lost two of their leaders to Count Zinzendorf's Moravian church.[35] The Brethren decided to meet these "encroachments" on their faith by establishing the Annual Meeting, "a yearly gathering of the entire membership for the purpose of spiritual renewal, mutual edification, and the united resolution of church problems and difficulties."[36] The first such meeting took place in 1742. Their goal was to shore up their faith by better defining its boundaries.

Brethren Migration

Despite these efforts to promote unity, doctrinal disputes, along with an overflowing farm population, pushed many Brethren southwestward. Yet in seeking to avoid conflicts by moving, the German Baptists found themselves in the middle of many. In the early 1740s, for example, they entered territory still controlled by the Iroquois and other Native American nations still under treaty negotiations with the British Crown. Trouble was brewing not only between the continent's natives and the newcomers, but also between the English and the French. In an attempt to wrest control of the open territories away from the French, the Crown's representatives negotiated a series of land deals with the Iroquois for trinkets and promises, all of which culminated in Pennsylvania in the Lancaster Treaty of 1744.[37] As with all the treaties that came before it, this treaty eventually proved false. Giving nothing of value to the Indians, the agreement made it possible for the British to grab control of all land east of the Alleghenies from the five great nations of the Iroquois, in an amazing act of diplomacy and treachery.[38] These documents not only forbade native hunting and trading expeditions, but also they opened the gate for the settlers, the Brethren and other Germans among them. Anxious to move on, groups of Moravians and Brethren left Pennsylvania in 1743, even while this final treaty was still in negotiation.[39]

Conflicts between English colonists and the French in the New World seemed to have little to do with the Germans. Yet by settling in territories in dispute, some Brethren were already living in the war zone when George Washington issued an ultimatum that the French remove themselves from the Ohio Valley in 1753. Instead of heeding Washington's orders, the French reacted violently and drove out the English settlers from the region.[40] The Brethren again found themselves in the midst of war, including twenty to thirty members in western Pennsylvania who were scalped in an incident known as the "Dunkard Massacre."[41] Some say the believers stood meekly by saying *"Gottes wille sei gehan"* (God's will be done).

In this violent climate, English colonists remained suspicious of their German neighbors, especially those looking for a place to settle. Some thought them spies of the French and their Indian allies because, as one Englishman accused, "Whenever one of you Dunkers had passed through here, a foray of savages followed immediately after!"[42] Sangmeister and Hellenthal, two Brethren members who had made it all the way to the New River (near the present-day West Virginia and Virginia border), wrote on September 17, 1757, "Some of our neighbors said we should all be hanged, others proposed to burn us and our house so that we really did not know anymore which side most danger lurked on, the savages or the so-called Christians."[43]

While most accounts paint a picture of the Brethren's extreme efforts to remain at peace with native peoples, even to the point of giving no resistance to attacks, on at least two occasions Brethren men reportedly fired their rifles at Indians. On August 17, 1763, John Martin of Juanita Valley, Pennsylvania, shot and wounded an Indian man.[44] On another occasion, Brethren member Jacob Neff shot two Indians, one from the window of his mill and a second face-to-face in a shoot-out on the same day. These shootings led to sharp rebukes. One version of the Neff story says he was excommunicated for his actions. Another version says that while he committed the act, he repented, and was admonished and excused by his congregation with the understanding that he would never engage in violence again.[45]

A few people on the frontier began to realize that the Brethren were not spies or enemies. In September 1757, Frenchman Marquis de Montcalm wrote of three people, probably Brethren, living in a hermitage in the Virginia woods: "They gave food indifferently to the English, the French and the Shawnees who liked them very much." He goes on to say that the Ottowas, then allies of the English, captured those men.[46] Some Englishmen also began to change their view of the German nonresistant people. Even George Washington himself spoke of the German Baptists in a sympathetic way. On September 28, 1756, he mentioned in a letter to Virginia Governor Robert Dinwiddie, "The Dunkers who are all Doctors entertain the Indians who are wounded here."[47]

Despite Washington's understanding, the war distanced the Brethren from the emerging national identity. As British colonists prepared for and fought the war against the French, they imagined themselves as a single entity under one military command organized across the lines of individual colonies.[48] Unfortunately for the Brethren, these imaginings of America were far from the pacifist and religiously diverse colony Penn the Quaker had beckoned them to the continent with in the first place. His peaceful holy experiment was quickly overtaken by booming guns of war.

The American Revolution

Those who relied on God as their only defense, turning the other cheek to anyone who might strike them, had no place in the America that believed in using armed forces against the British. As America's nationalistic forefathers began to take control of Pennsylvania, the Brethren saw themselves increasingly as outsiders again.[49] In fact, some English had considered Germans competitors to their identity all along. Benjamin Franklin verbally attacked the German settlers in Pennsylvania, particularly those who had made their settlements in German-speaking enclaves. In 1751, five years before the French and Indian War began, Franklin wrote,

> Why should the Palatine boors be suffered to swarm into our settlement and, by herding together, establish their language and manners, to the exclusion of ours? Why should Pennsylvania, founded by the English, become a colony of aliens, who will shortly be so numerous as to Germanize us, instead of our Anglifying them, and will never adopt our language or customs any more than they can acquire our complexion?[50]

In this passage, Franklin not only criticizes Germans for speaking their language but attacks their complexion as a racial problem, a posture far from the attitude of tolerance Penn had offered even the Native Americans. Despite his initial hostility, later Franklin seems to have been swayed by the Brethren theology. In his autobiography he writes that he suggested to "one of the Dunker founders, Michael Welfare [note that he anglicized his German name, Wohlfahrt] . . . to 'publish the articles of their belief and the rules of their discipline.' Welfare in reply: '. . . it has pleased God to enlighten our minds so far as to see that some doctrines, which we once esteemed truths, were errors; and that others, which we had esteemed errors, were real truth. From time to time, it had been pleased to afford us farther light . . . we feel that, if we should once print our confirmation of faith, we should feel ourselves as if bound and confined by it . . . to be something sacred, never to be departed from.'" Franklin continues, "This modesty in a sect is perhaps a singular instance in the history of mankind, every other sect supposing itself in possession of all truth, and that those who differ are so far in the wrong; like a man traveling in foggy weather, those at some distance before him on the road he sees wrapped in the fog, as well as those behind him, and also the people in the fields on each side, but near him all appear clear, tho' in truth he is as much in the fog as any of them."[51] That display of tolerance of modest faith was soon overpowered by the drums of militarism.

As the American revolutionaries forged ahead, the Brethren and other Anabaptists began quietly to formulate their stances against the war. In their first recorded Annual Meeting minutes of 1778, the Brethren specifically addressed the Declaration of Independence two years after its inception. They forbade one another from participating in oaths of allegiance to any government. Their ancestors had already lived through war's effects, and for the German Baptists, the American war allegiances were no less violent than European ones. From 1780 to 1781, as pressure for military enlistment increased, some Brethren tried hiring surrogate soldiers to fight in their place, hoping that this mild form of nonconformity would suffice. Eventually, however, the Brethren strongly forbade participating in the war in any fashion. They wrote in their 1781 minutes, "Take no part in war or bloodshedding which might take place if we would pay for hiring men voluntarily."[52]

Jacob Sauer II and eleven others wrote succinctly about their central reason for their nonparticipation in the war: "We must obey God rather than men."[53] There were, of course, other related reasons that the Brethren refused to support the war effort. The Brethren held a "deep gratitude" toward the British Crown for providing them with a safe haven when they were fleeing persecution in Germany. Indeed, contrary to their later written opposition to oaths, earlier Brethren signed the required oath of allegiance to the king in order to enter what they perceived a peaceful colony. They also noticed that the Pennsylvania Assembly was far from united around the war, and those who supported the war in the Assembly were the same men who had been the greatest opponents of the Quaker Party. Furthermore, the concerns with trade and taxation vexing the urban colonists most were not issues for the Brethren, who were largely rural residents.[54]

A basic concern supporting the Brethren's rejection of the Revolution was their understanding of the church and state. Following Romans 13 and 1 Peter 2, the Brethren believed themselves to be subject to the political authority established by God, and they saw no signs that God had shifted his authority from the English king to the rebelling colonists. In their 1779 Annual Meeting, they declared: "Inasmuch as it is the Lord our God who establishes kings and removes kings, and ordains rulers according to his own good pleasure, and we cannot know whether God has rejected the king and chosen the [American] state, while the king had government; therefore we could not, with a good conscience, repudiate the king and give allegiance to the state."[55] Such a principled stand put the Brethren at great risk as anti-British fervor rose. Most dangerous was the patriots' accusation that, by remaining loyal to the British, the nonresistant Brethren were as treasonous to the Revolution as the Tories actively aiding the British in battle.

The newly formed Continental Congress and the Continental Army demanded allegiance from all residing in the colonies, and the Brethren and other Anabaptists who opposed the war were considered subversives. Even as they turned the other cheek and refused to defend their own families or farms against aggression, they were ridiculed, and even imprisoned. Some Brethren had their property confiscated and sold at auction to pay for the war they did not want. Although most members paid taxes to the Congress, rendering unto Caesar what was his, if their taxes became delinquent for any reason, the American government agents seized clothes, furniture, livestock, or other property. As the nonresistant Brethren were reluctant to report any abuses, tax collectors, particularly at the local level, often exacted higher tolls from the Brethren and confiscated their land.[56] Also, some belonging to other Christian denominations joined in ridiculing the Brethren's position on the war, further discounting their peaceful stance in the eyes of the authorities.

Most Brethren remained steadfastly outside the fray. As they had during the French and Indian War, many members again took the role of physicians and cared for the wounded from the American Revolution—as before, they tended the wounded of both sides. Some were moved by the Brethren as they accepted treatment. A wounded American officer was taken to Ephrata to receive medical treatment. He wrote of the experience: "Until I entered the walls of Ephrata, I had no idea of pure and practical Christianity. Not that I was ignorant of the forms, or even the doctrines of religion. I knew it in theory before; I saw it in practice then."[57] For the most part, however, this kind of acceptance was a rarity.

War-related persecution pushed many Brethren out of Pennsylvania, particularly as revolutionary writers argued for God's sanction of their cause. Thomas Paine, for example, claimed God's favor for the Revolution in his pamphlet *Common Sense:* "The will of the Almighty expressly disapproves of government by kings." Ironically, as Americans declared new freedoms, the Brethren were left feeling less free.

Family cemetery where German Baptists are buried in Franklin County. The abandoned farmhouse and barns in the background were once a central part of the family's life. Photograph by the author.

Many Brethren lost all they had as they fled.[58] Most Brethren searched for rural enclaves to the south and west of their original settlements—new sites where they could reestablish peaceful communities and remain separate from government pressure to conform. An Anglican traveler commented on some early Anabaptists who had fled to rural Maryland, describing them both as separatist and nonthreatening: "Mennonites and Dunkers who seem to have broken off by so contracted a scheme of discipline as clashes with the common methods of government and civil society; not that they intend any disturbance or innovation, for they are remarkably peaceful and passive and therefore readily tolerated and excused."[59]

Among those who headed southward were Brethren traveling to a location in the Virginia Blue Ridge eventually named Franklin County. They followed the Great Wagon Road. As the Appalachian Mountains curved around present-day Gettysburg and turned southward, so did the narrow and rough trading path. It passed through western Maryland, entering the Shenandoah Valley of Virginia, and then snaked on toward the Tennessee border. While the road represented freedom and opportunity for many people, for the Brethren it was, ironically, also an escape from American persecution.

2 The Carolina Road

Along much of the great trading route through Virginia, the Brethren and other Germans were either the first European pioneers or closely followed the Scotch Irish settlers.[1] Yet, the German Brethren and others among them were far from the stereotypical rugged individualists or explorers seeking land for profit or power. Rather, they were a community of believers and farmers looking for a place to settle. Many had already farmed in Pennsylvania and had saved their own seeds and raised livestock on farms in Pennsylvania. Most were also skilled in a craft, from log-building construction to *fraktur* illustration of texts.[2] The Brethren sought neither individual isolation nor adventure, but an out-of-the-way place where they could build their enclave of faith and grow their farms in peace. This is how their community in Franklin County was to begin.

They walked, some with packhorses in tow or driving ox carts filled with their possessions. They traveled over both muddy and rocky terrain, some of it steep and nearly impassable. They passed forts General George Washington had constructed along the route during the French and Indian War, though many of these had seen little use since the French and Native Americans were pushed into territories west of the Alleghenies. In parts of Pennsylvania, small companies maintained the road in exchange for tolls. Yet as the road passed into the territory that is now southern Maryland and Virginia where no one maintained it, river fords, deep mud, steep mountains, and loose rocks made travel arduous. The journey was especially difficult for those who traveled with families and

Three Holstein cattle lounge near an old hay barn after their morning milking on a German Baptist–owned farm in Franklin County, Virginia. Photograph by Rob Amberg.

had livestock to feed on the journey. One Moravian who traveled this route in 1753 recorded a portion of his family's winter journey:

> At last [we] found ourselves at the end of a narrow valley, with the steepest of mountain sides to right, to left, and in front of us. To go back seemed futile, to proceed almost impossible, but we finally managed it by taking the packs from the backs of the horses. They then succeeded in climbing to the top, though by the time they reached it they were trembling from head to foot. We men scrambled up as best we could, dragging the packs after us, and when we had caught our breath enough to look around, we found ourselves on a ridge with a wonderful panorama of mountain peaks beyond the valley from which we had come. . . . It began to snow and turned bitterly cold. Soon the snow was so deep that our horses could not find forage, and almost as soon our supplies ran short. I have some skill with a gun, but there was nothing to shoot and starvation stared us in the face.[3]

The Brethren established their first permanent settlement in Virginia in the northern end of the Shenandoah Valley in the 1730s.[4] In 1765, Jacob Miller and others established their first permanent settlement in Franklin County.[5] Over the next decade, other Brethren joined

This rock, located at the Germantown Brick Church of the Brethren, marks the place members believe that Jacob Miller and William Smith preached together in German and English respectively, circa 1775. Photograph by the author.

Miller and his community. Both during and after the Revolution, the flow of settlers continued to increase as many sought access to land as well as refuge from mistreatment farther north.

When the English first arrived in Virginia in the seventeenth century, the king of England had made large land grants to aristocrats, taking much of Virginia's most accessible and arable land east of the Blue Ridge. By the mid-1700s little land was left for claiming outright, though due to the inflated land prices, squatters were common, particularly in the Appalachian Mountains. For travelers who managed to bring at least some money with them, it was often cheaper to rent or even to buy a working farm from someone who had worked it than to purchase uncleared land from absentee speculators.[6]

The cheapest and most accessible land for the German travelers lay in the Virginia Valley, particularly to the south, where, protected from eastern encroachment by the Blue Ridge, land had remained slightly out of range of the Virginia elite. To reach southern Virginia, the Brethren pushed southward in the Virginia Valley on the barely passable path toward Big Lick Valley (now Roanoke, Virginia). From there, some continued southwestward into present-day Montgomery and Pulaski counties and even into West Virginia near Blacksburg, Virginia, perhaps even moving as far south as Tennessee and beyond.[7] One early Brethren settlement in Pulaski County became known as Dunkard's Bottom. Today the site lies at the bottom of the Corps of Engineers Claytor Lake, an impoundment of the New River. Other Brethren settlers traveled southward from Big Lick and up to the plateau of present-day Floyd County, Virginia.[8]

The German Baptists who settled in Franklin County traveled first to Big Lick and from there took the Carolina Road through the Blue Ridge at Maggodee Gap at present-day Boones Mill to settle in the hill country that lies between the last two mountain ranges to the east. The countryside there was rolling and had plentiful streams of water. It was ideally suited to those who developed their farming skills in the rolling Rhine Valley or the Pennsylvania hills.

Western Franklin County near Magodee Gap is rolling land, entirely unsuited to large-scale plantation agriculture. Especially in the western Franklin County hills there are few flat acres and because of the abundance of streams surrounding them, the fields must be quite small. Also, the upland region is inaccessible to river trade on which much of the slavery-based cash crop economy depended. The land was better suited for interdependent, small communities with reliance upon long-distance trading. While the Blue Ridge had its own trade routes for moving droves of livestock, including the Carolina Road, the land there was predominately settled by subsistence farmers.

Though Franklin County was a land of subsistence farming in the 1770s, it was not entirely isolated. For example, some Franklin County men enlisted in the Continental Army to serve under George Washington believing their territory very much connected to national interests. Others supported the war financially instead of serving. Most likely, the few German Brethren who made it to the county during the war would have refused to participate as had their counterparts in Pennsylvania. Perhaps their isolation, or their status as renters, allowed the Brethren to continue farming despite their stance against all war. While Brethren suffered Revolutionary War land confiscations in Pennsylvania, no records have been found to show this happened in Franklin County. As pressures increased to either fight or pay, however, the nonresistant Brethren may have been subject to public ridicule and even persecution. This was probably particularly pronounced when the Brethren took a

The Carolina Road, once a footpath, is the route the German Baptist Brethren took to Franklin County, Virginia, in the 1700s. Route 220, a four-lane highway, overlays the path today. Photograph by Rob Amberg.

public stance nationally in opposition to the Revolutionary War in 1778.[9]

In 1786, four years after British General Cornwallis surrendered at Yorktown, Virginia, the Franklin County Brethren organized their congregation and elected Jacob Miller as minister. Also in 1786, Franklin County officially organized and a census titled the *List of Whit pepol and Buildings* took a measure of all existing farmsteads. It shows that the typical farm at the time housed six people, usually a husband, wife, children, and extended family members. Most lived in one-room log structures with a mud and stone chimney. More than 60 percent of farmers rented their land, surely hoping to purchase their own farms at a future date.[10] Many families owned only a handmade bed, a table and chairs, and some cooking utensils. Almost every family was dependent on crops and livestock. Few had any surplus goods to sell. When there were surplus crops, farmers usually traded these locally. Most families owned some hogs and occasionally a workhorse or mule, but few owned teams of draft animals. Half of the county's residents owned less than six cattle and only 5 percent owned twenty or more. Robert Hairston, the county's wealthiest man, owned a herd of only sixty cattle.[11]

After buying or renting their land, the Brethren worked together to build houses, barns, and fences. With a variety of skills between them, they worked quickly and efficiently to house one another under roof within the first year of their arrival. They shared homes as they worked to construct cabins for neighbors. Already living together or in close proximity, they met for worship in homes or barns. Keeping ties to other German Baptists, the Franklin County Brethren managed to send representatives to Annual Meetings even if held in Pennsylvania or other states. Through these plenary meetings they remained in touch with and accountable to other Brethren, and were able to set common guidelines by which they could order their lives. At the meetings, ministers from all the districts addressed issues of broad concern. Elders were elected to preside over the meeting with one acting as moderator. These presiding elders entertained questions of doctrinal concern by means of petitions and queries. All who attended these meetings voted. None were paid, and most of the ministers present were farmers. They boarded with one another in their homes and stabled the guests' animals, each helping the others keep the costs of travel to a minimum.

As is still the case, exchanges also took place on many other levels at these meetings. Young people met their future spouses. All shared language, foods, and dress across state lines. Though the Franklin Brethren lived far from Pennsylvania, by staying in touch with likeminded counterparts in other locations they retained a distinctly German American identity, more like that of other Brethren in distant states than their non-Brethren neighbors who lived nearby. Even by the time of the Civil War, the Franklin County Brethren were still known by their non-Brethren neighbors as the Dutch (a variation of *Deutsch*, meaning German).

By keeping the doctrines of the national denomination, the Franklin County Brethren found themselves starkly at odds with the prevailing wisdom of the region. Joining with the Mennonites and Quakers, the Brethren first recorded their stance against slavery in 1782. Following their Annual Meeting that year the moderator wrote, "It has been unanimously considered that it cannot be permitted in anywise by the church that a member should purchase Negroes or keep them as slaves."[12] Undoubtedly some Brethren owned slaves at the time and this decision was handed down as a result of a query regarding what to do about this problem. Also mentioned specifically at this meeting was the issue of one Brethren man from an unspecified location who fathered four children by a slave woman. The minutes say that he was instructed to give the woman her freedom immediately, and to feed, clothe, and educate the children until they turned twenty-one, at which time he was instructed to give them their freedom and a new suit of clothes. Fifteen years later at their Annual Meeting in 1797, the Brethren again rejected slavery, this time at a farm in Franklin County. This location was particularly radical due to the large number of slaves held in Franklin County, including most famously (and somewhat later) Booker T. Washington and his family. The minutes of the meeting read, "If a brother, contrary to this conclusion, would purchase negroes, and would not emancipate them, he would have to be considered as disobedient, and we could have no fellowship with him until he sets them free."[13]

The German Baptists also took a stand against making liquor. At the 1783 Annual Meeting those present concluded that any Brother with a still should "put it away," calling it a "very offensive evil which has endeavored to gain ground in the church."[14] Many Franklin County residents, as well as others throughout rural America, had found efficient ways to turn corn, barley, and even apples into good hard liquor to trade or sell. Liquor was an easy way people could exchange value over great distances. However, regardless of its efficiency and even its good sense to some, the church said no. This kind of stance by the Brethren church may have further distanced the Germans from those of Scots-Irish or English descent in the county, and perhaps exacerbating prejudices against Germans in general. Such animosities may have influenced even the formation of Franklin County towns, as we shall see below.

In 1782, the year the Virginia General Assembly was established, Germanic residents in Franklin County, at least some of whom were tied to the Brethren, petitioned the Assembly to grant them townships named Germantown and Wisenburg. Germantown was to be created on thirty-two acres owned by Daniel Lehman, laid out in half-acre lots for "divers Inhabitants, Artisans, and others."[15] On the heels of the Germans' proposal and perhaps in competition with it, English planters rushed to build up the town of Mount Pleasant—eventually called Rocky Mount—as the central business location for the area. Mount Pleasant already contained a courthouse, they argued, and they only needed entrepreneurs to make the town strong. To secure the location for businesses the developers forced landowners in town to sell their property to business owners. Despite some early resistance from residents, the town began to grow. By 1830, Mount Pleasant had 30 houses, 3 general stores, 2 taverns, 2 tailors, a saddler, a cabinetmaker, 2 blacksmiths, a shoemaker, a printing office with a weekly newspaper, and a tannery.

As Mount Pleasant grew, the German proposal languished. While by 1836 there were eleven post offices in the county—with the largest,

Mount Pleasant, acting as county seat and the central post office—Germantown and Wisenburg never gained even a post office. In fact, neither ever developed into towns.[16]

Despite the proposal's demise, in rural areas the German Brethren numbers continued to grow. According to local church records, around 1790, William Smith, a soldier sent from England to help put down the Revolution, converted to the Brethren faith, and was later elected to the Brethren ministry. Smith joined Miller as a traveling companion and fellow preacher in Virginia. Smith preached in English, mostly in adjacent Floyd County, and Miller preached in German in Franklin County, but always they ministered side by side. Through Smith, English-speaking Brethren with English surnames began joining the German numbers and their descendants remain in the church today.[17]

Despite the proposal's official failure, the name "Germantown" stuck. Under the branches of two great oak trees on a farm, the Brethren formed a congregation they called Germantown. There they built the Germantown Brick Church in 1848. The structure was made of brick fashioned from Franklin County clay with a roof of hand-hewn wooden shingles. There were two doors on the front of the building; women entered and sat on the right side and men on the left. All of the Franklin County Brethren who could make the trip by horse and wagon met there until 1870.

In 1861, just fifteen years after the Brick Church was built, the Civil War broke out. The Franklin County Brethren found themselves geographically situated within the Confederacy. As the war increased in intensity in central Virginia in the Shenandoah Valley and around Richmond, communications with their Brethren in the North was nearly cut off. Southern attendance at the Annual Meetings fell though the meetings continued to take place throughout the Civil War. Virginia Elder John Kline of the Shenandoah Valley refused to stay home and thereby became the only known Brethren casualty during the war. Though a Southerner, and technically a resident of the Confederate States of America, he was elected in 1862 as moderator of the Standing Committee of Elders presiding over the Annual Meeting. He continued in this role in 1863 and 1864, each time crossing into the North on horseback to attend meetings. Under his guidance the Brethren voted that all members should bear equally the fines either the Union or Confederacy levied against those who refused to fight. In Franklin County the fine was between $300 and $500 for each able-bodied man in a household. The Confederacy demanded participation from every man over the age of sixteen. Large Brethren families had exorbitant fees to pay and most could not do this alone. The Brethren nationally helped collect money to settle the debts.

In 1864, as in the previous years, Elder Kline and another elder named John Wine attended the Annual Meeting, some of the few Southerners among the 150 congregations represented that year. At that meeting Kline and other Brethren voted to forbid its members to wear any military clothing. Should one do so, particularly in preaching, they said, he should be admonished and even taken out of fellowship if he refused to change. Returning to Virginia from that meeting, Elder Kline, wearing nothing that might have identified him as a soldier was shot in the back and killed by Confederate soldiers. The Confederates, already angry at anyone who refused to back their cause, said they thought Kline was a spy and shot to kill on first sighting.[18]

Kline wrote in his diary three years earlier on January 1, 1861,

> It may be that the sin of holding three millions of human beings under the galling yoke of involuntary servitude has, like the bondage of Israel in Egypt, sent a cry to heaven for Vengeance, a cry that has now reached the ear of God. I bow my head in prayer . . . Secession means war; and war means tears and ashes and blood. It means bonds and imprisonments and perhaps even death to many in our Brotherhood, who I have the confidence to believe, will die rather than disobey God by taking arms.[19]

Surely most of the Franklin County Brethren agreed with Kline. However, a Confederate sympathizer in the county named T. B Greer wrote to his friend, Franklin County–born General Jubal Early, in 1861 that regarding secession, "even the Dutch are all right."[20] All right in what sense? The Brethren would not have fought against the Confederacy under any circumstances, but they were not "all right" regarding the cause of the war, or even with war itself. Perhaps in keeping with their stance on nonresistance, they were simply not vocally in opposition to the war and could be counted on to say nothing. Another possibility, though unlikely, is that Greer referred to non-Brethren German-Americans only.

As early as December 1799, sixty years prior to the start of the Civil War, the Franklin Brethren requests for exemption from military service began. John Beckleheimer and his son, John Boon, Joseph Flora, Henry Ikenberry, Peter Ikenberry, Jacob Kingery, Jacob Kinsey, Jacob Miller, Isaac Naff, Jacob Nave and his son, Michael Peters, and Stephen Peters, all the elders of the Brotherhood, signed a petition to the Virginia

General Assembly. Referring to themselves as *Tunkers* (Dunkers in English) they asked to be exempt from any military duty, though leaving an opening for participation should there be an invasion.

> The Petition of the people resident in Franklin Called Tunkers pray that for their Conscientious scruples they may be Exempt from performing Military duty but as they do not wish to shrink from Supporting Government they are willing that in addition to their proportions of the Revenue tax any thus Scrupulous and having a Certificate of Connection with said Church may be taxed Two Dollars each year as an equivalent for such Military Service Required of them but in case of invasion or insurrection they are then Willing to bear a part as other militia.[21]

The General Assembly rejected the request.

Again in 1813, during the War of 1812, the Brethren in Franklin and Montgomery counties united to petition the General Assembly and were again rejected. In 1826, a third petition came from "ministers in the Tunker Church" asking that they be exempt from Military Laws due to their "conscientious nonconformity." This petition arrived with a letter from many of the county's founders stating, "We do hereby express our conviction that such an alteration would be just and salutary in its consequence." Still, the General Assembly chose to ignore the request.

As soon as the Civil War broke out, the Brethren of Virginia petitioned once more for exemption from the military, starting anew with the Confederacy. This time, they achieved a small amount of success, particularly because of help from a few key individuals. Among them was General Stonewall Jackson, known for his own religious piety. He wrote regarding Brethren exemption on March 21, 1862, saying he would give his support, if "they shall act in good faith with me and not permit persons to use their names for the purpose of keeping out of service."[22] This letter led to the March 1862 passage of an exemption from service on the basis of faith.

Despite this, for the first months of the war, Brethren young men had a great deal of trouble with recruiters. Prior to 1862 some had to go into hiding in the mountains, returning home at night undercover for provisions. Some Brethren fled to the North to escape the draft, though some were caught by Confederates and put in prison as traitors.[23] Even after the granting of the exemption, hardships continued. By 1865, the loss of family members to the North and the heavy fines and confiscations had taken their toll on southern Brethren who had stayed behind to keep their farms going. That year at the Annual Meeting members announced that the Brethren in Virginia and Tennessee needed financial assistance. They collected donations and a brother from Maryland was appointed to take them to the southern districts.[24] These donations helped the southern Brethren survive the aftermath of the war, but even as the country began to heal and to rebuild, ushering in the Industrial Revolution, new issues of change and tumult lay in store for the entire membership. Worries about war would be replaced with concerns about members adopting clothing styles of the world. The mention of military-style clothing worn by some members during the Civil War, likely out of poverty and necessity rather than collusion, was only the beginning of German Baptist concern with worldly clothing styles. These issues would come back to haunt the Brethren as the Industrial Revolution began to take hold in America and wealth increased, making buying stylish clothing an option even for rural people. A conflict over dress and other issues lay on the horizon, even in Franklin County.

Following the Civil War the Brethren congregation at the German-town Brick Church continued to grow. In 1870, five years after the war's end, the congregation had increased in size so much that the elders voted to divide the congregation into three groups by geographical district, reducing the size so that each could minister to the others' needs and each person would have a direct role to play in maintaining the church and the community. At the time, one-third of the Germantown Brick Church congregation moved to Antioch Church and one-third to Bethlehem Church. By 1873 the two new congregations had completed two new meetinghouses in western Franklin.[25]

Economic growth began taking place on a larger scale in the county and nationally. By the 1880s the nation was in the midst of a major economic change following the Civil War. Railroads were becoming more common and by 1878 the first spur to serve Franklin County arrived. Also, machinery and manufacturing were beginning to replace hand labor in many sectors, including sawmills, textiles, and tobacco manufacture. For the first time in their history, the Brethren of Franklin County were in a position to capitalize on this economic improvement. German Baptists also faced the personal choice of whether or not to modernize. Many chose to change. About the same time, a new evangelical awakening began to spread through rural America by means of revivals and prayer meetings, and these had their effect on the Brethren as well.

Debates broke out between the Brethren hoping to retain old traditions and to stand against the modernizing forces and those who favored change and modernization in both religion and economics. At the base of the conflict were the facts that the Brethren were no longer being per-secuted for their difference, in part because they simply were no longer as different as they once were, and the growing economy and the rising middle class made Americanism all the more appealing. These debates, regarding the extent to which the Brethren would entertain change and accept parts of "the world," occurred at different rates of intensity depending on the district. The conflict reached a crescendo in the late 1870s in the North, when some members began to talk of splitting off from the main church.[26]

The queries about change first began in the Miami Valley of Ohio in the late 1860s, shortly after the end of the war. Conservative Ohio Brethren began meeting among themselves to air fears that some mem-bers were refusing to wear the Brethren garb. There was the impinging threat of Sunday Schools and missions these members claimed were nonbiblical and patterned after worldly institutions. Further, educating ministers and paying ministers salaries professionalized a role that had always been maintained by equals.[27]

For the first time in Brethren history, the lure of inclusion in the world rather than persecution threatened their faith. Adopting new beliefs and practices, even such a seemingly benign one as Sunday School, could only be the beginning of allowing the ways of the world to influence the church, with the old practices of the faith in danger of falling prey to the very forces they had always shunned. Threatened were the peculiarity and distinction that had always been their way.[28]

By the late 1870s some Brethren districts had already begun to hold "protracted" or revival meetings and evangelical-style altar calls, which the traditionalists believed were clearly fashioned after the emotional worldly institutions. The treatment of the Christian faith as a matter of feeling to be gained without sacrifice, hard work, and separatism was anathema to those clinging to the Ancient Order. Some churches had even started their own high schools, though education beyond the pri-mary grades was, according to the Old Order, a means of training students to join the world. Also at issue for the Old Order were church-centered social meetings and Bible classes, which appeared to have come from pop-ular culture and not from scripture. Meeting in homes, the traditional Brethren began their quiet campaign against the erosion of the Brother-hood. Then they turned to letters of concern and petitions to the Annual Meetings, submitting the first one as early as 1868. Continuing in this vein, the Brethren put forward to the Annual Meeting of 1878 the follow-ing: "A number of contrary things introduced problems in Upper Still-water Valley including 'altar calls' and the [progressive magazine known as the *Gospel Visitor's*] publishing inflammatory articles. . . . There was [also] some push to build a meeting house in town—a move which was felt by some to lead away from simplicity and humility."[29] Note that the members mention a town environment as problematic, if not anathema, to the faith of the Brethren. In this manner, the emphasis on Brethren distinctiveness had turned from hostile persecution to the subtler influences of lifestyles.

Two years later, at the 1880 Annual Meeting the conservative Ohio group submitted a lengthy petition asking for a return to tradition in order to "restore brotherly harmony and peace."[30] But the presiding elders returned an alternate understanding of the tradition: "While we declare ourselves conservative in maintaining what may justly be considered the principles and particularities of our fraternity, we also believe in the propriety and necessity of so adapting our labor and our principles to the religious wants of the world. . . . Hence, while we are 'conservative' we are also 'progressive.'"[31] Believing this act a deliberate reversal of their most basic precepts the Old Order "turned toward a separation."[32] On August 24, 1881, the conservative group met separately in Arcanum, Ohio, with members from various states in attendance, marking the beginning of the Divide. Those in attendance vowed to "hold to the Church which they had joined." Eventually two distinct denominations formed, the Progressives and the Old Order, the former choosing to adapt to change and the latter trying to resist it.[33]

In Franklin County, two Ohio Progressives arrived in their Boones Mill church in 1881 to explain the Division to the congregation and to help them take a vote on which branch of the faith the congregation would choose to support. This visitation hastened the local decision to divide Antioch and the other Franklin County districts. The power to hold the building apparently already rested with the Progressives. Those who voted to adopt the new rules of allowing seminary-trained ministers, missionaries, and all the rest were told to stay in the central meeting hall of the church. According to oral histories, those refusing the changes were asked to withdraw to the building's kitchen.[34]

A total of eleven people at the meeting left for the kitchen, including three of the five ministers in the church. Jacob Flora Jr., the minister who donated the land for the Antioch church, chose the Old Order, and thereby forfeited rights to the building. It is not clear how many remained in the meeting hall at Antioch, but eventually 25 percent of the overall Brethren membership would choose to hold to the Ancient Order. This number totaled between four thousand and five thousand nationally by 1882.[35]

The two groups initially called themselves "German Baptist Brethren" and "Old German Baptist Brethren." According to the Antioch Church of the Brethren literature, the groups in the Antioch community became commonly known as the "Brethren" and the "Old Order Brethren." Both groups today often refer to themselves informally as simply "Brethren," however, and both still have sizeable congregations in Franklin County. Later, in 1908, the Progressive Brethren adopted the official name "Church of the Brethren" while the Old German Baptist Brethren have maintained their name until the present.[36]

Substantive changes were slow in coming to the Franklin County Brethren church—so slow that during the early decades of the twentieth century the members of both groups continued to meet in the same building for nearly forty more years—though at separate times. In part this harmony stems from the fact that Franklin County Brethren remained generally more traditional than their northern counterparts. For many decades following the Divide, it was hard to tell the Old Orders and some of the Progressives apart. The Ikenberrys and others who voted to join the Church of the Brethren dressed in Old Order garb the rest of their lives. A few still wear prayer coverings today.

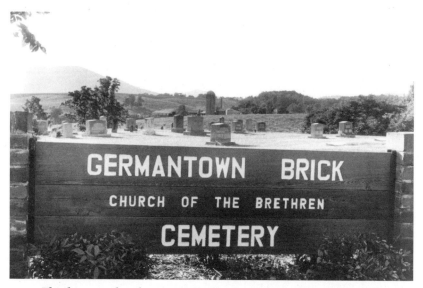

This historic church cemetery at the Germantown Brick Church borders a dairy farm and Cahas Knob, the landmark passed by many early Brethren settlers as they traveled along the Carolina Road. Photograph by the author.

*Samuel and Elizabeth Ikenberry and family posing in front of their
Franklin County farmhouse in 1901. Note that some, though not all, of
the members of the family are dressed as Old Orders. The author's
maternal grandfather is the infant on his mother's lap on the left.
Author's family photograph.*

In 1919 the Antioch congregation razed their simple meetinghouse
to build an entirely new church with a steeple. At the time, the Church
of the Brethren moved temporarily to a warehouse and the Old German
Baptist Brethren returned to meeting in homes. The new, contemporary
construction included both a formal sanctuary with a raised pulpit and
baptismal fount and Sunday School rooms. Later additions included a
fellowship hall and a picnic shelter.

These changes, directly conflicting with traditional doctrine, made
the building unacceptable as an Old Order meetinghouse. Those devoted
to the Ancient Order decided they had to leave. The Church of the
Brethren agreed to pay those leaving the inconsequential sum of $175
for their interest in the first building. With this as seed money, the Old
German Baptists started building a new structure called Pigg River District Meeting House, finishing it in 1923.

It is several miles and just a few minutes in this age of paved roads
and automobiles from the present Antioch Church of the Brethren to
the site of the meetinghouse of the Pigg River District. Pigg River
church is a large but simple white clapboard building reminiscent of the

Inside the Antioch Church of the Brethren is a glass case displaying a prayer covering and bonnet once worn by all the women in the church. Today German Baptist Brethren women continue wearing the same head coverings. Photograph by the author.

original Antioch Church that preceded it by nearly fifty years. It was erected in 1919, but there is no sign in front of the building giving its date of origin or its name. The building literally straddles the headwaters of the Pigg River. The stream, after flowing under the church, pours over a dam used to deepen the waters for baptism a few yards downstream from the building. Nearby there are outdoor restrooms neatly kept and without plumbing.

Two entrances in the front of the building, one for women and one for men, lead into a large, open room lined with unpainted solid white-pine pews. The room seats over five hundred people. The windows are clear and unadorned. The interior walls are also white. Pews line the room all the way to the minister's table at the end opposite the doors. A low table in front of the minister's pew is the only separation of the ministers from the congregation. There is no dais and no lectern. During their church meetings, the ministers—seven have that appointment in the Pigg River District—face the congregation. The deacons or the "visit brethren" sit on the front row of the congregation facing the ministers directly. All these office holders are men.

The women sit on the right when facing the ministers and the men on the left. The ministers' and deacons' wives normally sit directly behind the deacons. In the congregation, usually the older members sit closer to the front while the younger members sit toward the middle. Those who are not members and the older children sit in the final half-dozen or so pews near the entrance doors.

Hat and bonnet racks line the walls and are suspended above the middle aisles between the three sections of pews. Hats and bonnets are never worn inside and are left on these racks during meetings. As there is no Sunday School or nursery, and as the children are to be "trained by their own parents," the practice of remaining in the service for the entire two hours begins in infancy. Fathers and mothers walk outside with the children for brief periods.[37]

In 1993, Elder Ezra Rutrough, now deceased, recalled the demolition of the original Antioch Church and its rebuilding in 1919.[38] He was ten years old at the time. He remembered the $175 payment to the German Baptists and still grieved this division and cried when he talked about it. He said through his tears, "This is my neighborhood." He meant that his own neighbors participated in the Divide and though they separated, no one moved away. Elder Rutrough, the senior minister of the district, struggled to find a way to be neighborly and separate at the same time. A farmer and carpenter all his life, Elder Rutrough headed the Brethren carpentry crew that built an addition for Antioch. On March 28, 1960—he remembered these dates without hesitation—the construction began. His German Baptist crew set the cornerstone in November of that same year. Every time Elder Rutrough passed the Antioch Church, which is only a mile from his home, he saw a church that he had helped build, but that had originated from disagreement.

During Elder Rutrough's lifetime, spanning nearly the entire twentieth century, the German Baptists continued their rural lifestyle of simplicity, community, and quietude. World Wars erupted, but the Old German Baptist Brethren petitioned the U.S. government for conscientious objector status, and along with the Church of the Brethren, Quakers, and Mennonites, they received it. By World War II, many of the Franklin County Brethren served in Virginia work camps instead of going into the military. Meanwhile, Franklin County remained a predominantly rural county, even as tobacco warehouses, textile plants, and more recently furniture plants came and went. Though agriculture changed dramatically in Elder Rutrough's lifetime, farming remained a primary means of earning a living, particularly for the German Baptists.

On the Rutroughs' living room wall there was a painting of a now-defunct meetinghouse in Hollins, Virginia. Roanoke's urban sprawl long ago overtook the area and a shopping center now stands on the old church site. The loss is emblematic of the problems the Old German Baptist Brethren face today in Franklin County. All Brethren pay taxes now and they fully embrace their citizenship. Gradually, alternative service for conscientious objectors and general acceptance for those who are different religiously and culturally has made being German Baptist less threatening to the status quo. Today, however, another onslaught in the form of development and change in agricultural policies that favor ever larger farms threatens rural life in general, particularly those whose faith ties in with rural life.

At the turn of the twenty-first century Franklin County has joined adjacent Roanoke County in its fast-paced march toward change, and the Old Brethren look on without public comment. First, Smith Mountain Lake, built by the Corps of Engineers arrived and brought with it second home developments. Now Interstate 73 looms on the horizon, promising to bring with it higher land prices, more conveniences, and more challenges for farmers and rural life in general. German Baptists find themselves in the midst of a strange new twist on difference. They now provide local color, along with a reputation for honest living and good work, encouraging some outsiders to move to the area to enjoy their neighborliness and honest and skillful construction practices.

Even in the midst of these changes, the Pigg River District has continued to grow steadily, almost entirely due to the German Baptists having large families or through members from other places moving to Franklin County from other districts. Because of this growth, Pigg River members recently voted to divide the membership in two, creating a new district called Mountain View. This was an amicable separation designed to allow all members to have a participatory role in the fellowship. Loyd Jamison explains:

> Our district is divided into two. We have a meeting every Sunday at Pigg River, but two of those Sundays it's Mountain View, which is a new district that we formed from Pigg River. And then Pigg River District has a meeting every two weeks. After church, one-half of the district fixes dinner on one Sunday and the other is scheduled to fix it the other Sunday and then we invite everyone from church. If we have visitors from other districts . . . we try to make sure we invite all those. Sometimes we have just 2 or 3, and sometimes we have 25, 30, or 35 in

New house construction at Smith Mountain Lake. Note the old chimney nearby. Photograph by Rob Amberg.

our home. This is a custom that we have and we spend the afternoon in fellowship visiting. We like to think that we visit on spiritual things to some extent but we do visit on natural things as well. Maybe too much so sometimes, but it's an evening of fellowship. We feel like when we eat together and fellowship together we're drawn closer together and this is part of our way of life.

The newly built Mountain View Meetinghouse sits on a knoll not far from Cahas Knob, near where the first Germans came through the Blue Ridge at Magodee Gap. Looking from that knoll a scene unfolds that contains many of the images both past and present that make up the world of Franklin County and the lives of the German Baptists who live there. Numerous dairy farms—those owned by the Old German Baptist Brethren and some by Church of the Brethren farmers—surround the site. Not far away is a county park that features an original section of the Carolina Road with a sign explaining its historical significance. Also visible from Mountain View Church is a housing development on the old Ikenberry farm, a place that until the development started in 2001 was in continuous agricultural use since 1790.

As has been taking place since the first Brethren arrived in Franklin County, change has come, while tradition persists. Though the Brethren

Antioch Church of the Brethren in Boones Mill, Virginia. The church was once home to a German Baptist congregation. After the Divide of 1881, Church of the Brethren members retained possession of the building, eventually adding Sunday School rooms, a steeple, and other changes. Old Order members of the congregation left to build another simpler building at Pigg River, also in Franklin County. Photograph by Rob Amberg.

sought a place to remain apart, change has found them. For now at least, nearly all the cultural and historical markers of the Brethren story remain present in this scene, the old farms and new houses, the pastures with cattle and for sale signs, the simple church and the modern ones with lighted signs and steeples. Yet these juxtapositions of old and new that occur as change overtakes this place beg the question, how do people who cling to an Ancient Order continue their difference in the face of these alterations of the landscape? Which parts of change does one embrace and what is considered part of the world that one rejects? And if they cannot live their separate lives in the Blue Ridge, then where will they go? As Franklin County Brethren head through the twenty-first century, these will be some of their central questions. Knowing their history of weathering storms, we can be assured that they will face them with all the determination they showed as they first traveled and settled along the Carolina Road over two centuries ago.

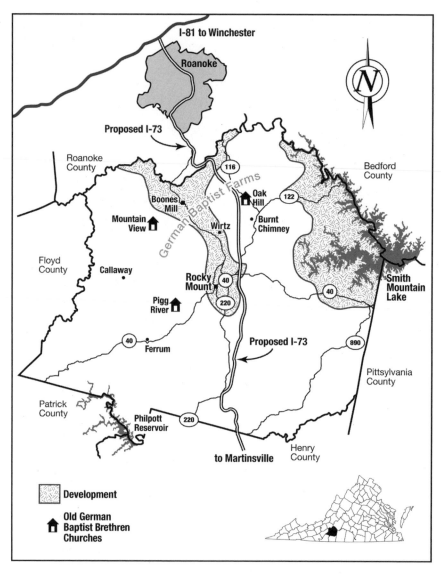

Franklin County in 2006. Note the close proximity of German Baptist farms and churches, encroaching housing developments, and the proposed Interstate.

PART II

Wilderness No More

For decades the Old German Baptist Brethren of the Pigg River District of Franklin County had charge of a small congregation in Clemmons, North Carolina. By 1994, the last remaining North Carolina district—called Fraternity—retained only two families: a couple in their late fifties along with their son, his wife, and their young children. Every other member had either died out or moved away.

The Fraternity meetinghouse, once located in the open countryside in a separate enclave of Brethren, was built by those who had traveled the Carolina Road to the vicinity of what is now Winston-Salem some two centuries before. Over the last half of the twentieth century, the numbers in the congregation dwindled as non-Brethren newcomers built houses around them. The rural land turned into subdivisions. Then, in the early 1990s, the Department of Transportation constructed the Interstate 40 bypass through Clemmons. They put an exit near the old meetinghouse. The two families' modest rural homes—complete with gardens, outbuildings, and even a tractor and equipment—suddenly looked out of place as a convenience mart and a KFC were built nearby. The church itself sat in earshot of the heavy Interstate traffic.

A few years after this change, the two families, along with the Pigg River District, voted to disband their Clemmons location and close it altogether. They sold the Fraternity church house to a lawyer and their homes to newcomers and moved to

Franklin County, Virginia. In North Carolina, the father and son had been carpenters on a crew that worked on luxury houses in Winston-Salem. Their boss called them the "black hats" and few understood their difference. In contrast, in Franklin County they joined an all-German Baptist crew. They say it is good to work among so many of their Brethren now.

In Franklin County today the Brethren still live in rural communities together. Following patterns in many ways similar to what happened in Clemmons, however, Franklin County is also changing. Because of proximity to southwest Virginia's largest city and booming development around Smith Mountain Lake, land for retirement homes and recreation is selling for prices higher than anyone could have imagined a generation ago. This makes for lucrative opportunities in the construction business for both carpenters and farmers who know how to operate heavy equipment for clearing land and building roads. But development also means that farming and rural living are increasingly hard to imagine let alone afford. At the same time, increased populations in formerly rural areas give rise to oppor-

German Baptist member and construction company owner Dale Angle surveys an old cemetery at the site of a new housing development on Smith Mountain Lake. Photograph by Rob Amberg.

tunities in niche farming., Located near Smith Mountain Lake, for example, is a new creamery specializing in direct milk and ice cream sales to consumers. Farms are struggling, but people are not giving up. Farmers are innovating yet again.

In the preceding chapters, we learned about the history of the Old German Baptist Brethren, largely through archival sources. Here we turn to Brethren farmers and their neighbors in Franklin County to understand their own words about what they believe about issues of faith, farming, change, in the past, present and future. For the sake of brevity, I have taken out the interview questions in most cases and shortened each response, while always endeavoring to maintain the cadence of speech as well as the context of all that was said.

The interviews contained here—recorded in 2001 and 2002—show us that these Brethren are nowhere near disbanding their districts as they did in Clemmons. In Franklin County the German Baptist community seems as strong as ever. Yet we also find that change is on everyone's mind. This has only intensified in the decade since I began my work with the Brethren in 1994 particularly with the proposal of Interstate 73 and Westlake, a retirement boomtown next to Smith Mountain Lake, quickly becoming the county's largest town. Through their words we learn what the German Baptists think about issues stemming from growth, new roads and developments, changes in farm technologies, farm subsidies, and so on. This, of course, represents only a snapshot, a slice of time. But as Brethren face change, perhaps even the demise of most of the family dairy farming in the region, what emerges here is a glimpse into their way of being, which is always pragmatic, faithful, and filled with hope—not hope that the world will improve, but that their community will persevere. Like the Brethren of old, the story of persistence in the face of persecution, and of staying true to the Ancient Order is central to Brethren identity, even as everything else around them changes. In the midst of these changes, German Baptists and their neighbors talk about how they raise children, how to be a neighbor, how to maintain a community, how to approach small farming, and what it means when farming and rural community life is threatened.

3   Raising Citizens

Farming not merely for the sake of producing food but as a way to build a life for a family and a community is a theme Old German Baptist Brethren return to again and again. They speak of religious beliefs and lifestyle intertwined, of clothing, cars, and business ethics all as part of living by example. They cultivate values, not just corn. They build community, not just barns. And, more important than cattle, they raise children to be citizens of the godly kingdom that is not of this world. In this chapter, four people, three of them German Baptist ministers and one the daughter of German Baptists who now works at a historic farm depicting a German homestead in 1800, talk of history, theology, and farming and how they are all interconnected in the Brethren story. They tie together their farms and community with strands of family and church dedication even as they acknowledge that life is changing in Franklin County and the world at large.

Loyd Jamison

*Our People Are Not Exempt from Losing
the Virtue of Small Farming*

In his seventies, Loyd Jamison is an Old German Baptist Brethren minister. He also runs a small seed business beside his home. Coming from Roanoke County, Loyd bought his farm in 1956. Now retired from dairying, he helps his three sons, who remain in the dairy business in

A young boy watches patiently during an afternoon milking at the Bowman dairy farm near Boones Mill, Virginia. Photograph by the author.

several locations in Franklin County. On the day of our interview, in June 2001, Loyd and many members of his extended family had planned to gather in order to slaughter and process hundreds of their own homegrown chickens. He told me, "Sometimes on Sundays when we have company from church, we might have fifteen to twenty people come in to eat with us and my wife will prepare one of the bigger roaster chickens. They're more like a turkey, and they're real tender. They eat good." Working together with women, children, and men, the family had nearly all the chickens readied for freezing by the time our interview ended.

I began our interview by asking about how the Old German Baptist Brethren understand their difference from the world today. Loyd explained both the basis of separation from the world and what happens if someone fails to live up to world-denying principles. We also talked about why small farming and faith are intertwined among the Brethren. Having been a farmer all his life and a German Baptist elder for decades, Loyd is articulate about both Brethren theology and small farming. In his lifetime he has witnessed the dramatic changes in agriculture that have caused the elders to veer away from offering their earlier recommendations that young Brethren families consider farming a primary choice of occupations. He knows that all Brethren farmers are feeling economic "pressures," and thus he admits, "we're not exempt from losing the virtue of small farming."

We believe we should be a separate people from the world and we believe the scriptures uphold living a low profile, in meekness. We certainly don't condemn anyone else for their beliefs, but we appreciate the fact that they let us practice and believe the way we believe.

We're not exempt from the fast lane. At times we don't cultivate our mind and thinking in terms of the scripture as we should, but trusting that we always come back to that when we get through the busy seasons, of course. But on Sunday afternoons, we'll get into an intimate conversation on issues that might affect us, like the things that we see within our own group—troubled marriages, for instance, or doctor appointments. And sometimes company will stay until 9:00 or 10:00 o'clock at night until we get these things talked out. And I think it does us good to know and consider each other's feelings. We just think it's pretty important really to communicate.

One of our church principles is the eighteenth chapter of Matthew, where it talks about if a brother would trespass against you. We read this to all applicants who come into the church, and they're asked if they're willing to abide by this rule that if your brother would sin against you, then it would be your duty to go to him and tell him his fault between you and him alone. And then if he won't hear you, then it's our duty to take one or two more. In the mouth of two or three witnesses every word will be established. And if he doesn't hear then, well, then we tell it to the church and let the church judge in the matter. If they won't hear the church, then they are to be disfellowshipped as a heathen man and a Publican. Not that we mistreat them, but they're not in communion with us. We term this a "golden rule of life," and this is a very important part of our fellowship because it keeps us united. We keep our differences worked out and it doesn't cause division among us and we think this is very important. The sooner you take care of these things the less difficulty you have. Sometimes a thing grows and then it gets so big it's hard to correct it. We find this system works between Brethren, between neighbors, and in business dealings.

We don't want anyone to think that we're better than anybody else, but we're only trying to live a type of life that will meet God's standard, God's will. Take radio and TV, for instance. The church has protected us from the evil that's on these things, and we realize there's a lot of good in them. But the church stands against this because we're in the flesh just the same as anyone else and we have the potential to be just as bad as anyone else, but yet we try to be led by the Spirit. We're willing to deny ourselves these things so that it doesn't affect us in our spiritual walk. We don't feel like we can rub elbows with the world. We're living in the world and we got to be part of the world as far as making a living and providing for our own, but we don't have to participate in the things that the world has to offer to pull the Christian walk down.

It's not that we are separate from our neighbors. We enjoy our neighbors. We couldn't do without them. We believe to have good neighbors we have to be good neighbors. We had two neighbors when we came to Franklin in '56. I was just twenty-one years old and we started operating a farm and they were old enough to be my daddy and they took me under their wings and we would build silos together. We made hay together. We ate together. One didn't belong to any church that I know of; he kind of believed in the Primitive Baptist faith. And they appreciated our way of life and we appreciated theirs, but we didn't try to convince each other. Any time they asked me, just like you here this morning, if you ask me something, then I feel like it is my duty to try to explain it to you. But we don't push our religion on anybody. We don't go out on the street corners and say you ought to do this and so.

We believe that our greatest mission is in keeping our own families in the faith, the older women teaching the young women, older men teaching young men, and to do it in a quiet, humble, and meek way. But I think this teaching process is breaking down. We probably don't see it cultivated among us as we used to because of the pressures of life, because of the fastness. We get busy and we don't instruct our children. But it has always been God's desire. Even Israel was to teach their children when they rose up in the morning, at noon, and in the evening. So any time we have the opportunity we feel that it is our duty to instruct children by word and by example. You have to live what you try to teach. And yet with all of that we still lose a lot of our children. I mean, the pressure of the world is still there and we encounter it just the same as anyone.

It's pretty evident that pride affects our people just the same as it would anyone else. About the time we think we're humble, we've lost it because that's pride. So we have to be careful, but truly we don't condemn other religions, other people's beliefs, and we appreciate the fact that we can worship like we feel. Of course, this is freedom of worship, but we can't say that we're free from all these different avenues of temptation, 'cause we're not.

There are some things that aren't consistent among us, and that is what we try to work on every year. We have our Annual Conference where all the German Baptist congregations take up a question that comes up that a local congregation can't answer. Take the Internet, for instance. That's something that's pressing hard on our people because the workplaces have more or less accepted the computer for bookkeeping and these kinds of things. We do have some big farmers, big businesspeople within our group, and they feel a need to have the Internet. But it seems like up until this point we have never accepted the Internet because we feel that it's too much. There are too many things on it that are not conducive to Christian living that can't be blocked out. I'm reluctant to say anything about it because I don't know that much about it. I don't even have a computer, but it's the things we hear.

The way we feel about it is that the apostles were ignorant, unlearned men. But the Bible goes on to say that the people understood that they'd been with Christ. And that's the way we'd like to look at it. We'd like to live a life so that we might be ignorant to some of the things that the world has to offer out here but we trust that our light goes out to shine forth Christ. Our lifestyle is not meant to bring attention on the German Baptist Brethren or on us as individuals, but it's just like John the Baptist. We like to show forth that we do live for Christ and that Christ is magnified in our lifestyle. I mean, if we fail in this, well, we failed it, but that's our concern.

We like to think that we are citizens of the United States. I mean, we believe in paying our taxes. We believe in being obedient to the laws of the nation unless they conflict with the laws of Christ, but we will have to say that we don't think that the danger of persecution is any less today than it was for our forefathers who lived in Germany. This is the reason that German is used in our German Baptist name. And there came a time that they couldn't go along with the state. We were persecuted and driven from one place to another because of our faith. We don't experience that today, but we think that we do experience some things that's just as hard on us or just as much a detriment to us as what they had. We're living in the terms of prosperity and really prosperity is probably a downfall to us as much as persecution ever was.

The gospel, according to the early church age, spread in the time of persecution. They would try to put the fire out—but everywhere, every time they would burn one at the stake, there would be other believers that would come forth. And possibly they showed a better light to the world than what we do in the day of prosperity. We're living in a time that if we're not careful we think we deserve anything the world has. That is one place that the Brethren have always cautioned us.

And I'm not saying that this is all good, but there's just a lot of pressures here to live and serve in the present age that our forefathers didn't have and we do the best we can and trust that God can be merciful to us. Take an Interstate coming through, for example. If I happened to have a pretty good-sized farm on a main road and a clover leaf would come in, then automatically overnight I would become a rich man. So probably this prosperity would spoil me. In other words, we believe in working and providing for our own and sharing with those in need, but how would you spend millions of dollars and never let it affect you spiritually? That's just some of the pressures we're under. As far as relocating and maintaining a lifestyle, that can be done. But naturally if an Interstate divides or comes through a district, we'd want a fair value out of our land, but we wouldn't take anything to court. We would accept whatever is given to us. But we would expect a fair share.

Our people are not exempt from losing the virtue of small farming. We're pressured just like everybody else to operate on volume and this is one thing that we've seen over the years. It's quite different than when we first started in the farming business. Well, now it's a business instead of a way of life like it used to be.

When I was a boy, I was raised on a little small farm and we had an orchard. We had peaches and I guess I never did enjoy orchard work. And so therefore I thought when I got old enough to be on my own that I would seek another type of farming. I had two or three brothers that were in the dairy business and I thought maybe I would like the dairy business. And so I worked for the state highway department a couple of years and then I decided I wanted to go into the dairy business and I had some of my brothers look around. We lived in Roanoke and my brothers lived over here in Franklin. Farming got to where it was pretty scarce in Roanoke County, so we decided we would come to Franklin to see if we could find something.

We'd always milked by hand. And so we learned under Mr. Rakes [the owner] for a month and then we took over January the first, and of course he still was there and helped us and we'd go to him for advice. And we just had a good relationship all along. We had his respect and he had ours and it proved out.

After the six years we had a pretty tough time starting up because our milk check wasn't very big. I can remember that I was working for $200 a month and we'd get a $600 milk check and we just didn't have money enough to buy feed and feed those cows. We bought twenty-

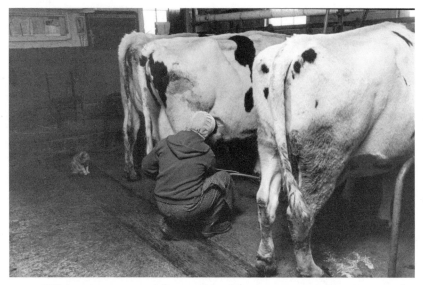

Milking time at one of the smallest dairy farms in Franklin County. The family milks fifteen cows with equipment in vogue in the 1960s. Photograph by Rob Amberg.

seven cows from him. But as time went on and we began to raise a little more of our feed and as we got accustomed to farming, it got a little bit better. So after the lease began to get to where it was going to run out, we got to talking to him about the farm. And so he said, "Well, now, I'll tell you, I'd like for you to have the farm." So he gave me a good opportunity to buy the farm and we bought the farm from him. And as time went on we got a little more familiar with farming, I suppose. We could raise a little more of our feed and we could realize a little more income and so we were able to make a go of it at farming. We had to learn a lot about farming and we can't complain at all about what farming has done for us.

I do remember one thing that Mr. Rakes said when we made the last payment on the farm. He said, "Now, when you came over here, you were just a kid. I didn't think you were going to make it." But, he said, "I'll be frank with you, I see that by the help of the Lord that you did." And we always appreciated that. Never had cross words. We might not have agreed all the time, but we didn't have a cross word.

The dairy industry has done a lot for Franklin County. It made it productive. But on the road that we lived on when we first moved over to Mr. Rakes's farm until the time we left, we counted up twenty-four new houses that were built on a three-mile stretch of that road. So that's how much it changed in the thirty-nine years that we were there. But we try to meet these changes and do the best we can.

Farming has considerably changed. At the time we started, we just had twenty-five milking cows. We sold our milk to a little small dairy in Martinsville and it was more of a way of life. I mean, we weren't pressured. But even the first year we were there, we began to see a change. By September 1956 we had to put in a bulk milk cooler. We'd been shipping in cans up to that point, but here we had to make a change. So we put in a 250-gallon milk tank. Well, the first milking that we milked in it we didn't even get the bottom covered. But from that stage we went from a 250- to a 400-gallon tank and then to a 800-gallon tank and now a 1,500-gallon tank is on the farm, and they're filling it up. So, this same farm has been pressured into more volume. They're milking eighty cows now versus our twenty-five cows. But now two families are living off of it where just one family lived off of it when I was running it.

It's hard to make payments. Your taxes are so much higher. Everything you buy is so much higher. So you've got to generate more income to meet it. Wages go up. So, the product's got to go up to meet it, you see, and we just keep going and there's so much more money involved today versus what it was when I started farming. I worked for $200 a month then. Now a farmhand makes $2,000 a month. See?

We have to modernize to meet these changes and again that kind of destroys the way of life and makes a business out of it to some extent. Farms are getting fewer but bigger. Every year we lose two or three farmers. That cuts down on our seed business but the farmers that are still in business a lot of times increase to the point that you don't see much difference.

My five boys that were raised up on the farm are all still farm-related. Once in a while I question if there's going to be enough for all of them to stick to the farm. Some of them will probably have to pick up other avenues of carpentry work or something like this, which is good experience. Some of my boys did carpentry work for a couple of years between the time they were thinking about marriage or wanting to leave Dad's house and before they got something on their own. This proved out well for them because they can use this experience back on the farm. But, you can take the boy off the farm but it's hard to get the farm out of the boy. Most of them do enjoy farming.

As a whole, we've always felt that working the land and farming is a good way of life, puts you close to your Maker, your Creator. Not that you are exempt from the temptations, but it's not like truck driving.

They meet a lot more temptation than you would out on the farm. And we don't recommend trucking. We don't say they can't do it but we'd rather for them not to do it. But we do have some that do drive trucks.

We still have a congregation at Roanoke that has met the changes. It has never grown much. When I was a boy we had about 120 members there and we still have about 120 members there. So they have pretty well maintained what they have had but they've lost a lot of people, like children, who have come over this way. Of nine children in my parents' family, six of them live in Franklin County because of the pressures there. We wanted to farm and so we moved over this way. And I don't know whether there ever will come a time that we will have to move on somewhere else or not. We do see a change in Franklin County. It's grown up just like Roanoke County did. But we just meet these changes and we take a day at a time and do the best we can. Trust God for the wisdom to guide us.

Rebecca Austin

To Be in Business with a German Baptist Person

Rebecca Austin, in her thirties, is the daughter of German Baptists in Franklin County. She works as a cultural interpreter at Ferrum College's Blue Ridge Institute and Farm Museum. On a sunny May morning in 2001, she gave me a tour of the farm. The exhibit represents a German American farm as it might have looked in 1800. We walked through the log house and outbuildings as she pointed out aspects of the family life that might have taken place in such a setting. Raised on a farm herself, Rebecca clearly loves this work. She is married to a full-time dairy farmer whose grandparents on both sides are German Baptist. Her husband now farms in partnership with a German Baptist man who took him in when Terry's own family was having problems. Neither Rebecca nor her husband Terry is a member of the German Baptist church, though they both remain in close family contact with members.

Rebecca gives us a unique glimpse into the family lives of German Baptists from the perspective of someone who has left the faith but who still knows it intimately. She ponders how being a child of German Baptists affects one's vocational choices. She is particularly insightful regarding communications between generations on the topic of vocational choices. She also speaks of nonfarming neighbors, newcomers to the county, and her own children's nonfarming classmates.

My husband's grandparents were German Baptist on both sides of his family. When Willmar, my husband's grandfather, was born, the Austin family adopted him. They took him in and raised him with their own children and they had four or five or six.

My husband's family life was not great either, and when he was about twelve he went to work for Howard Bowman, who was a German Baptist neighbor with a dairy farm. He worked for Howard and John Bowman until he was about twenty-three or twenty-four years old, at which point we had got married and had two small children. He bought half of the farm from Howard then. So Howard and John took my husband in as a preteen and he did sometimes live with them. They didn't adopt him or anything like that, but when his parents would go through a really, really rough time my husband would live with Howard and his wife. And so while Howard is only twelve or so years older than Terry, he's more like a father figure or an uncle or something. So they work very well together. Their situation has worked out pretty good. It's not usual for someone who's not German Baptist to be in business with a German Baptist person. We encounter surprise at that quite a lot when we talk about that.

Farming today is not just about food, clothing, and shelter for you and your family. It's about making money. It's about a living. It has to be a business. You have to make wise business decisions for it to work. I think the small family farm is—I don't know that I really want to say, it's on its way out—but a person asks me how many cows do you milk and I say eighty. And they say, "Wow, that's a lot of cows." But that's small. That's a really small farm comparatively today. The big corporate farms in Florida, and California, and other places out West, are in thousands of cows, and eighty is not very many compared to that.

We don't have hired help at our farm. It's a full-time job for my husband and his partner. It's interesting to find out what people's ideas about farming are. Some people find out that my husband and I have a farm and they say, "Oh, that is so much work." And it's not nearly as much work as it used to be. Seasonally, it is. You put in long, long hours, and it's just stressful work because you're under the pressure to get all your corn planted by a certain time. You have to get all your hay done before it rains. Get all this stuff done. Then my husband had somebody say to him one time, "What else do you do? That's not a full-time job." I think he probably wanted to punch him. People's ideas about farming are pretty mixed up sometimes.

It's changing. I'm married to a farmer and I work on a farm. So, farming is a pretty big part of my perspective, the people I associate with, the people I know, and my day-to-day viewings. But then when I look at my children, in high school, their friends are fascinated with it. They have friends who want to come over and go to the barn. They're like, "This is so cool." They're so full of questions and interest about this because they've not encountered it. Most of my younger daughters' friends live at Smith Mountain Lake. Most of them were not raised in this county and their parents were not either so farming is entirely new to them. They've come from various points north.

We have neighbors who are from Connecticut who are friends of ours. They owned a landscaping business up there and just wanted to get out of the city. Their perspective was that the Smith Mountain Lake area was not far different from Bridgeport, Connecticut. But they liked the area surrounding the lake and so they live real near me right now. They have land over on the Wirtz road and they plan to build a house, but they are waiting to see what I-73 is going to do before they actually start on that.

I think the Interstate coming through is going to have a pretty big impact on farming in this community. It's scheduled to go across the backside of our farm. I would just as soon it had taken my house. I don't want to live in sight of an Interstate. That's not to say I won't. You know, I'll either move away or I'll adapt, but it'll change things.

I think that kids today are completely out of touch about where their food comes from. I get groups who come and we look in the pig pen at the [Blue Ridge Institute] farm museum. When I'm doing the animal part of the tour I ask kids, "What do you think we have oxen for?" or "What do you think we have pigs for and why?" There will be whole groups of kids who have no clue what a pig is. They like bacon. They like sausage. They all raise their hands. "Yes, I like pork chops and ham." These are little kids. They have no clue. They might know that milk comes from a cow and eggs come from a chicken, but that's pretty much it. Maybe that's not fair because I remember the first year that my daughter found out that Thanksgiving turkey was actually a living animal; she wouldn't eat turkey that year. She was four or five years old. So that's just developmentally where they are.

A friend and neighbor of mine is the youngest son of a German Baptist man who farmed but by the time he reached the point that he wanted to get into farming his father was no longer operating his dairy. This guy worked for a number of years at Franklin Welding gathering information about farming. He renovated his father's buildings, leased the farm from his father, and began farming there. And he's made very wise decisions. It's so easy for a young man to start farming and get too

Grand opening sign at a new waterfront development on Smith Mountain Lake in Franklin County. Photograph by Rob Amberg.

overwhelmed by big new equipment and this wonderful stuff. Boys don't outgrow their love for big equipment. They can get in over their heads pretty quickly because of that. That hasn't happened to my friend. He appears to be doing very well with his farm right now. It can be done. Just like my husband buying in on the farm that we own. If you find somebody who wants to sell gradually to a younger person, it can happen.

German Baptists may be in farming because you don't have to deal with the outside world so much. You are your own boss. Also, the non-Brethren farming community is very much aware of the German Baptists and their customs and their way of doing things. So to continue being a farmer they don't have to face strangers, people who don't know their background and their customs.

A large number of German Baptist people have computers now. The church has ruled that they should not have Internet access and they do not have sound cards in their computers but they do have computers and they do have e-mail. My mother was in the grocery store just a couple of days ago and they gave her a promotional thing with Internet, the CDs with so many free minutes of Internet, and she got like four of them with the amount of groceries she bought. She was quite excited and was like, "Do you want these? You can have these. It says free." I have my Internet connection through the college so I really didn't have a use for them. She said, "Well, I'll just hang onto them. Somebody will come along that can use them." She laid them to the side and is going to keep them. They adapt. They adapt to the change just like everybody and the ones who see the changes coming too fast tend to be the ones who move away.

I have a cousin who is a minister in the Georgia congregation and things are simpler for them down there. It's much more rural than even what we have. My husband has a cousin who married a farmer whose family moved to Wisconsin. They're pretty conservative. The ones who tend to go off to these more secluded places are the more conservative ones.

If a young man wants to farm and his father farms, okay. As long as the two people who are trying to farm together can communicate with each other honestly and openly that works. Now I see communication problems and this is not just a German Baptist thing. This is a rural farming problem. I don't see farm families communicating with each other very well. My husband had to say to the guy he worked for, "I can't work for you for the rest of my life. I have to have something, an investment. I have to either go somewhere where I can make more money, or I have to buy in on this farm, and it's your choice. Which one do you want me to do?" And basically that's what almost always happens. It's not sit down and discuss in advance, saying, "Well, okay, when you're ready we'll draw the papers up and you'll buy half of this." But it's usually the young person that forces the issue. That's sad and I see that as a large reason for the failure of the family farm: the communication patterns. Now I'm a woman and I think communication is very, very important. A lot of men don't see it as that big a deal. But I see that as being a really big thing with rural people and German Baptist farmers.

Joel Jamison

A City Set on a Hill

Joel Jamison, an octogenarian, is a German Baptist minister like his younger brother Loyd. He lives, along with his companion, as the German Baptists refer to their spouses, on a knoll surrounded on every side by the Blue Ridge Mountains. Below their simple brick house is the dairy barn. From his yard he can see three of his children's homes. Though the house is small, the "gathering room" entered through the front door is large and furnished to allow fifteen or more people to sit in around the perimeter. Having no television, the room is laid out to foster conversation. Slightly off to the side of this room is the kitchen and dining area. The table is large and expandable to accommodate a dozen or more. Though the home is ranch-style, invented for a nuclear family, the Brethren have modified the style for community gatherings, a holdover from the era when they met for worship only in homes. In this living room, in June 2001, Joel talked with a deep reverence for his church and its history, how the members make decisions about lifestyle, and how livelihood relates to theology. After we talked, he took me to the old site of the Carolina Road, now preserved in a park, where we walked together for a half hour or more.

Joel speaks of separation from the world in the context of rural life. He weaves farming into the historical theology of the Brethren, including their stance as conscientious objectors. He helps us understand the Divide of 1881, and the reasons there are two main denominations stemming from the Brethren tradition and how the German Baptists interpret their maintenance of the Old Order in light of societal changes today. As a longtime delegate to Annual Conference, Joel explains both how decisions are made and how interstate travel to such conventions plays a role in keeping the brotherhood united. We begin with his response to my question about why the Old German Baptist Brethren and the Church of the Brethren are two denominations.

There were several things that were brought in that the old German Baptist Brethren didn't feel were according to the Bible. Well, they was a transgression of the scriptures. For example, you would probably think Sunday School is a great thing but there's nothing in the Bible that says we should have Sunday School. We feel like that's a man-made institution so we are opposed to Sunday School. We feel that the parents are supposed to teach the children and bring them up in the nourishment of the Lord like the scriptures teach. Prayer meetings or revival meetings and church-sponsored colleges and this type of things, we as the old German Baptist didn't feel that this was going to be good for the church.

Back there at some point in time, they established the uniform that both the brethren and the sisters wear. And this uniform was designed for specific purposes, one for identity and another to be modest and not reveal the shape of the body. And so that's one of the main reasons why we try to hold on to what we have had is both for identity and to have a modest uniform.

The Progressive Brethren wanted to move forward. I guess it was said in history that if they wanted to gain the world they had to be more like the world. So they laid down some of their self-denying principles. We put a good bit of stress on nonconformity and of course they have lost all of their identity, as far as dress. They dress like the world and they accept divorces in their churches. Some still believe in nonresistance and do not go to war. They are conscientious objectors. But as a rule I think their church has pretty much laid down most of those principles.

Back in the Revolutionary War and the Civil War, I have heard that some of the old Brethren just hid. Just didn't make themselves available. And I've heard how the officer would come, would hunt for them, and couldn't find them. Some of them were caught and put in prison. I had two great-uncles who were drafted in World War I and they saw it pretty rough. They didn't accept a [military] uniform. By being firm in their belief, this established—along with our Brethren and Mennonites and Amish and other nonresistant principle churches—the liberty that religious objectors now enjoy. And because those old Brethren were able and willing to stand and suffer for us, we never had to suffer for that. In World War II they had CCC [Civilian Conservation Corps] camps. They put the Brethren out there and worked them, and they'd work for practically nothing. They just did forestry work and worked in hospitals. They might have been given $15 a month.

During World War II, I worked on a dairy farm and I had a 2C classification all the way through the war. A 2C was a farm deferment classification and I worked on a dairy farm. The war was over in 1945 and I worked there until 1952, until I thought I could start on my own. I really had a good man to work for.

One scripture here says you are supposed to love your enemies. Do violence to no man. Christ said, "My kingdom is not of this world." He said, "If my kingdom were of this world then would my servants fight." Then he said, "My kingdom is not of this world." We're not supposed to do harm to our fellow man. The Bible actually says, "Thou shalt not kill." And it all fits right together.

Our Brethren has pretty much tried to hold on to agriculture and carpentry. Those have been our two main occupations. Generally speaking, with some exceptions, they like to be more rural and more out in the country. We feel like we can maintain our nonconformity a little better by being more rural than Brethren being in the city. Maybe older folks, once they retire from the farm life, move into town and just have a house and lot. But generally speaking, we live out in the country.

Joel Jamison's vegetable garden on his dairy farm near Rocky Mount, Virginia. Photograph by the author.

The church decides the issues. I mean, there's no bishop or no elder or nobody who makes decisions on their own. We have council. We put it before the brotherhood. As of now each district sends two delegates or two messengers to the Annual Conference. Then on a Monday all of these messengers come together, which is usually somewhere between 100 and 105, and they vote by voice on twelve Brethren to form what we call the Standing Committee.

If I'm a delegate or a messenger and if Pigg River happens to have a question that they want answered at this council, I turn this over to the Standing Committee. Then that Standing Committee takes these papers and they open them all up and lay them out. They try to come up with a biblical answer to this question. For most of these questions you don't have any specific word in the Bible saying exactly how it should be. And so we try to use the tenor of the scripture to answer these questions. Sometimes there's quite a bit of discussion, sometimes not very much. And sometimes we can come to an agreement and pass it. And sometimes if we can't come to a conclusion we'll defer it for one year and then reconsider it next year. If it's only two or three objecting, they usually go ahead and pass it, but they like to have as near a unanimous agreement as they possibly can. And the sisters don't voice, it's just brethren. The sisters sit on one side of the tent and the brethren on the other side.

I like farming. I can be with the family, bring them up and try to be with them more. I can be my own boss and have my own business. I can let the children grow up right here on the farm and teach them to work and labor. Before I was married, my father had a peach orchard. I guess when I was first married I didn't hardly know what I wanted to do. So when I got married the first job I got was on a dairy farm and somehow or another, those old cows just kind of fascinated me. And I had a good man to work for and he taught me dairying and I really appreciated that. I used his teaching and we come through real good. The Lord has blessed us.

I still go down here and wash the dairy barn and the holding area for the boy. If he wants me to mow hay or something like that a day now or then, I'll help him do that and maybe plant a little corn for him, just little jobs on the farm and tractor driving mostly. And I have my daughter over here. She's a widow and so I kind of help her and we've got a little orchard over there and raise a little fruit for the families, so, we kind of help look after her and her needs over there, I think, between twenty and thirty acres over there, I guess.

There are some German Baptists who are working in factories now. It's getting to the place where can't hardly everybody be farmers anymore and neither can they all be carpenters. I've got a son and his boys help him. There's three of my grandsons that are doing carpentry work and that's worked out pretty good but they're not at home quite like they would be if they had a farm. And we do have a few Brethren that are in the cabinetmaking business now. They're building cabinets for people and they're doing real well with that. And then there's Franklin Welding down here that's owned by our Brethren. He started that thing by building wagons back there when people wanted a wagon. Rather than go buy a new wagon, he'd just make one. The man who's operating it now is the grandson of the old original Glen Boone that started it.

In farming, it's getting to where you either get bigger or you get out and that's the way the trend is. Generally speaking, we haven't tried to be real big. Now there's been a few farmers that have been fairly good size, but generally speaking we try to be a family operation as much as possible.

We know who controls the future. We also know that the Bible tells us that conditions in the world are going to get worse and worse. We know that and we know that as time goes on it's probably going to be harder to maintain the nonconformity and all that we try to maintain. And yet we know that this is getting down close to the end. The Bible plainly tells us that Christ is coming one of these days to get his church, his bride. It says, "Wherefore comfort one another with these words." So we believe that the time is coming. The Bible plainly tells us that nobody knows when the end time is, but it does tell us to be ready for such an hour as you think not the Son of Man cometh. I've read where the old Brethren thought a hundred years ago that surely the Lord would come anytime, but we know we're a hundred years closer now than we were back then. You're going to see some changes that are going to challenge our faith more than what they do now.

It's going to be harder for us to remain in separation. But the Bible plainly tells us that we will be as a city set on a hill. It can't be hid. Not that we want to show off or anything like that, but you can't be a light to the world if you're in darkness. You'd be surprised in traveling across the country, maybe in the areas where you had no idea that there would be anybody that would know you, there'll be people come up and ask you questions and they'll say, "My grandmother wore a dress just like you do." It's amazing how many people will come to you, want to ask you a question and talk about it. But generally when people see somebody dressed like we do they take for granted that we're Christians, that we try to live a life accepted of Christ, a Christ-like life.

In the Bible it says that, "All that will live godly in Christ Jesus shall suffer persecution." And I have tried to think about the persecution my father and my grandfather have had to encounter. We haven't had bodily or physical persecution, but I have come to the conclusion that we are living in the most deceptive of times. Maybe we've just got a different type of persecution than when the Brethren had physical persecution, and old Satan, he's going about seeking who he might devour and he's working pretty hard to cause us to lose faith or become disobedient and tempt us.

My grandfather used to preach that whenever Christ comes it will be in prosperous times. And you know the Bible says as it was in the days of Noah so shall it be also in the days of the coming of the Son of Man. They bought, they sold, they planted it, they built it, they were married and were given in marriage until Noah entered the ark and the flood come and destroyed them all. In this prosperous time we're busy buying, and selling, and building and everything is going so good that we get so busy with our natural things that we forget the spiritual. And I think this is where we can be deceived pretty quick.

Now we travel back and forth as a people. Our family members are getting companions from maybe Indiana, Ohio, California, or wherever.

But in this very vicinity I know of old men who just passed away not very long ago with three boys who married three sisters over here, the neighbor over here. They didn't go very far to get companions. So we see quite a change in that direction. We have members here in our district from Ohio now and West Virginia, California, Indiana, and North Carolina. That is a change that we see and it's not all bad. Might not all be exactly good because there are some customs in some faraway areas that might be a little different than what we've been used to here at Pigg River, but they usually come in and work together real good.

When I was young, they would go on trains to Annual Meetings. Just a few would go. Now the money's more affluent. Most of us children stayed home and took care of chores and maybe my dad and mama would go. I was ten years old before I ever attended an Annual Conference and that was in 1933 and then '45 was the next conference I attended. So we didn't go very much then, but the young folks now they've got money, they've got cars, and they go.

Billy Boone

We're in the Business of Raising Citizens

Billy Boone, in his mid-fifties, is an Old German Baptist Brethren minister in the Pigg River District. He is also part-owner of Franklin Welding, a Massey-Ferguson tractor sales and repair business specializing in dairy farming equipment. I interviewed Billy in May 2001 inside his business as welders hummed and mechanics banged hammers on metal in the background. He talked of why ideally German Baptist Brethren farmers are in the business of farming and of what might happen if farming ceases to be an option for them.

As a businessman, Billy Boone understands the capitalist trend toward ever greater concentration of ownership, both in his equipment business and in farming. He is realistic about changes on the horizon but talks about ways that local communities can prolong their cohesiveness and their rural emphasis. Boone articulates the meaning of the term "conservative" as the German Baptists see it. This concept includes nonconformity to mainstream society, honesty, hard work, commitment to one's neighbors, human-centered business practices, staying within one's means, and, above all, raising good citizens to be members of a community dedicated to right living while remaining apart from society's mainstream. As with other members, when the conversation turned to the looming Interstate 73, Boone spoke of its usefulness for traveling to see relatives and other German Baptist members. We're a "transit people," he says.

Across the United States, our membership is probably around 5,500. Having "Brethren" as part of our heritage and our background simply means that we commit our judgments of how we live our lives to our fellow members, our brethren. Throughout the nation we tend to settle in groups, although there's no rule to that. You can live anywhere you want to. Our church districts are the central places where we worship and that we go back and forth to regularly. Here in Virginia, there's four districts, three in Franklin County and one in Roanoke County. The membership is probably around eight hundred in Virginia.

We have plural ministry [more than one minister] called from the congregation through an election process. They are unpaid. Whenever the elders feel there is some need for a minister we will have an election. And so I was called in 1983. Being that position is not paid, we have to have other occupations. I was born into this one here at Franklin Welding and like it and have made a living at it.

We practice nonconformity. A lot of times people look at the German Baptists along with the Mennonites and the Amish and they strictly look at our garb, our dress, and say that that's our nonconformity. But our garb is just for identity. Our nonconformity reaches much deeper and we use the scriptures as the basis for our faith. We don't collect debts by the courts of the law. The way that affects us here, of course, is by our accounts receivable and how we do business. In the farm equipment business, we just have to be more careful—as we extend credit—that we deal with people that are going to pay. And if they don't, we just write it off and go forward.

Nonconformity is also practiced in the way of nonswearing. We don't take the Bible and use it as an oath. Our nonresistance, of course, also relates to nonconformity. We do not go to war against our fellow man, although we do strongly uphold the government. We believe that they are part of the whole scheme of God's plan, although we believe in strict separation of church and state. We would be nonresistant as far as going to war, yet we believe that the government has the authority to have protection. I think there's scriptural basis to maintain the peace within the nation and the world.

I am on the national nonresistant board. We have a national board of seven of us across the nation. Six of us meet every year and periodically we go to Washington and meet the conscientious objector officials. There's where we get our government-granted blessing of a nonre-sistant classification. Back in the 1960s and 1970s, in the Vietnam era, there were a lot of protestors who claimed that because they were against that particular war. I'd like to make it clear that there's a differ-ence between conscientiously objecting to war or just a particular war. You'll see that rise and fall according to the political scene and whatever the purposes of the wars are, if anybody knows what that is. We are non-resistant to all wars.

It's hard to say that we stay completely separate because we do live in the world. We live in the nation. We are involved in government day-to-day situations, but as far as voting? No, we do not vote. That's where I would count it a very hard decision to choose between the worst of two evils in the political field—most of the time that's what we've seen. You just pick this candidate because he's just not quite as bad as the other candidate. But we do support the government through prayer and we believe God sets up and takes down whosoever he pleases. He will. So we do not vote.

I think in traditional religious circles that are based on good morals and a family basis that we would all agree that a rural environment makes community prosper rather than the cities, though our cities all were built up from country people moving together. The climate of training our children to be good, honest citizens prospers better in the country. Let me say it this way. Though we lose sight of this many times, we're not in the business of raising milk. We're in the business of raising citizens and children. But in so doing we have to have the money to keep our livelihoods.

The German Baptist Brethren were just a small part of the whole population of farmers when we came to America. At the time every-body were farmers regardless of religion or community. Our heritage, if you go back far enough with any American, is rural farm people. That's where we all come from. Probably because the ones that came over in the beginning were seeking freedom to continue farming rather than moving to the cities and adjusting to that environment. The city folks probably wouldn't have been able to make it. The farmers do. The rural climate does make people healthy and fit to survive.

If you look at the history of farming, at one time it really wasn't a business or a career. Every family had a cow and a horse and pigs and chickens. I suppose as the Industrial Age came along folks moved toward the cities, toward those centers, and gave that up. But I think the biblical background kept some people from moving to the cities. So therefore they stayed in the country and then adjusted to that change in

Billy Boone looks up the price of a tractor part on the computer for one of his customers at his agricultural business in Rocky Mount, Virginia. Photograph by the author.

the rural environment. As electricity came, the telephone came, the automobile came, the need for a higher standard of living made the rural environment change. The marketing needs of the cities concentrated as they grew bigger. They had to be fed and so farming specialized. Either you were a dairy farmer or you raised hogs or you raised other food products, such as corn and beans, to fill that need. That's just natural. As the market develops someone provides that need.

Dairy as we know it today was not known in those days before the Industrial Age. You just had a cow and that cow produced milk and from that you got butter and cheese and that was all produced in the home. But as the need arose and the city folks did not want to do the butter making, then it started to specialize. The first thing that happened was that farmers took on more cows to provide their families' needs and to ship cream elsewhere. Later as the farms grew in animal numbers they decided that it was easier to milk more cows at a time. They shipped cream in those cans and then they started sending the whole milk. When the ten-gallon cans came in, they were put into larger containers and shipped to larger processing plants. Later on that volume got so great that they went to bulk tanks in the latter 1950s and early 1960s.

When I was a boy, we were in the milk tank business and we took the can coolers out, put the bulk tanks in. And that's still the way it's handled today. Trucks go in and draw the milk out of the bulk tanks rather than handling milk by hand in small containers.

With the government giving people forty-hour work weeks compared to a farmer that gets up at four o'clock and goes to bed at nine, many people just don't choose that lifestyle. Why is it changing? Well, the reason in my opinion is because in America we look at the price of food as a political football. Our food prices are politically held down for the American people. If you'll look at the amount of dollars that the American income spends on food, it's a small amount compared to what it is anywhere else in the world. Then our government subsidizes that. We keep prices low on the local market and that's the reason we have so many problems on the national or the world market. We are outpriced.

Somehow or another you're going to have to get the farm profits away from the whims of the political people and get them on a real level of what a gallon of milk is worth. In the rest of the modern world the people pay a high price for food. So we're in a losing situation as we continue to move toward the world market in farm products and the income is just not there to maintain a standard of living compared to other jobs. As our children get a higher level of education, they very seldom ever return to the farm because they've got to pay for their education some way and they can never do that with farm income.

I'm not against education but I am against a diploma without a standard of accomplishment. In America, someone decided that everybody needed an education. But we don't have an education. We just have the diplomas. In European countries you are a privileged individual if you get an education. So therefore their graduates are much more knowledgeable about what happens in the real world. But somehow or another we need to get our standards up to the point so that those education degrees mean something.

I can tell you right now with Case New Holland Farm Equipment, the second largest farm equipment business in the world, they will not hire you unless you've got certain degrees. Although the service rep that calls on us was hired probably fifteen to twenty years ago and doesn't have a college degree, he is the best rep and the most people-oriented person that you'll ever see. So, somewhere along we lost the value of experience versus educational requirements.

To go back to the question, why do German Baptist and other plain people like the rural environment? We have said that being a millionaire or Bill Gates is not really what we're in this world for. Yet in our society, everything is based on dollars. People come here looking for a job and the first thing they want know is, "How much am I going to get paid?" They're not concerned about whether they can perform. We gladly would train them if they would just have a desire to learn. But somewhere along that line our government says that regardless of anything there's a minimum wage that we have to start them out at. There's no standard saying you need to be able to read, you need to be able to write, you need to be able to comprehend, or even with a desire to learn. Everything is money based from CEOs to the bottom level. Too much focus has been placed on the dollar value of things rather than basic values. And that all relates back to, we're just in it for the short term. We're not looking at the long-term effect and how that affects marriages and family life in general.

A little history on the business: it was started way back in 1945 by four brothers. It started out when welding wasn't very popular, and then soon moved into farm equipment, which was a fast-growing need. We do not do any welding other than just repairs. We don't do any fabrication or any other type of welding other than just what relates to farm equipment. We supply modern farm equipment and technology to the farmers. Our main business is to dairy farmers. Tobacco is slowly losing its position. And beef cows. A very small bit of wheat or corn is grown as a grain.

I was born into the business. My father and his three brothers started this business. I'm here because I enjoy people. I learned the business. I like it. In the early 1960s, there was Anderson Farm Equipment, Clemons Tractor, us, and Angle Implement—five farm equipment businesses and each community around us had the same thing. Gretna had a couple of farm equipment businesses. Moneta had one. Floyd County had three or four. And they're all gone. Everybody's gone except the two here in Franklin County.

We've had some small start-ups. People have tried to get into business and it just was not profitable enough to keep them. It's gone. The other Franklin business is the John Deere dealer, Anderson Equipment. They are much, much larger. They go anywhere east of the Mississippi. We have just chosen to serve Franklin County and the surrounding counties. We get out a little farther once in a while, but basically our business comes from Franklin County and the surrounding counties it touches.

Is there a level of farming that's just right? I wouldn't say there is a right size, but how large a dairy is affects how much income is generated. Being a perfect dairy farmer is only going to produce so much income. I think the average number of dairy cows per farm in Franklin County is probably around 80 to 100 but we have a few that are in the 30- to 40-cow range up to our largest with around 800 animals. Whether the average is enough depends on how many family incomes there are that need to come out of that. A 40-cow dairy would not support more than one family with 3 or 4 children, and you'd have to be really good to do that. So, if you've got 2 families, or if a son marries and stays on that farm, then they're going to have to go up to 70 or 80 to be able to survive, to be able to pay the bills.

I would think it would be a good rule in any business or any family to avoid having much debt. And that's part of the major problem today that either the educated people are deceiving us or they don't know. If you'll look at the national figures you'll see that the American people have a lot of nice things, many nice homes and nice vehicles, but we owe somebody for them. And that's unhealthy under any circumstance.

You have to understand the thing that we're dealing with is, if I was just going to say one word, it would be pride. I've heard that the Amish man said to the other Amish man if you wash your buggy over ten minutes then it becomes pride. Well, that has to do with cars, or tractors, or whatever. But that is a basic principle that needs to be dealt with and I think it has affected the American people. And you have to have a new SUV and it's not based on whether you can afford it or not. We're living in a time not of manufacturing or engineering, but we're living in a time of marketing, and that's done in mass advertising. All you got to do is convince six million people that they need one of these things and then all of a sudden you've been a business success. That's what happened in Bill Gates's situation. He had a good product but that market has now began to level off and I'm not sure what it'll be next. But the market is not in milk and meat and pork. It's in all this other gadgetry.

In our situation we just don't want the things that the world has to offer us to take away the integrity of being honest and letting our word be our bond or to destroy what I said earlier, about raising men and women who will make the world better instead of worse. We have been concerned in our business here that integrity is no longer a requirement to do business. You've just got to be a better merchandiser, marketer. And for a company to tell me that he promises me that he's going to deliver me a product at a set amount of dollar that's no longer a question. It's whatever he wants to charge me once I get it and depends on how many pieces of paper I sign and how much the fine print is.

Our whole world system has changed. I'm fifty-two years old and I can barely remember the old system, but at one time credit was all done with a handshake and the guy that borrowed the money always made sure that he went back and paid that bill or he was railroaded out of town. He was a crook. Then the credit thing grew to where all businesses send statements. How many of us would feel that it's wrong not to pay a bill if a businessman didn't send us a bill? We go in and get the product. We sign the papers. If he fails to send us a bill, do we have a moral obligation to go back and pay that bill?

I can remember a farmer, a dairy farmer, coming in and saying, "Don't send me one of them duns." That was a slam on his integrity. He borrowed the money and what he was saying was, "I'll be back to pay you. Don't worry about sending me a bill." Well, that's all changed today. Now we say, if we don't get a bill we forget it. But do we owe it or do we not owe it? And that gets back to truth and honesty.

We still try to teach in the church that you are responsible. I believe that all of us are going to have to meet a Judge someday to find out whether we're responsible or not. In other words, the question I have been asked recently in messages is does society dictate right and wrong? Or does what society accepts really change what is right and wrong?

The loss of farms will continue. And the reason for that is technology. Service stations, grocery stores, or any other segment, requires less of us. Last year there were ten billion bushels of corn grown in the United States. That's enough corn for every living person in the world to have a bushel or thereabouts. And where it used to be 60 percent to 80 percent of our population raised food, now it's less than 2 percent. Technology has allowed that to happen. The scientifically altered seed, I know where we're going. They will be accepted a few years from now without any questions. I mean, really they are already. I'm not sure why they happen to be in the forefront of our minds today because tell me what a genetically altered seed is. Everything we have is hybrid. We don't have any pure seeds. The same with cloning, all these issues become current but they soon fade away. So do you hinder technology for a cause, or do you promote technology? I don't know.

There's not enough working people to handle enough cans to take the milk that is being produced and bring the cans out of those seventy-five or seventy-four dairies in Franklin County. Probably when we were using milk cans the average production per animal was around four thousand pounds annually. Just recently I saw we have animals here in the county producing 32,000 pounds per year. If you would have told your grandfather that one cow was going to produce that! Now we've got a surplus. So to say that we want to keep dairy farmers, that would be ideal, but what are you going to do with their product?

The real question concerning technology is how much will God allow to happen? I don't know. What is the moral issue? I don't know. I can remember talking to an old dairy farmer of our faith who said that he was one of the first ones in Franklin County to use artificial insemination instead of bulls and it was a big issue. Well, it's the same issue today and nobody questions it. That's what we're talking about. Genetically altered, or moving genes from one place to another—the question is, how much will God allow? In my ministry position and scriptural faith I don't really think it's how the seeds will be altered, but what it does to the person.

Technology has always affected us as German Baptists. There will be some who get all excited about technology and will feel that the world's going to end tomorrow and then when it doesn't happen they're so shocked that they'll wander away from us into different places. They probably never will be stable. The belief the Brethren have always taken is we don't want to be the first to take on technology, but when technology becomes an everyday accepted thing then you'll see the Brethren start to pick it up.

Back to the finances: whether a man is Brethren or whether he's Amish or whether he doesn't have any faith at all, you show me a guy that buys the first new anything and I'll show you a man that can't pay his bills. He's overextended on credit. Some of those things become everyday articles, but a lot of them just fade out by the wayside. Technology is very expensive, so it costs to be on the leading edge. You have the first new automobile in town I'll guarantee you paid at least $1,000 more than the guy that waited.

So how will it affect the Brethren? We've probably maintained about thirty to thirty-five Brethren families in the dairy business. So that's almost half of what dairy farms you've got in Franklin County. Ten years ago it wouldn't have been nowhere close to 50 percent. So maybe we're holding our own better than other people.

The very things that we probably would frown on, we reap the benefits of. For instance, right now in Franklin County the building industry is just booming because of Smith Mountain Lake. I have a relative who's in the contracting business. I can't get him to put a roof on my house because he's too busy building these $3,000,000 and $4,000,000 homes! That's just a house for one man and his wife, no children. I don't know why you'd want six bathrooms with two people, but that makes profit. We reap that benefit because of that.

Brethren on an average have more children. So if those thirty-three dairy farmers have an average of four boys or four children, just the law of averages is going to say that there's more who want to go into dairy, depending on how well the father and mother has promoted the dairy. I know church members and farmers and I think this would hold true in any business: if a father decided that he wanted to be a dairy farmer, then he needs to be a dairy farmer to the best of his ability and sell the idea of farming to his children by living happily in that environment. That'll do more for the son than saying that God wants all good people or all godly people to be farmers. That's a myth, anyway. If someone is a farmer just because Dad wanted them to be then he overstressed it somewhere along the line. And that would be true in this business. I'm here because I chose to be here. My dad told me that it was my decision. I had to live with whatever I chose.

The farms have never had to have a succession plan because they are guaranteed that that land can be sold for building lots. Now all of a sudden they've never had any money all down through their lives and they're multimillionaires. But if you take a family that's got four heirs and one of those chooses to be a farmer and the other three decide that they want the high dollars, then that is almost a guarantee that farm's not going to survive, because the one son cannot buy out the other three partners at building lot prices. There's no way he can pay for it and he couldn't live long enough to pay for it.

There is a program that guarantees that your farm will be in agriculture from now on. Whether that's a solution, I don't know. These decisions that we make that are going to last forever. I'm a little skeptical of them too.

Building I-73 will hasten what the lake started many years ago. The Brethren who want to stay in farming were there a long time before I-73 was ever dreamed of. But this will be the hastening of it. Is it good or bad? If we're going to continue to make automobiles, we got to have somewhere to put them. People base their decisions on how it affects them right now, but Dwight Eisenhower was a very wise man when he saw the need for an Interstate system. That doesn't affect the Amish people but does affect those of us that like to travel. I can remember going from Rocky Mount to Chambersburg, Pennsylvania, where I have quite a bit of family. That was back in the latter 1950s or 1960s. It was an eight-hour trip. Last week we made that same trip in about four hours and never had a stoplight, never got out of our vehicle from one end to the other. We're a transit people. You got to have roads to travel on. The roads are going to take up farmland, but then we don't really need the farmland to produce the food. I think the question is, is the world ever going to slow down? No, it's not going to.

We got millions of people moving from one place to another. They're going to have to have service stations and fast food. Do we like it? I'd rather see us travel slower. I think we're in too fast of a gear, but that's just part of it. I enjoy the climate control that we have. If it gets too hot, we turn the air conditioner on. What that does for us as people? It certainly doesn't make us stronger. It just makes us more dependent.

I can survive in this business in my environment. I have already made the decision. I have people calling every day that want to tell me how to get more efficient, how to better manage the assets that we have and I know the answer is you got to get bigger. You got to cover a bigger area. You got to have multiple stores. And that just speeds everything else up. I can survive. Can my son? No, he can't. Twenty years from now my $4,000,000 farm equipment store is like a twenty-cow dairy. I know that, but at the same time I'm comfortable with my standard of living and why do I want the headache of another fifteen to twenty employees? So, it all really comes down to: are you satisfied with your standard of living?

We talked earlier about the nonconformity and nonresistant belief that we have as Brethren. I'll say this about the rural people as clientele: they're good people to do business with. Is it changing? Yes, but it is still the cream of the crop when it comes to integrity, when it comes to doing business with a handshake. Sad to say as you move into cities it takes more legal documents that don't guarantee a thing. But our accounts receivable loss is very minimal. If you decide to walk across America and you need to stay all night somewhere besides a motel, your chances at a rural home would be a whole lot better than it would be at a city home. Why it's that way, I don't know, but that's just the way it is. I'd like to preserve it as long as I can, the rural dairy, family life, but at the same time it's probably a vanishing breed. We know that. Just prolong it as long as we can.

4 Community-Based Agriculture

Family farming is not enough. To survive as a farmer on a small scale, one needs not only family members, but also neighbors. Neighbors help with work, creative financing of farmland purchases, and collective purchasing power. They swap labor and equipment, help one another with repairs, tend to one another's farms when someone has to be away, respond to emergencies, and encourage one another with camaraderie and moral support. Though on some level farmers are competitors, they also rely on one another for their survival. In this chapter, four farmers tell their stories. We learn from each not only as an individual but also as part of a larger community of agriculture. Included are two German Baptists who grew up on farms, a farmer who lost his agricultural community in North Carolina and moved to Franklin County, and the only African American dairy farmer in the county. Each in his own way talks about his reliance on family as well as on neighbors and the broader community and what this means for farmers in the twenty-first century.

Henry Jamison

Our Doctrine Is Solid, but Farming Has Changed

Henry Jamison is a German Baptist Brethren member in his early forties with four children living at home. He and his wife Gloria run the farm. They also operate a catering business specializing in barbequed chicken to help pay the bills. Henry is the son of Loyd Jamison from chapter 3. According to Sue Puffenbarger, the county extension dairy agent whose story appears later in this book, Henry's farm is one of the most efficient in the county. It is also one of the smallest, with just fifty milking cows. We talked in the middle of hay season on a day when thunderstorms threatened to drown any hay he might cut. Henry talked of families, of receiving help from his father, and of his son's interest in farming today. He also explained how the community shares labor. By the end of our interview, the clouds had blown over and I left Henry preparing his tractor and "haybine" for a long evening in the field.

Henry talks of how he raises his children and understands the process of passing a farm down to his progeny, particularly regarding the fact that likely only one family could survive on his acreage. He is eloquent about shared labor, both its concept and its everyday practice. He is a strong believer in small farms and believes that if farms that milk as few as fifty cows as his does have the right structural breaks that they can compete favorably even with the largest agribusiness operations. He also defines by examples and by narrative what a family farm is.

We've been farming here about twenty years. I was twenty-one years old when we moved here, just a greenhorn, but willing to stick my neck out and learn. We started out leasing the property for eight years and buying the equipment and the cows from the former landowner. We tore the old house down that was here and built this new one back. We furnished the labor. Our Brethren worked together on that type of thing. The landowner furnished materials for the house.

You learn the hard way when you do it that way. It's been educational. It's been a challenge to me, but I enjoy that and then some. Just trying to take nothing and build something out of it. We worked on our notes and then in early '96 we got three paid off. So we tore down the old bank barn that was on the place and built some more modern facilities. That's been a challenge too. I think we anticipated about $100,000 to do the two barns, but it ran over about 35 percent. It's worked good for us, though. We've had good luck.

I had to do a lot of milking when I was home growing up. You kind of get burned out on it, especially as a teenage kid. Coming along, Daddy helped us. There was five of us boys. Daddy helped us all. Talked to older farmers who were probably thinking about getting out—went with us and helped us talk to them and see if there's any interest there to have a transferal of the dairy. At one time there was four of us that milked cows. There's still three of us with dairies. My older brother started out raising hogs in Pennsylvania. He married a girl from up there and he's into raising vegetables and fruit now—still farming.

I think our biggest challenge as a farm family these days is to make things interesting enough for our children. There's jobs out there that pay a lot more and they don't have the challenge or the stress involved. I mean, we're pretty much at the mercy of the weather here. The challenge is to instill in my children to accept the fact that you've got to rely on the weather or the Creator. Farms in this county have diminished so much in the last thirty years and, of course, urbanization is part of that. But I think a lot of it is that children from farms can go in construction or something like that and don't have to work the weekends and still make good money. They can make a living there.

My son says he's interested now, but I'm hoping that he will wait till he gets on older before making a decision. I'd like to be able to form a partnership in a few years. We'll get ready and kind of slow down and make a possibility for him. I don't want him thinking that's what he's got to do. I want him to be happy with what he does. At the same time he needs to understand what's involved too. I don't want to paint an all-rosy picture or else once he becomes a part of it he'll get discouraged and we'll have wasted five years. I think he's got a pretty good picture of it. He doesn't work with us on the financial part of it and probably the second challenge of farming today is making it all work, financially. We're not incorporated so we just sign a checkbook and keep our living expenses separated out for tax purposes. We'll pay the bills and if there's anything left we'll go to the grocery store. If not, we'll go to the fridge. We don't eat out a lot. We try to cut corners, to be conservative as much as possible.

We were raised up knowing that there's the possibility to farm. And that's one thing I'm grateful to Daddy for. He tried to teach us to work in the shop. I mean, don't get in the way, but whatever we set our mind to, do it. And that was a big plus for us. There are farmers who think that a challenge is just like a wall. They can't scale it. It's just too much. They just don't want to deal with it. You wonder if you're doing the right thing, but accepting the challenge is the part of farming that I reckon makes us farmers.

Communication on the farm is probably not always as open as it needs to be. My wife accuses me sometimes of not communicating enough and it's hard for me to be open. I mean, when I'm thinking about what corn I'm going to plant this evening and what I'm going to be doing tomorrow and I'm trying to do so much planning. So, you have to work on yourself to be able to think about what you need to talk to your children about. You kind of have to train yourself to be open and communicate. It's hard for me to be always thinking about what I need to talk about. I need to take time to tell the children what we're doing, and why we're doing it, and be able to instill it in them.

Probably what's going to happen when my son Chris gets into it is he's going to have to learn the hard way just like I did in order for it to stick with him. Life's hard lessons are better learned by experience. It's hard for me to slow down and say, "Chris, this is what we need to do, and this is how I normally do it." To work and be able to teach him at the same time is sometimes hard.

If Chris is interested in it, I would like to form a partnership with him, work together, and try to let him learn in a way that he has some experience in decision making and all and won't have to go green like I did. Of course, let me clarify that a little bit. We had Daddy and we could always call back when we were younger and ask any questions. I'd like to do the same thing here down the road. When I get ready to slow

Henry Jamison unclogs the automatic flushing system in his cattle barn. Though small, his operation is one of the most modern and efficient in the county. Photograph by Rob Amberg.

down a little more Chris will be at the age that he's ready to take on a little more. I would like to just slowly transfer everything. I really don't want to retire, to be honest about it. I look at it as I have spent twenty years here so far and why all of a sudden do I want to quit? Chris has probably got ideas of what he would like to see. But even though Chris might be the majority owner, I could still work here and enjoy the improvements and the ideas that I'll have formulated over the thirty, thirty-five, forty years. I would like to slow down probably at that age, but I don't think I want to fully walk away from it. I'd like to keep active enough to see what I spent practically my entire life building.

Daddy told us if he wanted to keep his boys in farming he knew he had to leave something to them, and so, he kind of semi-retired. He still comes around and helps us all, like when we're building a silo and planting corn. We need an extra hand sometimes. He's not able to do a lot of physical work anymore but he does a lot of our shelling for us in the fall. And that makes a big difference when you need an extra hand. While he's shelling I can be unloading trucks. Another thing about my children is I'm able to draw on how he handles turning over his farm to my youngest brother. I can't imagine seeing my son starting up on a farm. To realize that he could go bust or he could make it—I can't imagine what that would do to a parent for them to choose that situation and just to stand back and watch and see what happens.

I think I have learned that the hardest thing for a parent is to know when to let the children make the decisions on their own. In the early years we're trying to instruct them in the right way. But there comes a point when they're going to have to become their own person and make their own decisions, whether it is religiously, financially, or in the business world. That's what develops their character and their personality. It's been tough for us. Of course, Chris has spoiled us. I don't say this in a boasting way, but he's been an ideal son. We've had to do some correcting in him, but he reads a lot. He picks up a lot. He learns fast.

Why do I want my children to go into farming? Probably the lifestyle, that and the very fact that somebody's got to do it. In the last thirty years the farms have diminished. I think in the last thirty years we've lost like forty-some farms in the county. The number of families is still here, but if we keep going like this, there's not going to be any food in the grocery store anymore. The farmers are the only people that know how to do that, provide that. And there's a whole number of reasons why it's that way. You've got environmentalists, you've got regulations. Don't get me wrong. I think the environment is important.

Being good stewards of your farms is important, and I want to pass that on to my children. But I think people, the world at large, needs to understand what farming involves, and the time and money and responsibilities involved of farming, and realize that the grocery store is not where the food comes from. That is going to be our toughest point in the next ten years. Our virtues are still going to be the same regardless of who our neighbors are.

We milk about fifty cows and we farm roughly 130 acres. We're probably one of the smallest farms in the county as far as cow numbers. And what I'd like to do is maintain something small so that when our children come along they're able to take it on, so that it's not such a large thing that one of them can't purchase it and be able to run it. I think it is important that we, regardless of what we're doing, keep our priorities in line because we got our children to raise.

It's a family-size operation and if it gets so big that one individual can't take it, well, you have to have a partnership. A father-and-son partnership works okay, but as far as a partnership between two individuals, it hasn't always worked the best. Therefore, I'd like to keep it small enough so that one of my children can have it, that it is something he can take on and not be too large for him.

The dairy industry as a whole has become basically a science. I still feel like we have a lifestyle. You can make it what you want to. You've got to be home for the families. I can leave out of here now, say, the middle of the afternoon, go plant corn. Chris, he'll come in and milk. I can stay out and plant corn until 10:30 at night if it doesn't rain. Well, at 3:30 the children's going to be home from school. Supper's at 7:30. I think it's important that the family meets together at least once a day, because they need that togetherness. Your family needs to be together some, share meals and talk, to keep the communication open. I think it's a good style for the German Baptists.

But let's face it; it's probably no different than any other occupation you choose. Just because you're a farmer is not an indicator that you're going to have togetherness and everything is going to be perfect. Because regardless of what you choose to do, you have to work to make time to be together. Make time to talk and all these things.

We're not dealing with the public. In a way, I appreciate the fact that I don't have to. I enjoy talking to people, enjoy doing business with people. We write checks for monthly bills and I'll just take them around, make a circle through town and drop them off. That way you've got contact with who you do business with rather than just sticking them in the mail. I got that from my dad. That's the way he did it. So that's the way we do it. And whether it's important or not, I don't know. I like the feeling of a face and the people see who they're dealing with.

We still do a lot of work together, like when we're building a barn or a house. When we were trying to add a fence around a paddock out in the pasture yesterday, I couldn't do it by myself. I called a church brother of mine that I'd been over and helped. If somebody calls, I try to look at it as a lot of people have been good to me so I'll just drop and go. I called them and they came over yesterday evening and helped me string the barbed wire up and in just a matter of four to five hours we were done.

Anybody can call and we'll try to go help out. If somebody's building a new house, we'll go. I like to go help anybody and everybody. I think it gives us a sense of community to be able to work together like that, and it saves a tremendous amount of labor. It might not be as perfect as a carpenter would do it, but a lot of us have done it enough that it's kind of second nature to us. You know what goes up next and you know what to do next. To me it's a good feeling to be able to help somebody get something done.

Sometimes you'll let stuff go at home, but you try to look at it as an unselfish act. You've got plenty of time to do what's yours anyway. It's kind of a trade-off. You're just trading labor is what it amounts to. We built this house, which is roughly 30 x 40, and we had the foundation in and the subfloor down and we laid the foundation out of block. We had a crew that oversaw it and they laid the block for the foundation on one Saturday. We put the roof on the following Saturday. That's how swift it can go.

I've noticed that the large herds within our group of Brethren members will tend to get a lot of hired help from Mexicans. And they don't ever call you about working on a barn or something like that. So therefore the smaller farms keep this community together. The others do good—I don't want to take any credit away from them, like on a house working or something, you get a lot of shared help—but the farmers are the ones that share labor.

It goes without saying that urbanization and farming can't occupy the same place. Roanoke is spreading out all the time. There's only three or four farms left in the whole county of Roanoke as far as active dairy farms. I've got a brother-in-law that lives in Roanoke, but he farms in Franklin. He drives back and forth. Since there's not much farming in Roanoke County, you don't see as much working during the week, therefore the workings are mostly building houses on Saturday. But everybody just comes together.

A real good expression of that is our Annual Conference. That is a four-day meeting that assembles in a day and disassembles in two hours. It's a little more involved, like the rest rooms and the nursery are done ahead of time, but it's a tent meeting and the tents are erected and the seats are put in them in just a couple of hours. 1999 was the last time it was here in Virginia. It was over right behind the Peter's Creek meetinghouse and a lot of the comments were in the local paper that talked about the speed that it was erected and disassembled. It's really amazing how much it makes a difference with a lot of help.

With money there's all sorts of temptations—it affects our lifestyle. The better off we are the less dependent on each other we are. We've had Brethren farms that the Interstate's come through. They sold land close to the city limit. Took that and went across the Interstate to the opposite side and bought whole farms for the same money. My wife's grandmother in Roanoke, for example, had Interstate 81 go right through her farm. Route 419 dissected it the other way, putting all the land they had into four corners. Of course, they had to quit farming, but it put a lot of money in the bank, whatever that's worth. That brings a whole different set of problems. I don't know what the answer is other than just make the best of it and keep going.

Within the church there has been a falling away. Doctrine issues have been questioned. The authority of the church has been questioned. There were divisions, differences of opinion. There have been a lot of members that have left the Old German Baptist faith and have started other churches. Thirty members recently left and started their own group. It got to the point that some of these questioned the decisions of the Annual Meeting. They were starting to either determine alternatives to old German Baptist faith or trying to rationalize their own thinking against the decisions of the Annual Meeting. Then, of course, that couldn't be resolved. Instead of trying to bring themselves to the decisions of the Annual Meeting, they say, "I'm just going to go over here and start a group that thinks like I do."

Our ancestors needed each other back then. They didn't have access of going back and forth as much as we do now. And they didn't have the means either. As long as we need each other it is a blessing. And in that respect today, we still have that responsibility to maintain what they had even though we've got all this other stuff: the modern conveniences, the time on our hands, plenty of money. Just like out there yesterday. I could have hired fence builders to come built my fence. I could have done whatever I wanted to do. But I really didn't have the money to hire fence builders, plus I cherish the fellowship we have, too. I wonder sometimes if our well-being and our luxurious lifestyles are not a tribulation, a test for us.

What I'm saying is, as long as we're dependent on each other, I think we'll keep together. I don't want to say that farming is the only way to do that. But I think it can be as good as anything else we could choose to do. And there's none of us that I know of that like to take less than a day's pay for a day's work either. We like to make all we can, and I don't fault anybody for that. But making money leaves us in a responsible position and luxury might make it harder to keep the church together.

I feel that there is always going to be a need for the family farm. Whether I'm just hoping for the sake of hope I don't know, but what I'm saying is I think we're as practical or efficient as any of the big operations are. And if we can find a way to effectively pass it on to our posterity, to keep the farm in the family, I feel like there's possibilities there.

I'm not sure if farming is as important to German Baptist lifestyle as it used to be. It's not like our doctrine. Our doctrine is solid, but farming has changed. It's more technical now. There's more science to it. You get caught up in it and it's easy to be doing the details of the farming operation and forget the details of the family. We had a real good discussion here two weeks ago right after our love sessions on Sunday dinner. One of the Brethren said that once we recognize our need for Christ and join the church, everything else that we do, all of our families, our livelihoods, people we meet, our contact with other people, all that becomes spiritual. How we treat our cows, our families, all of this. How we do our business. This should all be governed by our belief. It's easier said than done, to be a Christian all week and not just on Sunday. It is easy on Monday morning, when the cows get out, to forget Sunday's sermon. I think that's a challenge today, whether we're farming or carpentering, to bring it in perspective so that we can serve in a way that's pleasing to God.

To me it's a big challenge to be able to focus on the things that matter, but also to focus on the science of dairy farming, on the details it takes to be efficient at it and be able to do a good job. We're commanded to provide for our own. That's scriptural. But we also need to realize our priorities and try to remain focused. I think that's the biggest challenge of the Brethren today, regardless of what we're doing. There are so many distractions.

The old Brethren would go to town on court day, one day a month. Now if we need something we can be in town in five or ten minutes. Some of our members have moved to Wisconsin or Washington State. They had a desire to get away from these heavy influences. And they've got a good situation. The district is thriving. There are a lot of strong members there. I see the Brethren doing that more in the future as urbanization creeps in. I've seen more of our members moving to these less populated areas like the West, the Midwest. I see more relocations coming, not so much as to get away from the world but just to get to where there ain't so many people.

We still need to educate the people that don't know where their food source is. We need to do whatever it takes to help people realize that the farms of America are providing the food for the world and somehow or another we have to keep them alive. Europe's been in two World Wars and those countries see what the farmer does, and they're more protective of them. The governments take care of them. We do need to realize how America eats. Americans need to be educated about what is good for the environment, good stewardship laws, and that farmers provide open spaces. There's a lot more talking going to be done, but there's a lot more work going to be done, too.

Robert Rutrough

Faith, Family, and Farming—
They're All Tied Together

German Baptist member Rob Rutrough, in his early thirties, lives with his wife Freda and their young children in their house on fifteen acres. He farms his retired father's dairy, located about a mile from his home. A former carpenter, Rob worked with his neighbors to build his house. In July 2002, when we met for this interview, the fields surrounding his home were filled with corn seven feet tall. The family lived literally inside a cornfield. From his back porch, however, it was possible to see beyond the fields to a row of new houses being built on the old Ikenberry place on the ridge above the farm. In this interview Rob talks about life as a beginning farmer and the hopes and challenges of starting out in dairying.

Rob, the youngest farmer I interviewed, gives us insights into why a young person, particularly a German Baptist member, would want to farm in the first place and why he continues despite hardships. He gives us intimate descriptions of what it is to live in close touch with cows and crops. As young people with little equity, Rob, his wife, and their children had to find creative means to enter farming, including living in one place and farming in another. By working with his brother, who happens to like crop work, Rob has made a successful and necessarily conservative start in a business some experts say cannot work.

There were eighty-five acres of this place. We rented after we were first married at an apartment nearby and were looking for land. There just didn't seem to be anything in this area that anybody was willing to sell that met our criteria. I wanted to stay near the farm there at Dad's because of working there. I was doing construction work during the day and helping on the farm in the morning, the evening, and at weekends. So we were looking for something within a mile or so. We looked at some places, couldn't find anything; then this place came up. Didn't have a wide enough right of way for development, it's just a twenty-five-foot right of way, so the land wasn't as strong. It was eighty-five acres, which was more than we could handle.

Finally my mother, who had inherited some land in Ohio, was able to sell that to her brother and they put that money toward this place and we were able to divide off fifteen acres off of that eighty-five. And that's really the only way that we got anything in this area. There's plenty of land owned by older people—I guess it'll be sold when they pass away—but there's not a lot of people out here looking to sell to a young couple.

I grew up on that place about a mile to the west of here. We spent a long time trying to decide whether we wanted to be involved in dairy or construction. It was just a hard call. But we finally went up the road here to a man whose place had been sitting idle for several years, talked to him, and worked out a five-year lease agreement. I was thinking that that would give me enough time to decide if this is what I wanted to do.

My younger brother and I bought a herd and started business on our own. But just before I went and talked to the owner he had made arrangements with his children that they would someday divide the farm between the four of them, so we knew when we went up there that there wouldn't be much chance of a long-term thing. But we were looking for a way to get on our feet and get some of our cattle and equipment paid for, and then decide what we wanted to do.

During this time Dad liquidated his herd and so the home farm didn't have any cattle on it. He kept his heifers, so it was a year before all of his cattle were gone. We knew there might be a possibility that we could move our farming operation back down there. We made these improvements, put a manure pit in, and were able to comply with environmental regulations better. My younger brother wasn't interested in the cattle part of the farm—he was more of an equipment operator—and at this time he is doing custom work. He's bought a chopper and got a couple of manure trucks and he does custom manure hauling and custom chopping. So he wasn't interested in operating a dairy. That basically left it wide open and Dad wanted me down there.

That's about as good an arrangement as you can get. If I didn't have my dad helping, I don't know where I'd be. Dad's been a tremendous help because he understands where we're coming from. He's still got his machinery and I'm not really interested in buying a lot of machinery because of margins what they are. So, that's kind of the way it worked. We're back down there leasing from Dad. Not all of the equipment is Dad's, but most of it is. Really, Dad'd be better off to move the stuff, to sell it, but he doesn't have any intentions of it and that's part of his way of helping me out.

It's hard to get somebody to understand farming. As I had my own family, there's a sense of belonging there, a sense of involvement. Farming's just different than bringing home a check at the end of the week and kicking up your feet and going back to work on Monday morning. There's a lot of stress because it's always there. You can't get away from it. If you go on vacation there's a possibility you're going to lose money while you're gone because something might happen to a cow; but there's still a satisfaction there of seeing a farm grow. I mean, when you can witness life from the beginning, like a new calf that for no reason that we can explain takes its first breath. You've also got death. I mean, you've done everything you can do and they die. With animals there's always a mini-picture of life. The same goes with the corn plant coming out of the ground.

Dad broke his leg in '82—fell off a hay wagon. I was driving the tractor, the hay wagon was full, he was on the front, and kicked a bail up and he reached for it. I pushed the clutch in to help him but I threw him off the wagon doing that, threw him off balance and he hit the bailer cage kicker cage and broke three ribs and the big bone in his ankle was coming out over the top of his shoe. And he was laid up for quite a while over that. But after that accident happened, us children—my sister would have been fifteen, my brother would have been nine, and I was twelve or thirteen—we ended up helping, getting more involved in the farm. I mean, we had to help Dad. It was a situation where Dad couldn't do it sometimes, so it took a little extra on our part. And even when I started working away, I felt obligated if there was something at home that needed to be done. I mean, you feel like you're part of the farm.

We're kind of in a halfway situation here because we don't live on the farm. It takes an effort to get the children to the farm and get the children back home. I mean, the farm and home are not the same place. But the children have responsibility. And that's something I see lacking now. There's so many children that don't have anything to do. Dad's gone and he'll be back this evening. Maybe Mom is too. I think children need responsibility. They need to feel like they can make a difference somewhere, even in their childhood years, that there is something to do. Life's not all play. I can remember at home, we had play time but we also had work time and there was a certain amount of things we were expected to do. We were a part of the whole that made the family work—that made life what it was. We were expected to take our place. And I think that's good for children to learn that they do belong. They're not just something that's stuck here in the way until they decide to go away from home.

Faith, family, and farming—they're all tied together. The faith and occupation could be linked together. I mean, God's here. This is evidence of the creation and we work, we touch it. It's just different to work hands-on with something that you have a responsibility to steward but you don't really make it go. I can't imagine how you can be actively involved in dairy farming and deny the existence of a Creator. In any kind of agriculture, you have to realize that you depend on something else. I mean, it gets dry, you got to have rain, and we're not the ones to make the decision whether or not it rains. It's a yielding to something higher.

When Dad sold out, it was tough. You maybe helped the calf into this world because she started to be born backwards or maybe she got sick and you've done everything you can to help and she grew up and is now part of the production. She's helping make the payments and stuff and then you just have to load her on a truck and don't know what's going to happen to her. I mean, it's hard to see it. They weren't my cows. I had my own farm but I about cried that day. I mean, it was just like selling part of the family.

There needs to be a pairing up of people who are no longer interested in continuing to farm and young people who are interested in an opportunity. But there have been some young farmers who weren't successful. So say a man's got everything paid for and some young guy's going to come in here. It's hard to shift everything over onto somebody else. I think the young people have to be careful. I think they really need to go into it slowly and listen to what somebody tells them about it, listen to somebody that's been there, because looking at the amount of

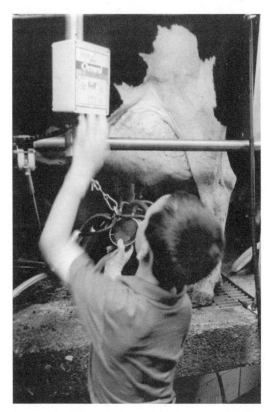

Rob Rutrough's oldest son helps out in the milking barn some afternoons. Here he places an automatic milker on a cow's udder and checks the electronic gauge indicating milk flow and pressure. Photograph by the author.

somebody's milk check is different than making a farm work. I mean, the margins are tight and you can't go out and spend a lot of money and make it work. It's just not going to happen.

Being conservative-natured to start with helps. I think you need a certain time-frame that you gradually work into it, instead of just going out here and borrowing a bunch of money and going full steam ahead because there's so much unforeseen out here, especially for somebody who's never done anything on their own. It's a business, and you've got your work that's got to be done. You've got things that you've got to notice that you've never had to look for anywhere else. They say it takes three to five years before things start smoothing out because there's just so many things that you've never been exposed to before. It takes time to get the knack of noticing things before they become a problem and fixing them early, specifically with the livestock. I can't go in somebody else's herd of cows and tell you what's out of place, but I can tell you when one of my cows comes into the parlor last when she's usually first. That is often a good indicator that something's wrong. And if I can treat her before she gets sick, it might make a difference in life and death. It might make a difference in calling a vet. And I can't afford not to catch problems ahead of time. That's what you can't run from.

There's some that say they want to work away to support the farm so they can continue to farm, or maybe start another line of business. With all due respect to those people, there's a certain amount of work that has to be done at the farm. If you're not there, it's going to have to be hired done because it's got to be done and why not pay the wages that you're going to put on somebody and support yourself and stay there because they don't have the concern. And again, not in every situation, but there's a chance they're not going to have the concern. They're not going to notice things like the one that's paying the bills. It's hard to hire that feeling into somebody.

Even here locally there's some tremendous cow people that can make things go, but I'm not interested in trying to search out those people. Basically, you're talking about riding around in a truck, managing farmworkers. You are no longer actively involved with the livestock. You're involved in making sure that people are doing their job taking care of the livestock. So you've just added another step to the process. And, personally, that's just not the way I want to operate.

You can't put someone on a farm and make them like it because the wage is usually not going to keep them there. And it's just different from an employee perspective than what I feel. I wouldn't want to be an employee on a dairy farm. You just don't have the same sense of belonging, the sense of making a difference. It may still be there, but if all I'm doing is making money I might as well be somewhere else making money and not be exposed to the hours and the constant responsibility that we deal with. I was reading recently, they were talking about operating dairies as a business, as strictly a business. It's kind of the shareholder attitude. You want the corporation to make money but the corporation will never be yours. It's just going to generate you something to live on. And that's fine, but that's not what I desire.

I would like to be debt-free and able to slow down. The big corporations talk about doubling their size every so many years to try to keep up. They want to keep putting out more and more and more and more product and there's never a satisfaction level. It's always something. And we all deal with that to a small degree. You've got to want to improve or you're not much of a businessperson but to me improvement is not necessarily iron-cast.

Who else in America has to continue to put out more and more and more and more? The guy working the forty-hour week might get overtime and work fifty hours, but they're not telling him in ten years he's got to work eighty hours. Why can't we reach a level that we can be satisfied? I think it's probably greed and also the attitude that you have to get bigger. That in itself is fueling this expansion, then flooding the marketplace, and it's just a vicious cycle. Keep in mind what's in it for the banker. They're wanting to loan money, so why not push expansion. They have to loan money to survive. But that way everything's got to belong to somebody else.

I think a lot of the older farmers that don't have somebody interested in taking over their farm are overly intimidated by the environmental issues. I think it's definitely something that we need to be concerned about, but I don't think we need to be overwhelmed by it. Somebody's going to have to work with them and I guess we just have to hope that somebody can make reasonable regulations that we can follow. Also, most nonfarmers have no idea what we're doing or why we're doing it, and all they know is what somebody's told them. And you take somebody like that and spread manure near their backyard and they just don't understand. I think the public has become more and more isolated from agriculture and it would be nice to see somebody giving tours or somehow welcoming the public. But with our schedules like they are there's just not a lot of spare time to tote people around the farm.

They just don't have any connection. Nobody in their family's in it anymore that they know. The older generation, at least the grandparents of those people, possibly the parents, were directly tied to agriculture. They knew where food came from. Now you see it on a truck or in a store and nobody thinks about how it gets there.

Like our Smith Mountain Lake down here, for example. Most anybody that's living down there or has a house down there has very little connection with anything we do. Anytime bacteria shows up down there or somebody says it shows up down there, they immediately think we're the ones that are the criminals behind it. I think agriculture is getting unfair blame for some of it because as they do TMDLs, Total Manageable Daily Loads, of coliform in the water, wildlife alone in a lot of areas puts it beyond what they have set as their threshold. So agriculture's not the one pushing it. I mean, if you would do away with every bit of agriculture in the county the bacteria would still be there, and that's why I say it's an unreasonable goal.

Farmers have a lot more concern for the environment than we get credit for. We can't afford to let our land wash down the river because what's washing away is your top layer that grows your crops. I think for the most part—and there are exceptions—we want to be good stewards. And we're going to do what it takes, within reasonable levels, to prevent pollution. We have a responsibility to take care of what we've been given. It's kind of like throwing trash out on the road. Nobody likes to see dirty roads, but I see people throw trash out all the time. If everyone would take care of their attitude, the whole picture's going to look better.

I think we'll see the day when development becomes more of a problem. There again, if people can just realize there's more to the country than open space. If the farmer can't afford to keep that space open, what else are you going to do with open space? I mean, farming is a way to utilize it. You could let it grow up with grass and trees and it would still be open space, but I don't think you can have that.

I would like to see a farmland preservation of some type where you could sell your development rights. I think that's really the only hope we have in an area like this for keeping it rural. I'll never buy land in this area to farm. I can't afford to. I like the sound of farmland preservation because that's the only protection I see that we have, and the farmer does get some compensation without having to turn it over to somebody that's going to split it up and put houses everywhere.

I'd rather see another farmer than ten houses. With farmers, there's a feeling of community there, there's an infrastructure. We've got a lot of veterinarians and different things it takes to support farms. In other rural areas, take northern New York, for example, they have beautiful country and cheap land, but they don't have any infrastructure. They don't have the feed store down the road; they don't have the veterinarian that can be there in thirty minutes. They don't have the milk hauler that's four miles away. And so it's hard to survive unless you're a megadairy that can generate all that off its own farm. It's hard to survive as a small farm in a place like that.

There's a feeling that somebody else is in this too. There's somebody that if I see him at the store and I've got a question or maybe just want to talk about what we're doing I can stop and talk. I mean, it's kind of a moral support group. It's a little bit like what makes a home. If you're there by yourself, it doesn't feel much like a home but when somebody else is there you feel like that's kind of what makes it.

It's all tied together. Just like I can't identify what makes me interested in being in dairy, I can't really identify how I'm going to instill that in my children, how I'm going to instill this sense of appreciation for the necessary things. It's hard to explain something you can't see.

Talking the talk is one thing, walking the walk is something else. I mean, it has to be a part of your life; it has to be within you. There's no such thing as a separation of your professed religion and your occupation. It's all got to work together. If it's really coming from within, it will work. Working with people's emotions is the easy way, but it's not always the lasting way. That would probably be the feeling of the Brethren. Let it come from within. A man who has a heart like he should have will show it in his life.

Farming is lot more quiet than some other professions. There's a lot more time to think, and maybe not as much time to pretend. I read a quote the other day, "People spend what they don't have to buy things they don't need to impress people that don't care." I think it's easy to get caught up in that. Our own life is our responsibility, not trying to impress somebody else, and trying just to be comfortable and satisfied. You go through life thinking something's got to be better than this and you never reach that feeling of contentment.

It's one thing to look at a new tractor and want one, but it's something else when your first payment comes in the middle of a tight time. I think there's still enough margin that a young fellow can make it if he can find a banker that will work with him. But he's going to have to do it without buying a lot of stuff and gradually work his way into it. Keep it simple.

As a young dairyman, I would like to see more of those interested be able to give it a try. If they can start into it without taking on a whole lot of debt, it's not impossible to give it up and go back to something else. For the most part, if you take care of the cattle you're going to get out of them as much as you pay for them, at least, so there's room for somebody if they can find somebody to work with. There's room for that. If people are willing to keep it simple and can work with a landowner and do without, I think it'll work.

James Cook

A Very Strong Sense of Community for Agriculture

James Cook and his wife are farm partners. While he does the field-work, she does the milking. In 1996, the couple moved their cattle and their entire farm business from near Charlotte, North Carolina, to Franklin County, Virginia. In part, their relocation was to avoid development pressures they faced from the recreational impoundment, Lake

Norman, near Charlotte. Now they find they have similar pressures from a rapidly developing Smith Mountain Lake in Franklin County. We talked just two weeks after the terrorist attacks of September 11, 2001. This event colored how James saw the future of the United States, but he remained an optimist. On the day we talked, James was cutting corn silage with his silage chopper. Two Latino men drove tractors hauling wagons of silage back and forth to the silo on the farm. He talked to me quickly between loads.

James has lived elsewhere and learned about Franklin County from afar. He chose to join the dairy-farming community in the county because he saw it as a vibrant and supportive place, different from where the Cook farm had been before. He talks about losing his farm to development near Charlotte and of his decision to move his cattle from one state to another. He talks about society's loss of appreciation for farms. James also discusses why he considers the German Baptists an essential part of the community he and his wife have chosen to locate their farm in. Yet, he also sees all too many signs that Franklin County could suffer the same fate as his previous location.

It's a 550-acre farming operation. We've got five hundred head of Holstein dairy cattle, two hundred and fifty milkers, and two hundred and fifty young cattle. We have four employees. My wife and myself also work full-time on the farm. The farm provides the sole livelihood for everyone who works on the farm and for their families, so we take our job seriously. Everyone understands that. People realize that the farm has to make it if they're going to make a living, so the employees have a little different attitude with that in mind.

We purchased this farm in 1996. We were originally from Mecklenburg County, North Carolina. Our farm was in the city limits of a little town called Huntersville, which is a suburb of Charlotte right off I-77. I've had ties in Franklin County since the mid-1970s. I'd served on the Cooperative Board of Directors, and its office was in Rocky Mount, Virginia. So for twenty years I visited this area and got to know a lot of the people through those contacts.

In my situation, I felt like I wanted to prepare my own path and I didn't want my path to be dictated by someone else. My choice was to relocate my whole farming operation in another community. After about a year and a half search through the three or four states in the eastern United States, we decided we'd call Franklin County, Virginia, home. So we moved our complete farming operation, our cattle, our equipment, all of our employees, everything we had on the farm. Even tore down seven or eight of the buildings, disassembled them with the help of friends and neighbors, and moved all that. Our farm was going to be utilized as a urbanization sprawl community, which it is today.

One thing I liked about Franklin County was its location in the state of Virginia. In North Carolina, we were in the rolling hills of the Appalachians similar to where we are in Franklin County. Soil types and the climates are very similar too. We're just a little bit later here. In the area where we were born and raised in the mid-1950s, they established a hydroelectric generating facility in the Catawba River basin that flooded our family farm. Our family moved a couple of miles away, and after that point, Lake Norman gave birth to growth in that part of North Carolina. Today, Lake Norman is a very prominent residential and recreational community, and I find myself in Franklin County, Virginia, with a lot of the same parallels. My farm is within a half a mile of the shore of Smith Mountain Lake, which also evolved from a hydroelectric generating plant off of the Roanoke River, with similar timing, in the early 1960s. The only difference I can see is that Smith Mountain Lake is in a more rural environment, Roanoke and Lynchburg being the nearest major cities, with nowhere near the fast growth area of Charlotte, Winston-Salem, and Hickory that perpetuated the tremendous growth pattern in Lake Norman.

Another thing that drew my attention to Franklin County, Virginia, was the immense agricultural community that Franklin possesses, not only with the farming community, but with the establishment of the Old Order German Baptist community. Within Franklin County about half of the dairy farmers and the farmers in the county are of the Old Order German Baptists. They possess a very strong community for agriculture, and they have also created some entities in the community that are vital to agriculture. We felt like down the road for a long period of time that community would be strong and we would be in a community where agriculture would have an important place within the area. Some of our major suppliers are Old Order–owned businesses. There's a tractor dealership, a dairy equipment dealership, and feed manufacturers. I felt like they would be in place as long as the community's in place.

Our society has got people thinking, play hard and work light. I think somewhere along the way that will create some hardships on the American people because they might have to sacrifice. It's hard for people to understand where their goods or services come from, and by and large the American farmers provide those goods and services at a very

An employee on a German Baptist farm carries a newborn calf to the barn for caretaking. Latino farmworkers are increasingly important on dairy farms, particularly as the farms increase in size and local labor grows scarce. Photograph by Rob Amberg.

cheap price for the consumer. Those days will not always be as they have been in the past, and I think what has taken place in the last couple of weeks [since September 11, 2001] is a testimony to that.

This region of Virginia is appealing to a lot of people, and people from the northern part of the country like to come to this region for retirement. They've got four distinct seasons of the year. They've got recreational activities. There are areas within the Smith Mountain Lake community that are catering directly to the retiree. They're coming in here excited, because it's so pleasant. But that pleasantry that we see with smiles on their faces is not always so pleasant once they get into our community and dictate increases in land values. Most of the farm community land being sold today is not going back to agriculture. It's going into other uses, residential or commercial. Investment people who've seen development in other regions of the country and made money know that this region is just on the break of dawn for growth and activity.

A lot of the farms in this area are century farms or several-generation farms and in order for them to continue it'll require some difficult decisions for those families to pass on that type of system.

Sure, the land values will be higher and the estate value will be higher. But one thing the government has done in the United States is increase the right to pass on properties due to a change of the state and federal tax laws. Farmers are able to maintain the farms as a unit and pass them on to the next generation without being charged the estate taxes due to the hardships of passing a farm from generation to generation. It used to be for estates of $500,000, and it's gone to a million. It sounds like a lot of money but a farm that's 250 acres that has dwellings and farm buildings and what not in this area can be valued at that level and it's still hard for a family to make a living at that.

If you're in an urban area, you're paying more of your fair share for the county tax revenues because you own more than an acre of land and a dwelling. They're basically taxing your property on a per acre basis plus some of your other assets that you have. So sometimes in a growth area like we were in, you're paying an extremely high amount of taxes, and sometimes that can be a burden. Particularly as you get older and your income and earning potential diminishes.

My goal was to continue a farming operation. I had to find the time and the energy and the ability to transfer an operation of magnitude from one locality to another and never miss a milking, never miss a crop, never miss anything. It takes a lot of planning. You have to plan a lot to milk the cows this morning, move two hundred miles away, and milk in another location that night. The cows' lives are not disrupted except for that move just like you are when you go to visit your grandmother three hours away. I farmed in two locations for a year and physically did the work myself to prepare ahead to have feed available, the facilities ready, to be able to transfer the whole operation and do it in steps.

Every part of the country is facing the same situation: it's the flow of people out. Some of the most productive land is being taken away for urbanization, because it's got the best septic drain fills. Every house can have a sewage system. You've got water, and you cannot farm on property that does not have drainage and water. Plant life and animal life necessitates the need for water just as much as people do. So we're competing for the same land. The housing projects don't want to build on the mountainside, and you can't farm on the mountainside.

The farmer today is a highly skilled businessman. He wears about every hat possible. He has to be a banker because he deals in large sums of money on a daily basis. He has to be an investor because he's trying to invest those large sums of money to get the most return out of that money because every farming operation takes cash to operate. He has to be a veterinarian because if he's got animals, he's got to take care of them. If he's got machinery, he's got to be a mechanic because he has to be able to maintain and operate his machinery every day of the week, seven days a week of the year.

If he's got a family, he has to be providing for the family, be the man of the household or the woman of the household. There's a lot of women in agriculture, and they're just as important as anyone else. I've seen that there's an opportunity for women because of their skill, their dedication, and they're probably a little more dependable sometimes than the man is. Another thing in the farming business, the farmer has to be a negotiator because he's negotiating his goods, he's negotiating his services, and he's negotiating with his employees. He's doing all this on a daily basis and we can name a few more. Just one of those things alone is a lot, but the farmer wears many hats every day.

Irwin Ward

I Was Always Fascinated with Farming

Irwin Ward, forty years old in 2001, grows tobacco and rents a dairy near the Mountain View Old German Baptist Meeting House. The county's only African American dairy farmer, he was raised by his aunt and uncle who, along with other neighbors, helped him get started in farming near Rocky Mount. Today his home sits just over the hill from the Wal-Mart and he realizes that development pressure is bearing down on his community, too. Now he only rents a dairy barn and pastureland. He hopes for a government buyout of his tobacco poundage so he can use the money to make a down payment on a different farm farther from town. Yet prices for nonfarm uses are rapidly putting land out of reach of farmers, particularly those who say they are already heavily indebted like Irwin. After we talked, I rode with Irwin in his pickup over the mountain to the dairy he rents. On the way, we passed a number of houses being built on a farm he used to work, including one owned by his sister. Even with all this working against him, Irwin was optimistic, even jovial, about his life on the farm.

We learn here the challenges of buying land and paying for it with farm income, particularly for someone who starts with very little investment capital. Irwin talks of always wanting to farm, of knowing what he wanted to do as a boy, and of the challenges he faces trying to make his dream stay alive, particularly as real estate development continues to encroach near his farm. While Irwin is committed to staying in farming, he also describes just how difficult it is for him to remain in business in an increasingly unprofitable and isolated community where there are few farmers and many newcomers. His reflections on family inheritance juxtaposed with the pressures of selling out are striking.

I was born in Pennsylvania at my aunt and uncle's place. And basically the farm I'm tending and some of the land I own or lease now is land that is actually on my aunt's side, but just through marriage. They've taught me a whole lot of good values. As a kid I was made to work on the farm and I don't regret it a bit. I'm really glad I was made to do it because as I got older I understood it more and I reckon I've done a decent enough job that they trust me with the farm they worked for years. It's a hard life but I enjoy it. You get into that mode where you're used to going all the time and I like to go and to be doing things.

When I finished school I was seventeen. And when I was sixteen I raised tobacco on about as good tobacco land as there is this far north. An elderly fellow had something like two acres and he asked me if I would help him raise it. He would supply everything and I would do the work. Oh man, sixteen years old back in 1979 and being able to make $2,000 or $3,000 clear money! Man, I was on top of the world. And I didn't even like tobacco.

I always liked milking cows. My uncle milked ten or fifteen cows and was selling C Grade milk and I always liked fooling with the cows and I always wanted to milk but I didn't want to ever fool with tobacco. But I raised tobacco that one year and I got hooked. I think the next year I raised it and a couple of years after that. Then he passed and I still actually raise that tobacco that he had. He never married and didn't have any kids and he just liked farming. He worked at J. P. Stevens fifty-three years. He was not a poor man. He had some extra money and he would do everything he could to see you succeed. He bought the farm, and I think it was about fifty acres of it, and he said, "Well, here it is. Do whatever you want to with it."

From the time I was big enough to know anything about it, I was always fascinated with farming. I always thought it was fun. It's a whole lot of hard work but it's still fun, just being outdoors, doing something different all the time. For me especially I reckon it was something or another for me and my soul to do.

In school, my goal was farming, and also the goal for a whole lot of my friends. A whole lot of them were working on farms at the time, even milking. Back in those days about the only place you could get a job was working either on a dairy farm or in tobacco. I had some close friends who raised twenty to forty acres of tobacco at a time. Back when we were in school if you raised that much tobacco that was a big crop. And they never started to school until they finished tobacco. I mean, it would be late September or October before they even came to school. And when they finished the crop up, then they would come to school and most of the time they'd have new pickups. And that's the time four-wheel drives got to be pretty popular. They would be able to buy a new four-wheel drive pickup on their share of that crop. The tobacco had helped the family grow.

I didn't like going to school. I was made to go, but now I'm glad. One thing that got me through school and graduated just when I turned seventeen was my mama, what I call my mama, my aunt anyway, was always telling me, "Well, you can't quit until you're sixteen anyway." That's what she always told me. She said, "You go on and study and when you turn sixteen you're about ready to come out anyway," which was very true. And I finished up and actually did right well in school.

The way my uncle told it, most of the land in this part of the county was owned by black people. They either farmed it or sharecropped. And, you know, if they had ten, fifteen, or twenty acres of land, and some of them had more, they got to thinking the city life was better than having to farm. Their parents did it, their grandparents did it, and they had to do it too, so it was better to leave the farms. They sold what land they had and moved to the city. My in-laws managed to keep their farmland, but a whole lot of people at that time sold theirs and moved to town and either worked in factories or something else that they could do. A whole lot of them moved north and some of them even went to the coal mines. From my understanding, a farmer didn't make that in those days. People said they raised a crop of tobacco and didn't even make their expenses. Only when government support came about did tobacco get to be profitable so you could make some money with it.

My uncle actually started selling milk in 1952, I believe it was. Whatever you got that morning you had to get to the processing plant that morning. They finally came along with the old ten-gallon can milk coolers and then went from that to put in a three hundred-gallon bulk tank. He milked in pails on up until then. I just helped do some of the fieldwork at the time. He put in a pipeline system when I was a freshman in high school. I expect he was close to sixty years old when he bought the new system. I watched him put it in and he said, "Well, Irwin, I'm going to have to get you to help milk now."

He was an elderly fellow and didn't catch on real fast. The salesman showed us how to sanitize it and wash it, but I think that my uncle was tricky. I think he knew what he was doing—that was a way to get me out helping him. That morning I got up about five o'clock and went out there to help him sanitize and ended up helping him milk and I've been milking cows every since. I milked cows for him for thirteen years before I owned any cows myself. I was planting his crops for him and I had some equipment. I'd bought a tractor and a chopper and I had a truck that I'd bought with tobacco money. With what little he paid me I was crazy to stay there, but it paid off in the long run.

After that he bought a few more cows. Also at the time he drove a school bus. He started driving the school bus the first year I went to school. So he drove the school bus and raised tobacco and milked cows and we did a little logging to create income. And that's how we got along through those years. I mean, thirty cows with two families living off of them, and selling C Grade milk, you would get nowhere fast.

At one time, everybody had a cow or two to milk and sold a little milk and raised an acre or two of tobacco. Some of them went to bulk tanks and milked a little after that and finally decided to get out or either got older and quit. But it got more modernized and things got tighter. In other words, when I first got in this thing I was told if you work hard and paid your bills you'd be all right. Now you've got to work hard and pay your bills and do a whole lot of management too.

Some farms are handed down from generation to generation. I had plenty of opportunity, but nothing has actually been given to me except for seed. We bought a farm about four years ago that had seventy acres in it, and like I say I'm heavily indebted, I mean heavily indebted. I'm not ashamed to tell you how much.

There were three black dairy farmers in this county at one time, up until a few years ago. And right now, as far as I know, my family and I are the only ones in the county. It got where we were the only ones left here shipping C Grade. It was getting tight where we weren't making any money, and come to find out, we remodeled this little stanchion barn for only $5,000. I mean that's all it cost me to upgrade. I didn't know any better. An individual loaned me the money to make that purchase and I paid him back in less than a year.

In the 1980s, the government had a buyout of dairy cattle. All the cows had to be branded and slaughtered. When you put your bid in you told how many milk cows you had, how many heifers you had, and all that. And if they accepted your bid, they started at the lowest bid and went up and I think it took something like three farms out of this county, might have been more. But they took the bids and they paid you for how much milk you could produce in five years. And you couldn't go back in the dairy business for five years and none of your farmland could be used. I mean, you couldn't house anybody else's heifers or nobody else could grow silage for other dairies on your farm. And that's when a few went out. And actually the number has been going down ever since. Dairies have been getting bigger and the cattle numbers stay the same. It's just the number of people operating dairies in the county that's been going down.

We had a Mexican fellow to help milk for four years and he found another job. Then found another who helped milk for two years and he went back home and I didn't have anybody milking. I'm milking sixty cows and raising tobacco and doing fieldwork and all that. My son fed the calves and my daughter helped do the milking night and morning until finally we got somebody to help. At that time I was working twenty hours a day on the farm. When that sun got going down, my eyes got to going together. I was scared to drive. I just dozed off. We got through that time and got somebody else to help milk.

I'm the type of person that if I can't do it right, I don't want to do it at all. I ain't saying I'm out for looks, but I get satisfaction in doing a good job at what I do. And most crops we grow most of the time are pretty decent. Our tobacco crop is most of the time as good as most anybody's around. And I take pride in doing that. If I want to plant something or another, and then it's got to take care of itself, I don't want to do that.

Just a hollering distance over there is some of the crop land where we raise tobacco. It adjoins Wal-Mart and they gave $25,000 an acre for that land. And the land that we got over there lays so good that it's just a matter of time before it's going to be bought for apartments and for whatever else.

On the east side of Rocky Mount, which is the Smith Mountain Lake area, I gradually see farming getting slimmer, like right around us here. If somebody comes by and offers some nephews and nieces $15,000 an acre and they didn't have to do anything for it and some don't really realize the value of owning, they might just sell it. I mean, they'd rather have the money and go on and enjoy life and be done with it. So that's the point where we're going to be in the future. Now me, I don't know. Would you take say $500,000? If I had that kind of money I don't think I'd be interested in farming. I mean, I enjoy farming. But if I had that kind of money, why would I want to invest it back in farming as risky a business as it is and then have to work sixteen-hour days most days?

Irwin Ward, Franklin County's only African American dairy farmer in 2001, drives by a house under construction on former farmland near the dairy he rents. Photograph by the author.

I think land needs to be set aside for farming in certain areas where farming is going on and people want to do it. In the United States, you can buy food cheaper, better-quality food, than anywhere in the world. And if you keep doing away with your farmers, you're going to be importing more food that ain't got restrictions about what pesticides they use on it. And there ain't going to be enough food to feed the people. That's the way I look at it. The world's getting more populated every day and more land is taken out of production for what I call growing houses.

They're selling land up around the Callaway area we call the dairy section. They've begun to develop pretty heavy in that area also, so ain't nowhere safe! I mean, if you're farming here and your neighbor over here's got a three hundred- to four hundred-acre farm and he says he doesn't want to farm anymore and his kids don't want to farm so he decides to sell it, they can develop that three hundred acres right there beside you. And when he sells it he can get $3,000 an acre. How many farmers want to take and spend a $1,000,000 on that three hundred acres of land joining them? Now if it was down reasonable in the $1,000 range, they would consider it. What I'm saying is if a farmer is in a farming community and wanted to buy a farm, it ought to be subsidized some kind of way where the fellow selling it can get his $1,000,000 and the other fellow can put up his $400,000 and get that particular farm. But it has to stay in farming and not be taken out. We're talking about getting money out of the government again, but that 300 acres will always be there for farming and we'll all have food for this country and other countries too.

5 *Adversity and Perseverance*

Though Franklin County is still rural and has more farms than any county in the southern Virginia Blue Ridge Mountains, agriculture there is in jeopardy, and so are its farmers. The pressure mounts from a variety of sources both local and national, even international, including the low prices farmers receive for their milk and other products, the rising costs of farming—which includes land costs influenced by the lake and other development—the extra psychological strain on people in debt, a proposed Interstate, and a general lack of understanding and support for farmers from nonfarming neighbors, both those who have recently moved into the county as well as those who make the laws in state capitals and in Washington, D.C. Another problem is the start-up costs that young people face when trying to take over a farm. And sometimes young people simply no longer want to milk cows, and that is true even of German Baptist youths.

One German Baptist family I talked with continue to live on their farm though none of their three children are interested in taking it over. Dean and Martha Taylor Bowman, talked with me at their picnic table outside their two-story farmhouse in August 2001. Dean is the youngest of six children. Since he was the last one at home, he inherited the family farm, as is "usually the way it works" among German Baptists, according to Dean. "In 1970 I began in partnership with my daddy after getting back from selective service," having declared himself a conscientious objector for religious reasons. He continued, "My daddy and I ran it as a partnership for five years. At that time I bought the rest of it." His parents continue to live just down the road.

"The 1970s were the best years I had," he says, "for more than one reason." First, the dairy business was very good during those years. Second, "I was in partnership with my father." After Dean and Martha bought the farm, his dad continued to help milk. Then, in 1976, Dean's father had a fall. "He had a night light on the side of the garage and lightning hit it. He went up and took it down. When he got it fixed and went up the ladder to put it up again, he forgot to turn the current off. When he touched the two wires together, it knocked him off the ladder and broke his skull and his hip . . . He didn't have any interest in milking anymore. He put one milker on one morning and that's about all he ever did after the accident. He went to town to get parts, but no more milking help."

Though Dean and Martha had built up a beautiful farm with Dean's parents, none of their children took an interest in dairy farming. "They didn't mind farm work," he says, "but they didn't care about cows. My feeling is if you don't care about cows, you won't make it in farming in this part of the country. The oldest son wanted to increase the herd and hire somebody else to milk, but I didn't want to. I'm not a personnel manager. We would have had to increase the herd, add more land, more crops, and more equipment, and so I wasn't interested." I asked him if the dairy had paid more, the children might have been interested. He replied, "You're onto something. That's probably true there."

"I decided if the boys weren't interested, then I wasn't either. We wanted to visit our oldest son's children in Ohio. So we decided to get rid of the cows. I didn't push my sons because I know if you're going to make a farm work, you've got to like it. I'll continue to rent the land to someone else for now. I've got no other plans. Somebody said, why don't you sell it, but I know what would happen if I did and I don't like to see that."

Dean and Martha Bowman continue to live on the beautiful rolling hills with their well-kept barns and outbuildings. All the grass is kept mown and the fences painted. It is an idyllic scene. All that is missing are the cows, and of course the farm income. This picture is repeated in numerous locations across the county as many farmers retire and have no one to replace them. Many farms like this appear to be in operation, but are in fact idle. Many are just waiting to be sold.

Farmers and their supporters in this chapter speak about the trials of farming and the adversity they face. They also speak of their willingness to persevere in spite of these hard times. Farmers must live with both pessimism and optimism, the result of the continual contradictions that accompany agriculture. Farmers keep breeding new milking heifers and keep up their farms, even when they do not know if their farms will be taken by development or by an impending Interstate highway. Farmers keep setting an example for their children, not knowing whether the children can ever be farmers.

The German Baptists who spoke with me were not openly worried about the Interstate. Instead, they talked generally about farming becoming too difficult for their members. They do not define themselves by a reference to their closeness to nature or any of the usual trappings nonfarmers assign to rural life. Rather, farming for the Brethren is about being physically close to multiple generations in their families, and living faithfully apart from the world. Though they guard against feeling any nostalgia for anything worldly and material, losing a farm must be as hard for the Brethren as it would be for anyone. What is remarkably unique about them, however, is their ability to remain steadfast in spite of this threat and faithful in the face of hardships, even losses.

Bruce Layman

All of a Sudden It Was Different

Bruce Layman, an Old German Baptist Brethren member in his thirties, once owned and operated a dairy farm. Under duress, he sold his farm in the early 1990s and bought half interest in the historic, Rocky Mount–based feed mill called Exchange Milling Company. A strong farm supporter, Bruce pondered during our interview how to create an economic environment conducive to farming even as he realized his own reasons for getting out were unavoidable. His story is particularly poignant because he put all he had into farming and received much encouragement from his community, only to undergo tremendous financial pressure and near emotional collapse from doing so. Now entering the feed business he has traded one form of stress for another. Here he talks of having to leave home early in the morning and returning late in the evening and of the trade-offs of working away from home in a nonfarm job. We talked in late September 2001, in the break room of the business as feed grinders hummed on the other side of the thin wall and the fine dust of grain wafted through the air around us.

I first started selling feed in '93, and at that time there were 124 dairies in Franklin County. There were about 11,108 cows. Then this one sold out, and that one sold out. I more or less thought, "He's been paid good anyway." I just sort of expected that. But after a while it got to be 99, 98, 97, instead of 127 dairies. Then it was eighty dairies. So then I said, "Wait a minute!" There are still pretty much all the cows, there's still 10,700 or so. We are still the second or third largest dairy county in the state.

Until they got to that point, the losses wouldn't bother us, because our feed tends to be a little higher-priced and we get a little better production. But in the last two years, the customers that are excellent managers, the customers that have been here for forty or fifty years, can't pay. They're old, they're getting ready to retire, and there's no problem with management and no problem with anything, no problem with our feed. There's nobody left to take over.

They couldn't afford to. The people who were raised on the farm have not had enough financial incentive to stay on the farm. It's just not there. The people that already own a farm and have got it paid for can make a living, but the guy trying to buy land now and buy everything that he has to buy, it's like he's crazy. And I don't know what the answers are.

When they built the Smith Mountain Dam, it did provide power, but it also provided a whole lot of shoreline for people to move in and build houses on. So people moved from New York and Chicago and New Jersey. They could sell the place up there, move to Franklin County, buy a tract of land on the lake, build a house, and put $1,000,000 in the bank, and they didn't have to do anything else.

So local people started getting more for their land, saying, "I'm going to ask for another $10,0000." That didn't slow them down, so they asked for another $10,000. Now they've got lots down there selling them for a $150,000, $200,000 for a lot on the lake. And they're just snatching them up.

As things progress along and land's sold all around it for a high price, then you start saying, what is this really worth? I mean, why do I need to be raising crops on this land and making $200 a year when I could sell it and make $20,000 on this acre of land? The problem is, after a while the $20,000 is gone. And you ain't got that land either.

Why am I selling feed instead of trying to promote a way of life that I see going down the tubes? I'm not farming. I'm selling feed to farmers. You can justify that by saying that's supporting our ag industry, but if everybody supported the ag industry, there would be no ag industry. Somebody actually has to do the work. But everybody can't be farmers either. The main thing I support is Exchange Milling. I mean, I've got to get a profit for this mill in order for this mill to stay here, so that profit is coming out of the people that I say I'm supporting.

But some of these farms now are struggling, I mean, for money. I know nobody's going hungry, but they can't pay the bills hardly and the more I think about that, how do we help them pay? Well, I could sell feed at cost, but that's not helping me and that's not really fair to everybody else.

I think we have to help them understand that farming is different now than it was thirty years ago, twenty years ago even. Back then, you could bank on milk prices going up every year. So what's happened is we've got a generation that grew up under steadily increasing milk prices. And so you just always thought, well, if milk was bringing $13, you can go to the bank and borrow money on $13 milk. You cannot do that now. Now, it's possible to be in the dairy business and make money, but you have to figure making money off of $10 milk or $11 milk and base your payments on that rather than $13, $14, or $15, because if you're at $15 and go to $13, you've lost money. And what happened was that generation of people, and wasn't any fault of theirs, when they had extra money, they had to spend it back into the farm to keep from paying it all to Uncle Sam. So as their children came on the scene, guess what? The bottom goes out in the milk price.

In the 1970s we started out milking cows. We started with one tractor and blade and a few pieces of equipment and a few cows. And as we got that paid for, we bought another piece of equipment to save taxes. We ventured into going from raising corn silage for forage to raising corn for grain. Grain is not a cash crop in Virginia. The Midwest cannot possibly raise corn for $2 a bushel but they do it regularly because of the government subsidies to the grain farmers. So what happens is we can buy corn here for $2.50 with the freight from the Midwest. All right, the grain farmer out there will make his money off the government. So we pay $2.50 here. It's ridiculous for us to pay $3 for corn that's raised right next door.

Before a lot of those support programs went into effect in the Midwest, the farmers here were milking cows and they got into raising grain. Put up grain bins, bought combines, bought trucks to haul their grain, bought haulers, and the boys my age were watching all of this. Boys love to get outside on the combine. And so what happens when Dad gets ready to retire, the boys buy him out. The land prices have gone up because of the lake. Because of the government subsidizing grain in the Midwest, it stayed the same. So now, you got a young man

that's following his dad at today's land prices. Plus, he's got to pay interest. Even if his dad might finance it, he still pays interest. So he's got
three things against him right there. Then, milk prices go haywire, and
every way you turn it's bam, bam, bam.

Another thing that's changed is the number of pounds of milk cows
give. In the 1970s, cows milked 45 pounds. Our daddies pretty much got
them to fifty-five pounds, and the boys went from 55 to 60 and 60 to 65.
But raising it ten more pounds to seventy-five is only for the over-
achievers, people who've got to topnotch management, and the will
power to push the cows as much as they can. Well, to get eighty pounds
of milk, you've got to be on the cutting edge.

Our [German Baptist] people as a whole tend to be more laid back.
We don't stay on the cutting edge. Now there have been some examples
of creative financing. In place of buying a whole chunk at one time,
maybe the farmer will just buy the milk cows and a few of the tractors.
The dad could finance that and pay for that, and then he can continue
using the other equipment, renting it or something, but he's not obligated if it's not making any money. There's a bit more of that going on
in the last few years.

When you ride down the road and see a silo and you see a painted
barn and see the grass all mowed and you see the fence all painted white
and it's beautiful, what you've got to remember is there's a guy who did
that. Now, the guy that's doing that farm, he's getting up at four o'clock
every morning and milking cows—every morning, Monday through
Sunday, the whole week long. And he milks them every evening at four
o'clock, because he's got to do that. He has to mow his hay when it's
time to mow. He has to plant his corn when it's time to plant corn. He
has to chop corn when it's time to chop corn. He has to watch his cows
till they come into heat so he can get them bred. He has to watch them
when they get sick. He has to keep his heifers. And at the same time
he's painting all this fence and mowing all his grass and painting the
barn. He works all the time.

I didn't grow up on a farm. I wasn't used to that. I'm lazy, I guess you
would say. I worked at Franklin Welder's from seven-thirty to five and
at five o'clock I got home, and we'd go fishing. We might have to mow
the yard one evening or might have to work in the garden one evening
but that was it.

When I got in the dairy business, all of a sudden it was different. I
was used to a much faster-paced lifestyle than what a dairy farmer is,
doing this, doing that, going here, going there, going fishing. All my
friends there were from farms, so I assumed that everything was just the

same. Well, they had to get their work done before they could go. Even German Baptists have to learn the mindset of what it takes to make it work.

Farming is one way of staying further away from the world. In other words, the way that we look at it is if you rub shoulders with the world sooner or later you're going to do some of the things the world does. I work in town and I see all these people in town. I get to know them, and I start thinking, well, what really is wrong with what I'm doing? But that ain't right. I have to be careful what I start justifying in my mind, because you can justify yourself right into pretty much whatever position you want to be in.

I've wondered really what my children are picking up, because Daddy goes to work at eight o'clock and comes home at five-thirty, six, and we go where we want to on the weekends. In other words, really, the only difference between us and most of the world is we dress a little bit different. And we don't have a TV, and we don't have a radio, but that's the only difference they can really see up front. But if I was farming, I'd stay a little bit further away from the world. It tends to preserve the flavor. I mean, it just makes it so that you're a little more close to each other if you're at home every day, and have all three meals together and you pray together at every meal.

The other thing is it seems houses grow up around our people and not just Old German Baptist but Mennonites, Amish, Quakers. Houses grow up around them. I feel like you wouldn't feel uncomfortable living beside Old German Baptists. You wouldn't be worried about somebody coming out and robbing you. You'd feel safe, and that's the way people feel around all these types of people. And so when they move out of the city, they see these people that look like religious people, and they say, "Look at this beautiful land right here, and these people. They ain't going to bother us. These are nice people. Let's move in here."

The future just doesn't look like it's good for the type of lifestyle we've been used to. That doesn't mean that we can't serve the Lord in a different lifestyle. I don't think we can do anything but adapt. There are already so many of us who are carpenters, electricians, and plumbers. We've already started going into all kinds of different avenues, and none of them's wrong. But you know, every time it happens, they weaken that picture a little bit. After a while it'll just be that these are a group of Old German Baptist Brethren, and there's two or three farmers there and the rest of the people will be working in town.

I've thought about that particularly because I just bought in to the feed business, and I owe quite a bit of money, and the farms are going away. I've got to pay that money some way. So I might have to get into some other business. I mean, I might have to buy bulldozers to put in the foundation for houses. I have to do whatever it takes to meet my obligations. I got away from farming, and I'm not blaming anybody, I'm just telling the facts.

My grandfather was a dairy farmer. My father worked as a book-keeper in a dairy farm. Now I am a partner in a feed mill. We're all tied to farming, but we have got two steps away from farming, you see, and my boys come along and they do whatever they do. We're three steps away from farming and as the next generation comes, we lose that farming heritage.

When you're on the farm, you are at work, and when something happens, you are the guy that has to figure out how to make it work. In other words, you have all the headaches. When I tried farming, if the fan belt came off and the water pump went bad, I had the headache of fixing the water pump and I had the headache of figuring out how to do the water pump plus doing everything else, way more than I ever dreamed it would be. What I'm saying is part of it was a mind thing, and you start worrying about things because you know the consequences.

Exchange Milling Company in Rocky Mount, Virginia, sells feeds and grain to local farmers. German Baptist member, Bruce Layman, is part-owner. Photograph by the author.

It's sort of like saying, if I don't turn the wheel, then I'm going over this cliff, but there's no option to turn the wheel! See, he's just going over a cliff. Those kinds of things got to me and they just piled up one on top of another and I got to where I couldn't handle it. I got to where I couldn't sleep. I'd wake up in the night sweating and thought I might have a nervous breakdown. I had a lot of verbal support from my family to stay in the dairy business. A lot of people come to me and were glad that I had decided to come out of the world, so to speak—out of public work and into farming.

I ain't never woke up in the middle of the night sweating like that before. I don't mean just sweating. I mean, the bed would be wet and I lost thirty-five pounds. I said, "This ain't worth it to me every night." They said, Well, you can take some medicine. I said, Yeah, but I didn't need to take a medicine before I starting to milking cows. So why do I need to take medicine now? I mean, I need to get rid of the cows and then if I need medicine, well, I'll get the medicine. And so, that's the way I did it.

I sold it to another boy. I just sold it for what I had in it. I told him if he'd pay me what I had in the cows and then the crops and everything, he could have it, and I'd give him the feed that was in the silo. He was a young guy, younger than me, and I warned him when he started. "Milk prices are bad right now," I said. "But they look like they're going to go up this fall."

So, I told the boy, "Whatever you do, don't spend this money. If you do, you're going to be in trouble." What happened is they were at $12 per hundred weight and they went all the way to $19. It's hard to understand what that really does to a milk check, but when you're shipping 100,000 pounds a month, you get $7,000 extra in your monthly check. It's like you got money. Man, I'm going to go buy a truck, I'm going to go buy something. But that money needs to be put away, because next year, it's going to be $12 and with $12 you've only got $200 left after you've finished paying your bills.

But he didn't come through. All he saw was the $7000, and so he put in a whole new milking system. He bought a hundred fifty horse-power tractor and a new skid loader, and then, he went and bought some more cows. The next year it went back to $12. And he couldn't make it. He stayed in three years, but he borrowed from Peter to pay Paul and he backed up. In the end, his daddy who had co-signed for him to get in to start with had to sell two hundred acres of the farm to pay off the debt. He was a German Baptist when he went in it. He went bankrupt, left the church, left his wife, and he lost everything. It's feast and famine and he wasn't ready for that $7,000.

The other problem is you've got two kinds of people. You've got the people like the farmer who went to New York [see Introduction] and no one knew where he was for two or three days. It bothered him bad enough that he couldn't stand it. He had to get away from it. And the other kind of guy says, "Oh well, so what," and he just keeps on going till somebody else shuts him down, till somebody forces his hand. But what happens so many times is the guy gets in bad shape, and he owes everybody around the table.

There's three or four vets in town. There's two or three farm equipment dealers. There's six or seven feed people that come into the count. We all stand around trying to figure out who's going to pull out first, and some new guy comes in, say, Purina. Well, they're nationwide and so they come in and sell some feed to this guy. Then, everybody else at the table is upset, and the reason is, they know that Purina doesn't know this guy. Purina doesn't know this situation, and so, what's going to happen is once the guy gets thirty days past due or sixty days past due, Purina's going to turn him over to the collection agency. They're going to start doing research and say, there ain't no way, and so, everybody at the table gets dumped on. As long as the farmer will stay in the community, they're okay.

I think the person closest to God that I can remember in the scripture was the thief on the cross. So he wasn't a farmer. I ain't saying we need to be thieves. I'm just saying that he guaranteed right there that he was going to be with him in paradise, and so, as far as to say a certain occupation is better than another one, I don't think you could back it up scripturally.

The family farm used to represent more of a community structure even among people who were not German Baptists. In other words, fifty years ago all the farmers in this area got together and thrashed wheat, and then they'd go in and sit down, and somebody would say the blessing, and they'd eat at that man's house, and maybe, none of them were Old German Baptists. They were just raised up to do those things. This morning, I went to work and didn't sit down and eat breakfast, didn't ask the blessing, and ate dinner (lunch) and did the same thing. And what I'm saying is my kids are going to start doing that, and it gets to be a habit. I don't think you're condemned to hell for not asking blessing. I'm just saying that that is one step, and then, after a while it's late eating supper, "Y'all go ahead and eat, I'll be on up there after a while." I've got caught up in the world enough that I went all day without ever returning thanks, and that is what we lost when we got away from the farm. That's a way of life, and you can't buy that with money. At the same time, we can't all farm, and so, that's the part we've got to guard against.

It would seem to me that if we want dairy farmers, we need to educate the children or encourage the children or show them there is real hope in the dairy industry. But there's no real hope in five hundred cows. I mean, you can't tell a guy out of high school who's eighteen years old and who's got $8,000 worth of savings, you need to borrow $4,000,000 and put down a five hundred-cow facility and milk five hundred cows. The guy's going to laugh. He'll say, "I'm out of here." But you show the guy that if you buy ten or fifteen cows and milk on them, and build your herd up, in ten years, you'd have $50,000 worth of cows. All of a sudden it is different.

Melvin Montgomery

In Corporate America, They Can't
Take Their Sons to Work

Melvin Montgomery, a dairy farmer in his fifties, is the son of German Baptist parents, though he is not Old Order himself. He is known in the community as a person who speaks his mind. Several farmers, including a few of his German Baptist neighbors, told me I had to go see Melvin. One reason is that he is an expert on the dairy industry, including such issues as milk orders for interstate marketing, the use of bovine growth hormone, and the Virginia Milk Commission. Quick to say he wants to farm and to have his son follow him, Melvin was also strongly opposed to giving up his development rights to the farm. In fact, he once had a surveyor mark off the land for a subdivision and then later decided against selling it, temporarily at least. We spoke on his front porch in August 2001 as yearling heifers grazed on the hill in front of his house. In his front yard among old cedar trees is an old cemetery containing the graves of ancestors who first farmed the land. Up the road are new houses overlooking his beautiful land.

Melvin describes the complexities of dairy marketing in simple terms, making clear that small farmers often take the brunt of governmental policies locally and nationally. He is able to keep a sense of humor, describing Interstate 73, development pressures on land prices,

dairy marketing, and other serious topics with a contagious wit. He is a
man who is able to speak his mind, often in blunt and biting tones, and
still have people laugh with him, despite the seriousness of his topic.

If we could have kept pace with the cost of living that the government gives everybody, you know, 3 percent, 5 percent a year, we'd be getting about 60 percent or 70 percent more for our milk than we are right now, and we wouldn't have this competition from the developers. It is not the roads and development who are putting us out of business. It's the cheap food policy.

Milk can go up three cents a gallon in the grocery store, and people will walk away and leave it. Beer can go up $2 a six-pack, and they'll take an extra one. And you know the problem with all of it is what I call the American Cheap Food Policy. My synopsis is the consumer has the right to steal food and that's about what they're doing. How much has milk gone up in the grocery store, and not only milk, how much have all these other things gone up in the grocery store in the last fifteen or twenty years?

Milk is the same price it was twenty years ago down on the farm. But that pickup out there has gone from $3,000 or $4,000 to $30,000 or $40,000 now. You used to buy a tractor for $8,000, $10,000. Now, they're $100,000. So the consumer's getting a good deal at the farmers' expense and the farmers are going out of business. These green spaces and the pretty green fields that we have are disappearing and the consumers are getting upset and they want to regulate that. They want to keep us, they want to keep these pretty green spaces, but they don't know how to do it.

Probably our biggest enemy is the tax structure. I'm not picking on anybody but the CEO of Norfolk & Southern or the congressman in Ohio can come out here and buy two hundred acres of land. He can buy a $100,000 tractor, he can buy a $30,000 round bailer and a haybine and a pickup truck and all that stuff, and he can write it right off his taxes, and it's called hobby farming. His taxes are basically the reason he has it. For every dollar he pays out, he ain't paying but fifty cents. And that guy is not feeding John Q. Public.

We've got big business guys around here that have come out of Roanoke and come out of Richmond and bought in and are milking six and seven hundred cows in the last five years. He's the guy who's putting five livelihoods out of business. He came out here and decided every dollar he spent is only going to cost fifty cents, because it keeps

Uncle Sam from getting the other fifty, and that's what he's doing. They've got it down so they can make so much per cow a year. And that'll service the debt and the feed and leave them 8 percent return on the investment. They're using somebody else's money, and they're not farming. They're managing people.

I've visited some big five thousand-cow herds in California and visited some in Florida, and they do a pretty good job. They've got enough people. They've got the people there who just milk cows. They've got people who feed pigs. They've got people who bed cows. They've got people who take care of sick cows, and they've got people who scrape manure, haul manure, and that kind of stuff. Well, we do all of that here. The ten thousand-cow dairy ain't no different from an assembly line at General Motors.

The only thing wrong with that is when you get 10,000 cows, you're putting manure in a lagoon out here that covers two or three acres. If you get a 10,000-cow dairy that has a 10 percent spill, that's equal to 10 of us dumping everything in the river every day. So your risk factors go sky high with the mega-dairies. Would you rather live in this community with ten 100-cow dairies or one 1,000-cow dairy?

I have a problem with the EPA because we're pointed out as being the problem. The only thing that's changed in numbers is people. There's ten times as many people in this county as there was fifty years ago. So where is the problem? The Roanoke sewage treatment plan last year dumped 173 million gallons of untreated sewage into the Roanoke River and it went right straight into Smith Mountain Lake. If every dairy farmer in Franklin County pushed every bit of his manure in the closest stream and it all went to Smith Mountain Lake, it wouldn't be 173 million gallons.

We want to do the best job we can. We don't want it to run off, we don't want to make a mess, because if I spill it out here in the road, I got to run through with it on my vehicle. I got to smell it in my house. And the more I can get on the field at the opportune time, the less fertilizer I'm going to have to put out that comes out of my back pocket. Absolutely, the farmers are the best stewards there are.

The whole problem is just like I told them at one of the EPA meetings. I said, "If you pay us for our milk, you wouldn't have to worry because we'd take care of it. If I was getting twice as much for my milk, hey, I'd be happy to put a buffer zone up. I'd have a paved road to my field. You wouldn't have to worry about erosion." But the money ain't there.

We've got 130 cows here on over four hundred acres. But if they come along and say, "We're sorry, we're going to put you out of business!" What do they think I'm going to do with this land? I put a plan together many years ago to build a road in here. And I can put in 335 houses on this same amount of land. Now, which would pollute the underground water and aboveground water the most? I told them at the EPA meeting, "If you can come here and shut me down, I'm not going to keep the pretty green fields for the people to ride down 116 and Peter's Pike Road to see. I'll put the houses in. The ground and surface water are going to be a whole lot worse off. We're going to have to build two more elementary schools right here in Burnt Chimney. You're going to have to build another fire station, another rescue squad. You're going to have more police officers. You're going to have to upgrade the roads. Now, what do you want?" I told the Board of Supervisors the same thing.

Dairying in the Southeast is different than it is in the Northeast or the West or the Midwest. Basically the concept in Virginia is we raise our forage and buy our grain trucked in, and we truck our milk to the market, 100, 200, 300 miles. In California where the big dairies are, they haul hay in from Idaho, which is 300, 400, or 500 miles there up the valley. And they haul the grain in, and they haul the milk. Their efficiency is in cow numbers, and they can compete well with us, because they've got one guy out there that's milking 300 cows a shift, and we milk 100. But as the fuel price goes up, that's going to kill that efficiency and it'll level the playing field a little bit. It's indirectly going to cost us all, but it's going to affect them more than it does us because we're a little more efficient and we're using less fuel.

Six years ago we had seventeen guys in the dairy business from Franklin County that graduated from Virginia Tech, and there's only four of them left in the business. And any of the guys that didn't go to Tech and were on the farm are still in business unless they just decided, heck, they were ready to quit. It's called experience. Here you've got to be able to identify sick cows. If the gate falls off the hinges, you've got to fix that. If you've got a calf that needs to be pulled, you've got to do that. If the truck runs out of fuel that you're feeding with, you've got to fix that. If you have a flat tire on the tractor, you've got to fix that. You don't have time to think twice. It's got to be almost automatic.

My parents are German Baptist and my wife was raised a German Baptist. They have a lot going for them. I mean, a lot of people perceive some of these notions that are a little strange, but we don't have a TV. We weren't raised with a TV and still don't have one. Really it's an insult to your intelligence. I mean, when you look at some of the commercials and some of the programs on TV, you don't have to wonder where all this violence comes from.

The German Baptists have their own little hot-line. If somebody's sick, the whole community knows about it in a little while, and they go in and do whatever they need to do. They're their own therapists, if you will, to an extent. And they still go by the old adage that you do an honest day's work for an honest day's pay. And that's the reason the guys in the cabinet business and the carpet business and that kind of stuff are successful.

They're good at whatever they do, farming, carpentry, whatever. But, what's happening in Franklin County is what's happening in Lancaster, Pennsylvania. They all can't farm so they're going into other walks of life, but they're not getting into corporate America no more than they have to and this is my opinion, but corporate America doesn't

German Baptist carpenter installs a door in a home on Smith Mountain Lake in Franklin County, Virginia. As farming has declined, many German Baptist men have turned to cabinetmaking and carpentry jobs. Photograph by Rob Amberg.

have the respect for family and family life that they do. When someone dies in a German Baptist community they're going to basically show up at the funeral whether it's immediate family or not. In corporate America, you don't get a day off to go to a funeral unless it's your own or your spouse or a child.

In corporate America, they can't take their sons along with them to work. A lot of these German Baptists in the carpentry business take their ten-year-old son with them and he's out there in the shade and if he can hand up 2 x 4s or if he can fetch them nails or bring the water, that's what he does. And when he's sixteen years old, he has more of a concept of how a house is built than a lot of forty-year-olds. He was there. He may have been out there under the tree playing in the shade but you bet your boots he was observing a whole lot of what was going on. Corporate America doesn't allow that.

You'll find kids in the German Baptist community mowing yards and working in the garden, and they're not getting an allowance except when they go to the table or go out to church on Sunday and somebody's home to visit. That's their pay. That's their allowance. It's a little different concept from giving the kid an allowance, and they sit in front of the TV. The Brethren kids are taught pretty early they're part of the show. This household runs for everybody. It's the whole family thing. You're part of it. You participate at your capacity. When you're four years old, you do this, and when you're eight years old, it's this, and you don't question it. As I look back, we worked hard, but I didn't consider it work then. I mean, that was just part of everyday life. We went out and bailed hay but when we got done, if we had time, before it was time to start milking, we'd go to the river and take a swim.

Franklin County is going to become a bedroom community. I-73 or no I-73, with Smith Mountain Lake here, Roanoke there, it's inevitable because they already filled up Roanoke County and Botetort County and it's coming to Franklin County. It's inevitable, and that's where it's going to put agriculture at a disadvantage, because you can't farm a $10,000 acre of land. And like I said, I-73 is not going to destroy as many farms as the cheap food policy. If the money was here, it's a good living—if you didn't have all of this pressure from all these outside forces. My old saying for a long time has been, "We're in the dairy business, but we're milking the wrong animal. We need to be milking these Yankees coming in!" When I meet somebody out here and they say, "Well, I'm so and so and I moved in here from New York or New Jersey," my first question is, "What brought you here?" It's the beautiful mountains, the wonderful climate, it's a little cold in the winter but it's nothing like the North, it's hot but not that hot in the summer, it's four hours from any-where. Four hours you can be in Washington, D.C., you can be at the beach, you can be in the mountains, you can be wherever. Low taxes, wonderful people. I get it over and over again. And we pick at them and give them a hard time. We call them "Damn Yankees" and say, "Why don't you go home?" And we say we're going to put a bus stop down there with one-way tickets, and you know, they just laugh and say, "Hey, we love it. This is a bargain." They sell a little hut in New Jersey for $500,000, come down here and buy a huge spread on Smith Moun-tain Lake and put money in the bank and love it. And I guess you can't really blame them, but why don't they go somewhere else? What's so special about this area? But it's about a fifty-mile radius in here that people are just swarming into.

Of course, they advertised Smith Mountain Lake a long ways around, and people come down here and they just love what they see. I mean, it's rolling, beautiful country. You get out on some of these mountains and the overlooks and these high ridges. It's beautiful coun-try, ain't no doubt about it, and for the most part, the people are just kind of laid back, the German Baptists, the easy-going, slow-paced, laid-back society. That's where they want to be. That's what happened to Lancaster, Pennsylvania. That's what happened in Holmes County, Ohio. That's what happened in Harrisonburg, Virginia, and we got the lake here on top of that.

The county administrator, he was standing right out there, leaned up against that cemetery fence about six years ago, and said, "We're working in the county on farmland preservation. We were thinking about paying the difference between land use and the value." They wanted to pay us the $600 difference. I said, "Thanks, but no thanks," not when they're selling lots up here for $22,000 an acre. For those two lots between here and the highway a guy paid $45,000 for two acres and three-tenths, cut it up, and put two houses on it, spec houses, and sold both of them before he finished them.

Hey, I'm dedicated to farming, but I ain't that dedicated. And where would they come up with the money to buy? I mean, you're talking about what, $15,000 an acre here? Say, it's an average of $10,000. To buy at $10,000 an acre all the cropland and farmland in the county, the tax would have to go up 2,000 percent. I said that ten years ago at a Board of Supervisors meeting. I said, "Y'all talking about the growth, and it's get-ting to me." I said, "What you need to do is put a $10,000 fine on it.

Anybody comes in the county, if they don't go out the other side, charge them $10,000 up front."

Jerry Anne Bier

The Whole Place Will Be Transformed

Jerry Anne Bier lives in a small, rustic house nestled at the foot of a mountain near Ferrum College, where her husband teaches. An avid environmentalist with a strong attachment to her community, Jerry Anne started an organization, Citizens Concerned About I-73. She has written numerous letters to the editors of area papers and organized her neighbors to speak out against the proposed highway. We talked about her motivations for action inside her quiet home, interrupted only occasionally by the shrieks of an orphaned baby squirrel that she fed periodically with an eyedropper.

Jerry Anne talks of the value of farmland to the county, the rural character that drew her and her husband to Franklin County. She argues that the county should be preserved as a unique agricultural community. As with many who oppose growth, Jerry Anne is passionate about her opposition to Wal-Mart shopping centers and similar developments that often overtake rural areas with little regard for tradition or the lay of the land. She and her organization strive to preserve the rural character by opposing the new Interstate and offering alternatives, such as making the current Route 220, already a four-lane highway, into a limited-access road.

The goal of Citizens Concerned About I-73 is to prevent an unnecessary road project, a real pork barrel activity, that would destroy the integrity of this community. I never thought much until maybe ten years ago about road building being an environmental issue. You drive down the roads and you appreciate the resource, and we do a lot of traveling. But I had been to a program in North Carolina and one of the issues was with how roads, unnecessary roads, really are kind of on the top of the list as far as damage to communities and to the environment and I started thinking about it.

The existing U.S. 220 can be upgraded to a safe and very functional highway. It's been known to have safety issues for years and years. There's been no response. They've done spot improvements, but that's all. So now in order to support the I-73 effort, the powers that be would say, "Well, safety on 220 is such an issue and economic development is such an issue that an Interstate is a way to solve it." And our contention is that neither of those two things are going to be served well by building a new Interstate. In fact, it's going to have such negative impacts on the whole character of life here.

The whole place will be transformed and the reason people live in Franklin County, come to Franklin County, cherish this area, will be gone, and it doesn't matter if you're in the path of the Interstate or not. You can be right next door, you can be on the other side of the county, but it'll change life here. We've done a lot of research. We've studied the Virginia Department of Transportation documents.

We say, don't build a new Interstate and destroy a whole community. There isn't justification. I just get so disturbed because it's very hard to convince people to study it hard enough to see what the report really says. It won't be an economic lifeline. It'll change things but it's not going to mean that everybody's going to have a great job and it's not going to offer them employment in meaningful ways. I think the basic question to me, and it's said over and over by citizens who've come to the public hearings, is, "Why don't we start with what we really want our community to be first and then ask, how do we get there?" Let's define what progress is.

There are a lot of people coming into this end of the county to escape, for peace of mind, for a good place to raise families, for that sense of serenity and security that just isn't available in a lot of places. And those are the folks who are in the hearing tapes, saying, "I came here," whether it's five years ago or whether it's twenty-five years ago, "because I thought this was a beautiful place to live. I feel safe. People are good neighbors. People are supportive. It has everything I need to live a good life." And what this road promises is nothing but the opposite: bringing in more people. Do we want more industry? What kind of jobs do we want? What kind of security do we want? Statistics do bear out that drug trafficking and crime follow Interstates. That whole sense of trust in the community will be lost. Sure, bad things happen here but you feel safe, you feel secure. I don't know where the keys to our house are. You go to any larger metropolitan area and there's always the tension, and you can live in this community and feel comfortable and appreciate things. So I think people who've come here from New Jersey will say, "Let me tell you what an Interstate will do to your community or at least what it did to mine. I lived in a farming community. Yes, New Jersey has farms and a farming community, and they said this Interstate was going to do this and this, and let me tell you what it did. You know my kids couldn't go out. It took me twice as long to get to

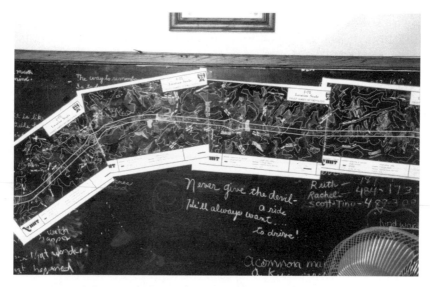

Maps of the proposed Interstate 73, a road whose swath would take farms and homes in the German Baptist farming community in Franklin County, taped on a chalkboard in a German Baptist kitchen. Photograph by the author.

work." And the list goes on, so you have people coming who have experienced something different.

It's so beautiful here. The natural landscape is just awesome. It's very nourishing. But even now at the Highway 220 interchanges it's already changing. You could be anywhere in the U.S., with Wal-Mart, Wendy's, Kroger's, all the Shoe Show and stoplights, the pavement, and there it is. For a stretch of a mile, you could be anywhere in the country, and it has no character. It has no individuality. It has no sense of community or anything. But that's what I see that comes with development if you're not careful, if you're not conscious, if you don't ask people what's important to them in the long term and respond to the average citizen and not just to the moneyed citizen.

The Interstate is a choice. Development's likely to happen, but an Interstate propels us, like whamo! It blasts us off into the atmosphere in a very singular direction. But what's in the community's best interests versus individual rights? There's a lot more discussion about that and we're hoping to get citizens educated to look beyond their own self-interest. Once the commitment to an Interstate is made, everybody zips into high gear, all the developers, the land speculators. There's no turning back. The Interstate just takes it out of proportion. It's out of whack. It's something like using a chain saw on the little toothpick or something, and that's not right because there are consequences. You're in deeper than you can get out.

The original concept of the Virginia Department of Transportation is of this being a high-priority corridor from Detroit to Charleston, and that's how it started in the federal legislation. One of the first documents we had, the mayor of Charleston declared that it'll never come there. So they changed their terminal to Myrtle Beach. In West Virginia, they were already constructing or looking at 52, the King Coal highway, and that would be Virginia's or West Virginia's stretch of I-73. That is being worked on, but it's not to Interstate standard, so it will not carry the I-73 shield, which is what we're proposing for 220. Michigan [meanwhile] has scrapped the idea. There was a citizen outcry, and they've put it away. Ohio doesn't have the money or the interest. North Carolina will say, "We have no plans. We haven't got it on the calendar on our long-range plan, but it'll be signed as 'Future 73,' so if we decide in the future to make it an Interstate, we can." So it's in limbo. Now, South Carolina is also not building, but I don't have the documentation that indicates what their status is or what their reason is. I imagine it's similar to Ohio. This isn't worth it. We don't have money. What's the point?

At all the meetings—and this is including the German Baptist community—there has been an excellent turnout. Visibly you can distinguish if they're Old Order. They don't speak publicly. But those who speak publicly are but a fraction of the comments that have been made about the road. I has a summary sheet with eight thousand comments. A number of them are from farm people. Mostly people have said, The quality of life here is important to me. They haven't really identified even what they do so much. They just say who they are, and they don't want it. Maybe five hundred came to the hearing in Rocky Mount. The whole middle school auditorium was packed and people were coming and going at it. They had about thirty-five speakers, and that's good for this community.

The German Baptists had a very subtle presence in the hearings. They were actively inquiring for information, studying the maps. I think there has been an awareness particularly in the Wirtz area, in Callaway too. But it's clear the German Baptists as an agricultural community care about the potential impact on them and their way of life. The opposition group has been aware of them but it's very difficult to connect with them because of their beliefs and because they do not participate in public life, and so it's hard. If people choose not to speak out publicly then you can't expect to utilize that sentiment in any way because that's not how the system works. It seems unfair in a sense that they would be so drastically affected. A friend of mine who's visited the Pigg River Church says, "You know, some of them really want I-73 because they think it'll give them a quicker way to get to Ohio, to visit communities there." I was quite taken aback. You have this expectation that they're all going to be in opposition.

But it's important to recognize there are different perspectives. What's important is how people form their opinions. Is it out of real information, or is it just a thought like, "Oh, it'll get us there quicker"? Will it really? Where's the balance? What will we be paying for it? People say, "Oh good, now I'll have a way to get to Myrtle Beach." But will getting that cost us in terms of our communities and the environment?

Mark Barnhardt

Trying to Stay in Business
as Long as We Can

Mark Barnhardt is in his mid-thirties and operates a seven hundred-cow dairy in Franklin County, along with his wife, semi-retired father, and full-time employees. It is the largest dairy in the county, perhaps in the Blue Ridge region. Mark and his wife live within a hundred yards of their large dairy barn in a cluster of houses and trailers where many of his employees also live. They had just recently had a new baby when we talked. This gave our talk of farm size, hired help, and particularly the future of agriculture a wholly different meaning. Though their farm is a corporation in terms of its fiscal structure, Mark convinced me that his farm operation is still part of his family structure in many ways. A number of Mark's neighbors strongly recommended that I talk with him. Rather than worrying about the size of his dairy, known as "Barny Bay," Mark's neighbors see his large cow numbers as a county asset helping them all. They worry that if, for some reason, he and his family and his employees cannot make it on his dairy, their loss would adversely affect all farms in the area.

Mark talks of his education at Virginia Tech and his decision to grow his farm into the sizeable operation it is today. He also discusses the hardships and rewards of working with a sizeable crew of employees, including newly arrived Latino workers. Mark is articulate regarding the challenge of having a large farm in a hilly place. His farm is already as big as it can get but he talks about whether even a farm of that size might fail to keep pace with economic trends, regardless of his good management abilities. Many believe that the Barny Bay is the linchpin in the county's dairy industry, and that whither it goes, go the rest of the farms. But then again, even Mark talks about the attractiveness of small operations with some wistfulness, though clearly downsizing is out of the question for him now.

My dad bought this place in 1952, and started off with about twenty cows milking. He built it up from scratch. There was an old farm house and that was the only structure here. He built everything else and it's just been growing ever since. We've maxed out. We've grown as large as we can get, and we've been there for six years now. We really don't feel like there's anyplace else to go. So we're kind of stuck at our situation right now. We're just trying to change and adapt and stay competitive and stay in business as long as we can.

Back in 1952, there were probably a half a dozen or more farms in this [immediate] area. Of course, everything was on such a small scale then, and since then, I'm sure that a lot of the smaller farms gave way to larger growth and that kind of thing. Right now, you're having the Midwest and Far West mega-dairies going up. They're transitioning from the seventy-five to a hundred-cow herd to a thousand plus-cow herd. That transition was going on to some degree even back in the 1950s, going from five to ten cows. Of course, a lot of people had hogs and poultry and were diversified, and they became more specialized over the years. So, cow numbers now are for the county as high as ever, maybe higher, but farm numbers are smaller than ever.

The technology and equipment have changed too. Now you have the capacity to farm larger acreage because you've got the equipment that can handle it. You can do it more efficiently too. There's no comparison to the way it was in 1952 or even in the 1960s. You can do two or three times the acreage in the same amount of time now that you could then. I would say that it would have a lot to do with your ability and your geographical limitations as to how big you can get. Some parts of the county have a good grade of land. Some parts of the county are more suitable for agricultural purposes than others, especially for tillage. We are at a disadvantage in that area because we do require a lot of acreage for the size herd we have, so we are spread out. We have land all over the county that we farm just because there hasn't been land available here close by. So we're required to go farther away to find the land we need.

This terrain also brings on growing environmental pressure. You can't go very far in this area without crossing several streams. We're now required to fence cattle out of creeks. And, of course, we have to apply manure on all of our land, so we're strictly regulated on our use of the land adjacent to streams because of manure running off and that kind of thing. So the general lay of the land and growing environmental pressure makes it real difficult to farm here. I'm not saying it's impossible. Of course, it depends on the current state of milk prices and how good things are going.

A low point was the year 2000. A lot of people went out of business when the price for milk dropped. There was a neighbor here that just went out, the guy that was farming right across the hill here. You see where that new house went up? We had another neighbor that sold out. A lot of those guys are close to retirement or are able to retire, and they've gotten to the point where new regulations, new restrictions, environmental pressure, and that kind of thing just made it so they couldn't justify making the changes that were required to stay in business. They just decided to get out.

Too small can be disadvantageous and too large can be disadvantageous, and that depends on your management skills and this and that, but when you get to a certain size, you've really got to have the ability to manage people, and you've got to have a good labor source. We've really struggled with labor for several years. Up until the past year or so, the national economy has been booming, and we just couldn't find help. So we were just scraping the bottom of the barrel. Then we decided to go with Hispanic help, and that's been a whole new revelation for us because we've got an unlimited source of labor now. But that doesn't come without its disadvantages.

A lot of people think that Mexicans will work for anything, but that's not true. They're very intelligent people. They have a good idea of what their time and what their level of skill is worth in this country. They make a big effort to try to get what they think they deserve. They don't see a lot of value in housing for some reason. We've always had our pay system set up so that if we have to provide housing for an employee, we have to deduct a certain amount from their hourly wage to allow for that, to make it equal to the people that we don't provide housing for. But the Mexicans don't understand that. At least, they don't appreciate the expense of housing.

There's a little bit of a communication problem with Hispanic help, of course, but for the most part, they all seem to have a real good work ethic, and they're very respectful. They won't look you in the eye, if you're in a position where you're the owner or you're a supervisor. They're very humble and respectful, and they make a good effort. They try to do things like you want them done. I think they see their opportunity here as a big chance and that they're fortunate to be able to have a life in this country outside of Mexico. I know living conditions in Mexico can be pretty bad, and so, in that respect, they're eager to learn, to do the right kinds of routines, and do the right stuff. For the most part, they do a pretty good job with it.

If we have a position that needs to be filled, usually all we have to do is make a suggestion, and they'll have a brother, a brother-in-law, or a nephew the next day. There's always somebody in the grapevine that will get the word and show up, and so it's kind of a relief to have that kind of backup. Then, the other challenge that comes along with that is to work between Hispanic and non-Hispanic help. That can be a big problem, and most other farmers that we know of have eventually gone to all-Hispanic help because they haven't been able to work out those differences. It's kind of hard to explain. I guess there are cultural differences that maybe Hispanics and non-Hispanics alike have a hard time understanding. There is just some jealousy there, especially for the non-Hispanics.

To be honest with you, we probably do tend to give them a little bit of a break because when we first started working with Hispanics, I used to try to put myself in their position. I was thinking if I was in Mexico working and I didn't understand the language or not very well, and I didn't know exactly what was going on, I would hope that whoever my boss was would have a little patience with me. I think that was interpreted by the non-Hispanics as preferential treatment, and so it's a hard thing to balance. There's still isolated cases of jealousy and mistrust from time to time. And there's probably a little bit of prejudice.

My dad is seventy-two and he's mostly the "gofer." He'll go and buy supplies that we need or whatever. Usually, I will go down first thing in the morning and meet with the herdsman David Cox; he and I have a real close relationship. He has as much or more responsibility than I do, to be honest with you, because he's responsible for all the dairy. He's got two other assistant herdsmen that work under him that he can shovel some responsibility off on to. He takes care of the cattle, the milking system, and more or less the employees involved specifically with that. We have two milkers on each shift, so we have four milkers in the course of the day. And then David looks after all of the reproductive records and milk records and everything that's involved with the cattle. That aspect of it is his responsibility. Then I focus more on crop work

and maintenance. There are probably a half dozen guys that work outside in that kind of work and so I supervise them. My wife does all the
paperwork, payroll, all of that.

Learning to be a manager is probably my biggest challenge and it's
still a learning process. I went to school at Tech, and we discussed some
labor management issues, but there was nothing there at the time that
really focused in-depth on dealing with people. I think when I was in
school, this mega-expansion mindset hadn't really kicked in. It was
probably on the verge at that time. That was back in the mid-1980s. I
graduated in '87 so it was kind of just pre-mega-expansion. In the Dairy
Science Department, most of the kids were representing seventy-five-
to a hundred-fifty cow dairies. I'm sure that they probably taught with
that mindset. That was the target audience. I don't think they really
were pointing you in the direction of a big operation.

I think farmers in this part of the country have a real tough road
ahead. I can't say that I've been too terribly optimistic for the past few
years, anyway. We're an old operation. We don't have a lot of room here
to make a lot of other changes, and our setup is outdated in a lot of different ways. I mean, we require a lot of labor for the amount of cows

*Mark Barnhardt, right, coaxes one of his cows to stand following an
operation by a local veterinarian, also pictured. Photograph by Rob
Amberg.*

that we milk, and there's just no way to get around that. But I think our biggest challenge is environmental right now because every year it seems like the EPA regulations get tighter and tighter and this watershed, the Black Water River Shed, is already above the state in terms of fecal coli bacteria in the water. So we're pretty closely regulated now and we're only beginning to get into that, and so it's looking to get a lot worse before it gets better. I think that is going to be a real challenge for a lot of people around here that have been around for a lot of years and have an old operation that maybe would require a lot of expense and a lot of change to meet these new regulations. We're talking about lagoons and new fences.

The dairy industry's definitely heading out west: California just exploded with new dairies and now they're the number one dairy state; New Mexico; I heard that South Dakota is providing some kind of a dairy incentive. These are huge ten thousand-cow herds. There are two big reasons for that: less population and less environmental impact in the sense that there's less rainfall. You don't have the streams there to deal with. Of course, their big disadvantage is the distance from population. So that's kind of a two-edged blade. You've got to truck all the milk to the East Coast, because that's where the market is. But you're away from all the people, so you don't have the big conflict. I think that's where the future of dairy will be for some time to come.

It makes sense if you've got a market on the East Coast to have your production as close to that market as you can have it so that it can be distributed more efficiently. This particular area has been a real good dairy county. It's second in the state but it's not real good in comparison to Rockbridge, the number one county. You just don't have the best-laying land. But I think the fact that we have a lot of farms has a lot to do with the long-term use of the agriculture land here.

Our farm is incorporated, so you can consider it a corporation, but one family owns all the stock in the corporation. How do you define a family farm? Does it refer to the people who work there? Or does it refer to the people who own it? Or does it refer to the working relationship between everybody that works here together? Or what? I really feel that we are a pretty tight group as a working unit, and we try to have some social events together. We'll have a cookout occasionally and get together and play some volleyball or do some activities together from time to time. I feel that we operate pretty much as a family. The herdsman lives in the house right here next door to me and we're right here on the place. We're on call twenty-four hours a day. I have a pager that I answer twenty-four hours a day. Everybody understands that I can be reached whenever needed. I'm sure that there's a dividing point. I'm sure that you get to the point where this place could be operated from an office, away from everybody else, and I'm sure that some people do. But I feel that we're a pretty tight group. There's not a single person down there that I can't call on. If they're off duty and I need them for something, there's not a single person down there that won't come give me a hand if I need it. So, I think we're as close to a family farm as we can be and not all be related.

Richard Jamison

I Don't Want to Be Negative, But We're Losing

Richard Jamison, the son of Loyd Jamison and a member of the Old German Baptist Brethren, started out in the late 1980s in partnership with his brother on their father's farm. Following three lean years, Richard left the farm and ventured into selling milking machines and other dairy equipment. His brother remained on the farm. Now in his early thirties, Richard is a friendly and articulate young man and, for those reasons, a good salesman. He travels all over the region and knows every farmer within several hours of his home. He sees those farms decreasing in number each year, however, and he knows why. We talked in August 2001 in the Jamison home that he and his fellow Brethren built on the corner of his family's land. His son mowed the yard on a riding mower as we talked, while two daughters helped their mother prepare garden vegetables and home canned goods for a supper of garden produce, homemade bread, and beef that we shared afterward.

Richard understands the intricacies of dairy management on dozens of farms. He speaks of the challenges of farmers as an insider and a roving sales representative who knows the latest inventions in the industry. Even as he encourages people to stay in the business of dairy farming, he looks at the business he runs and wonders whether he will have a clientele in the future, and whether if he had known when he first started what he knows now whether he would have ever begun. Even in this context, he is quite eloquent in describing the value of work for children and how he learned his own values of honesty and fairness from his experience in farming and through his faith.

I was raised on a dairy. Before I'd go to school each morning I had to get up and do chores and be back to the breakfast table in time to eat. We had a good old country breakfast by that time. Then I went off to school. After years of that I guess that's about all I knew. Then my dad had a few health problems. When he got to fifty-one years old, his arthritis was bad enough that he was ready to get out of the dairy business. There's five of us boys and we did the majority of the milking. Soon as we got to be twelve or thirteen years old, we'd milk cows. But his arthritis was acting up and he offered the farm to my younger brother and I. We're the youngest two—eighteen months' difference. And so he made us a deal for the farm equipment and the cows and the feed. We bought him out. That was in 1986.

1986 was a dry year, so we ended up having to buy a good bit of feed. We made expense, but it was kind of hard for us. We had a lot of help, including getting hay and corn donated from our Brethren from out in Ohio and Indiana. It was just coincidence, I reckon, but in 1987 we had a better year and they had a dry year. So we turned around and sent hay back out there for those guys. But that's kind of how our church works.

1986 to 1988 were the three years we farmed together, and it was hard for us to generate enough income to furnish both families with enough to live on because we were both just married. We were only taking home $500 apiece and we both had a child and were trying to make trailer house payments and buying the lot and stuff like that. We just couldn't do it. So we had to grow. We had to increase the herd. Well, we increased the herd up to 65 to 70 cows from 45 to 50.

But we're sitting right in here beside of the town of Rocky Mount. We're a mile out of the city limits and we just couldn't buy land. We finally came to the point that we figured there hardly wasn't enough here for two and one of us would move off. So for a whole year, 1988, I looked around at neighboring farms trying to see if there was one that I could lease or something. We could have two herds and share the same farm equipment to keep expenses down. While I was looking, we decided we needed a larger parlor down here to milk faster. We were milking four and five hours per milking twice a day. And so we pursued that and it just so happened that we asked Henry Fralin, who was the Serge Milking Equipment dealer, to put this barn in. He had one man working for him and that man was quitting at the end of the year. And so we got our parlor done on December 23, 1988, and that first year I started thinking in my mind, you know, that would be a pretty nice business to be in. We work with dairy farmers. We're always out on the dairy farms. Just about as close to dairy farming as you're going to get and not be a dairy farmer. So I went and talked to Henry and he offered me the business. He was sixty-two at that time. He was retiring in three years.

When I took over Mr. Fralin's business in 1992, there were 126 dairy farms in Franklin County and as we speak today it's in the upper seventies. That's how many we've lost. We lost 20 percent of our farms in Franklin County from January 2000 to today. Twenty percent!

We furnish milking equipment—the vacuum pump, the pipe, stainless steel pipe, the milk tanks—to the dairy farmer. We sell to about all of the Franklin County dairies. But we cover fifteen counties now, not just Franklin County. We even get three counties in the Greenbrier Valley of West Virginia and then all the counties that surround Franklin and a few to the west of us. It keeps us hopping.

In the 15 counties there's a total of around 210 dairies. In Franklin County we've got in the upper 70s. Then you take the other 14 counties and divide the other 140 into it. Then that drops the numbers per county on down, where you see an average of ten farms per county. Montgomery County is still a fairly good sized one, with about 30 dairies. Galax has got about 12 or 15. Floyd's got about 15 or 16. Then you're getting on down in single-digit dairies per county except for three counties over in the Greenbrier Valley in West Virginia. That's about how it stacks up.

Franklin County also is a conservative county. There are a lot of German Baptists. A lot of the farms that are left are German Baptist farms. And if you go to Harrisonburg, Virginia, you'll see the same thing with the Mennonites and Amish. The smaller farm is run by the conservative people. The great big mega-dairies are more investor-type dairy farms.

By conservative, I mean that the kids are held a little closer and they get a lot of labor from the children. That's how they can make it with 45 to 50 cows. Of course, a lot of the 45s and 50s have grown up to be 70- and 80-cow dairies now. They still get a lot of help from the children. The children help on the farm up till they're 16 or 18, when they're old enough to go out and seek occupations somewhere else if they want to. There are some circumstances where the kids want to farm, so a few family farms keep going because one of the children wants to farm.

Now I don't know how you teach children to want to work and want to be a dairy farmer because we lose a lot to the outside industry. We don't keep them all in dairy farms. It's probably impossible to do that. When I was growing up, I didn't have much choice. I had to go out there and do it. But really I have to appreciate that. That's what I try to teach our kids. We don't have a farm, but just like mowing the yard and stuff like that.

As a boy, as soon as we were able to put our feet on the brake pedals of those tractors we were wanting to drive them. That was just the drive in us. Of course, about all boys are that way. My boy's like that with the lawn mower. So, you just get that feel and you're out there and you hook the plow up to that tractor and you start plowing land. You just watch that, you know, God's creation, just watch it turn. It's amazing. It's just something that gets in your blood.

Sorry to say, farming is just going down. I don't want to be negative but we're losing. I gave you those numbers a while ago. If somebody would have told me in 1992 when I had 126, 128 dairies, that I'd been in the upper 70s in the year 2001 I don't know if I'd have bought the business. It's been good to me. It's still good today. The dairy numbers have gone down. The cow numbers per dairy have grown but we haven't kept all the cows here. We don't have as many cows in Franklin County now with 78 dairies as we did back in '92 with 128 farms. Of the 20 percent we lost last year I bet you only 5 percent of the cows stayed in Franklin County. In other words, in the last year and a half that 20 percent dairy loss has meant that 95 percent of the cows left here too.

One farmer in particular I can think of had two daughters. They both married young men in Roanoke. They both had good jobs, paying higher than farming did. So the farmer didn't have anybody to take over. Another farm that I remember going out was owned by a sixty-four-year-old man. He had a son on the farm but the son didn't like to milk. He didn't like to spend the time in the parlor. He liked to do the farming work and so the dad had to do the milking. Well, sixty-four years old, day in day out, morning and night, it wore him out. So he decided they would just raise feed for other farms and use the land. Since his son liked to run the tractors, he would just raise the feed for other farms and sell his cows. Out he goes. That was a year and a half ago. He had another son who was leasing a place somewhere else. He has come back home, brought his cows back home, and is renting his dad's place now. But we still lost that dairy. Our largest account was two brothers. They sold out in January 2000 and they were milking right at a thousand cows. Remember my percentages, 950 of the cows left here, probably fifty of them stayed in Franklin County. That was a big hit for us. They were young boys that took over their dad's operation and they had a lot of debt and debt just ate them up. They just couldn't swing it. So that's how those went. I can think of three more farmers that retired and nobody was there to take it over. And I can think of two more that went bankrupt. That's all in the year 2000. We lost fourteen dairies in the

Three Holstein heifers nearly ready to start their lives as milking cows on a farm in Franklin County. Photograph by Rob Amberg.

year 2000 right here in Franklin County. So that's how it's going. As development takes over, you can hardly blame a guy that's retired.

When I was a little boy, ten or twelve years old, we'd often hear preachers preach sermons on how the farm is a better place to raise kids because they're not exposed to all the stuff in town. It's just a better life out there. Of course, here I'm one of them. I was raised on a farm, but I've got my business in town now. And of course, it makes a difference.

It makes a difference on my kids because they go to school, they come home. We've got to find something on this little lot for them to do. We do raise a big garden and they help a lot in that. But on the farm we had to plow and we had to chop corn and plant corn and make hay. That's schooling you can't get anywhere else, if you follow what I'm saying. You watch these crops grow. You see that God's got a hand in it and that's the reason we raise a garden.

The kids don't like to pull weeds. They don't like to pick beans any better than we did back thirty years ago, but it teaches them. It teaches them a lot of values. It teaches them how to appreciate food and when they've got to sit there and shell beans out, when they dip out beans in their plate at suppertime they eat those beans. They don't throw them down the garbage disposal. That's the thing we're trying to teach.

Even as we speak today there's two robot milking systems going on in North America. None right here in my area, but there are going to be robot milkers and that's more farm labor that's got to go somewhere else to look for a job. This robot milker gets the cow in the habit of eating six times a day. Then the cow has to come up to this feed station to eat. She wears a transponder around her neck that IDs her. When she comes to this feed station to eat, the computer says, this cow has not been milked in the last six hours. So, while she's in there eating here comes this robot down. He's got heat sensors to find the teats and it pulls up under there. It milks that cow while she's eating. When her milk flow gets low, it retracts the milker. She's done. If she's done eating it turns her out and she goes on. They got forty or fifty of these robot milking systems over in Germany. But as far as technology, we've come from the late 1950s to the early 1960s with the old strap across your back with the bucket milker that you used to the milk from the cow and dumped it directly into the tank to the glass pipeline, to stainless steel pipelines, and now to robotic milkers. That's all in forty years.

We German Baptists want a simple life. If you get over in the cities and whatever it's just hustle and bustle all the time, a lot of lights. Of course lights catch everybody's eyes, even the German Baptist kids' eyes. They're drawn to lights, just like all the other kids. If you ever notice at a fair or carnival all the lights going around in a circle. You know what that's for, to bring them in. So we stay back here in the rural areas so we can have little better tabs on our kids. Keep them closer. Keep them where we want them. As a general rule, as a group of people we believe that agriculture, and even carpentry, is still a good lifestyle.

The farms are getting larger. Poultry and the hogs have gone corporate. We're told dairy is going to do the same thing. We'll just have to wait and see. Really it all depends on the milk prices. When the milk prices are headed down farmers are in despair and when the milk prices come up you can hardly tell because they don't say anything. It's just when they're not complaining, it's good, if you understand what I'm saying. That's kind of where we're at right now as we speak.

Of course, the reason I watch and I'm so concerned over milk prices is because it directly affects my business. When it comes time to replace an old twenty-year-old vacuum pump and the milk price is down they keep chugging that thing, pouring the oil in it or whatever it takes to keep it going. But when the milk price is up, they'll call in and say, "Well, you know that old vacuum pump is smoking a little bit and maybe it's time to update to a new pump." That's how business is when the milk prices are good. But it just seems like it is very unusual to hear of an optimist dairy farmer. All they are looking at is bills, bills, bills. You can about tell it when you go out there on the service call. If they're really upset because something broke down, you know they're in a bad way. But then you've got the good guys out there that really make our job enjoyable. If they even have a breakdown, they go out there and they smile and they shake your hand and they're glad to see you. And they thank you when you get done. We appreciate those guys thanking us because we feed off of them and they feed off of what they get for the milk and it's just a big old cycle.

As a dairy equipment dealer I'd hate to see us go to robotics myself. But that's kind of a hard question because man can't do anything alone. He can't invent the robot unless he gets knowledge. If God don't want us to know something he'll stop it. He's infinite. He can do whatever he wants to do. We don't control him. But now I really believe that God intended for man to put himself to use, not sit back on the porch in a rocking chair and watch the robotics do it. I really think that we've got a little obligation to, as the Bible says, "Occupy until I come." He means for us to stay busy. He means for us to prepare as though there is a tomorrow. Don't get on the stool of do nothing and sit there and wait because we might get hungry waiting.

If we keep the people in the field, we'll know where our food comes from and our source. And just look at the hands-on connection you get with creation being out there like that. You won't get that connection sitting around and driving back and forth from the grocery store.

Allen Layman

People Quitting All the Time

German Baptist farmers Allen and Dena Layman, in their mid-thirties, and their children lived and worked together on their dairy in the rolling hills near Wirtz, land first settled early in the Brethren's tenure in the county. Having farmed elsewhere, they live in the brick house on the farm where Dena grew up. Several others of their extended family live within sight of their home on the same farm. All this could soon come to an abrupt end, however, as Interstate 73 is slated to pass directly through some of their barns probably taking the whole farm. Amazingly, Allen exhibited no sign of anger or remorse about this fact as he explained it. As with so many other Brethren, his goal is to live a life of honesty and integrity, allowing the affairs of the world to go where they may. This, however, did not keep him from saying that if

the Virginia Department of Transportation would move the road just a
little and provide a tunnel for his cows to pass under, he and his wife,
and perhaps later his sons, could probably keep farming.

I wasn't born into the dairy. My dad was a carpenter and I don't really
know how I got into dairy, except about half a mile down the road from
us, a great-uncle had a farm, and I worked there for a little bit during elementary school. I quit when he sold out. My great-uncle called me up one
night out of the clear blue and said he'd decided he was going to rent his
farm out, and that was only half a mile from us. He said he was going to
build a house. So he let me have the house and everything. That was in
April or May and then we ended up getting married in September.

So I started renting up there. I bought thirty cows or so. If that
hadn't have happened, I don't really know what I would've done. We
were there twelve years, and then we came to Dena's dad's place here.
Her brother had been farming it but he sold out and started doing something else. So the farm sat here about a year, and then her dad agreed to
sell it to us. It's three hundred and some acres.

We thought we could do it. We would just buy this and move down
here. Her grandpa started milking cows here, so it's been three generations. I guess if her brother had stayed in business, he'd still be here, and
we might be somewhere else, but it's just the way faith had us. Dena's
ended up back in this house she was born in.

People are quitting all the time, so there are a lot of opportunities if
you want them. There ain't too many young dairymen left. I told my
great-uncle, "Yeah, I'll go ahead and buy the farm. But when corn cutting comes around"—for some reason, that's the most stressful time—I
said, "Will you help me get in the corn at least until the boys get a little
bigger?" He said he would, so he's been good help ever since. I can usually handle everything else, but corn cutting takes three people. He
doesn't milk or feed or anything like that. In fact, I don't see him sometimes for two or three weeks, except at church and corn-cutting. He left
this morning to go to Ohio to a church meeting tomorrow and Sunday.

From what I can read, the average age of the farmers is going up all
the time. I think it's because the younger generation's not interested,
and I really don't blame them. They can make more somewhere else
without the investment. There are some family farms that are passed
down from generation to generation, but as far as the ones like me that
come in out of the far blue, it doesn't happen real often. Maybe the new
ones try harder. You could rent like I did, but as far as what you get back
on your investment, I see why people don't.

Allen Layman rides his four-wheeler home for lunch after the morning chores. His farm pictured here is in the path of proposed Interstate 73 and would be completely destroyed if the new road is built. Photograph by Rob Amberg.

If you had to buy the land and cattle and machines and everything, you couldn't start a hundred-cow dairy for half a million dollars, hardly. Not the way real estate is in our area. I would say somewhere around $1,500 to $2,000 an acre. Another problem is they don't want you to finance cattle but for three years. Machinery, they won't want to go over seven years. Right now cattle are high. If you bought a hundred head, $2,000 apiece, that's $200,000. No, you can't get into farming for half a million. I messed up. You're getting closer to $750,000. Cattle prices in the last eighteen months have gone out the roof because dairy replacement cattle are so scarce. I hate to say the reason people are not farming is because of prices, but maybe it is. I don't know how much it'll take for them to be interested. If you had to pay $750,000 you wouldn't break even. You'd go broke. It couldn't be done, not if you had to set your cattle up like the bank wants to do it.

I've got one son who's fourteen and one who's eleven. I'm not going to push them into farming by any means. If they want to, that'd be fine. From what I've seen over the last few years, I'd rather see them go out and rent a farm and do it on their own than come in with me. I would help them if I could or if they wanted me to, but I just think they'd learn more on their own than they would being here under their old man all the time. I just think that they'd be a lot more independent. They can do what they want to up to a certain degree, be their own managers. There won't ever be a chance of falling out or anything like that. They could do things kind of like they think they ought to do them, and it just looks to me like they'd almost do better than the ones that are actually in partnership.

If I was fifty-five instead of thirty-seven talking now I might be saying something different. Yeah, I'd be ready for a partner anytime. But maybe by then they won't even want to stay. I have no idea. They mentioned a little bit about college, but that's too far down the road. They don't know. They do well in school, so I don't know if that's good or bad. I definitely don't want to push them into farming because I don't think that's good at all. If they want to farm, that'd be fine.

In dairy farming, either you make it full-time, or you don't do it at all. You can go out and get a job, most likely a part-time job, but you can't make $200 or $300 a week at a part-time job just working a few hours. In a month's time, that's $800. That's a good little bit, but during that time you would've missed a few heats, gotten two or three less pounds of milk production, and lost out. But if they had just stayed there and worked with the cows, they wouldn't have to beat themselves near as hard. You just can't spread yourself but so thin.

We haven't gone places a whole lot. You have to stay at least until you have somebody to take over. I did find a guy that's called "Temporary Relief." He's really good, and he'll come in and take over just like it was me. But, of course, he costs you. He gets paid to stay here. We went to the coast, down to Nags Head, last fall for a week, and he just took all of it over and it was nothing to him. He'll breed and do everything just like I would do it. But you go a year or two of mismanaging, a little bit here and a little bit there, and it takes forever to get caught back up.

I guess one of my major reasons for going into dairy—I haven't never really told anybody why—is that I always really liked cows, good cows, registered cows. When I was at home and worked on that farm when I was still in school, I had a little money saved, and I bought one cow, a registered cow. Then my dad helped me buy the next one. I think he helped me buy a third one. But I always liked registered cattle and I guess that's the only reason that really kept me. As far as the tractor part, I don't mind doing it to break it up, but it gets old after a while sitting on that tractor. Of course, milking gets old to people too, but breeding good cows is always something that really intrigued me. I love to milk. I have to say that. The farming part I don't mind. I'd just as soon milk if I had my pick. You won't find that in too many places, because some people will tell you that they don't really like to milk cows, that they're just doing it to farm crops. But those businesses are going out now. They're slowly winding down.

We farm more now. This farm is twice as big as the one we rented. We've got all we want to do farm-wise, really too much. I ought to cut back on it just a little bit. We milk between sixty and seventy cows most of the time, and that's about enough for one person. If you get any bigger than this, you need to go with at least one employee. With just sixty to seventy head, you really couldn't justify paying a man $22,000 to $24,000 a year. I'm sure that's what he'd want to make and then he'd need housing. You really need to go to ninety or a hundred to justify hiring somebody. So the only advantage to staying my size is one man can do it.

There ain't going to be many more with just one man doing it all. In fact, you don't see many of those around at all anymore. Most everybody's here has got a partner or an employee. The average herd size is a hundred and twenty now. So that's telling you right there, there's more than one person running most of them.

I've never had a full-time employee except in the summertime, but actually, I feel like I'm less worked if I don't have an employee than if I do, because if I have an employee, I've got to keep him busy. If I don't have an employee, I ain't got to worry whether he's doing anything or not. It's got its good and bad points. Of course, if I had an employee he could be up there doing something now but it doesn't bother me. I don't mind doing it so far. But like I said, you come back in ten years when I'm getting tired.

I think I-73 will take out my stall barn, my manure pit, and my hay barn. It would mess the dairy up. They were digging down here at my hay barn, and that's where the route looks like it's going. I don't know how strict it is. If I can just get them to move it down thirty feet, I think I could stay in business . . . maybe if I get them to put a little crossing down here at the creek where I could get from one side to the other.

The only bad part about it is we're kind of in limbo. I mean, there ain't no use in going out here and spending a bunch of money improving if they're going to take it. It's just a matter of what to do right now. I don't know how long they can draw it out until they decide for sure. Until they buy a right-of-way, you really don't know, do you? Once they buy a right-of-way, that'll be it.

I'm not for or against it, whatever they want to do. It would be an interesting experience if I do get to see it. I ain't going to go out here and try to stop them or try to hold them back if they want to build it. I sure wouldn't want to drive a two-lane road all the way to Pennsylvania. That'd be a slow go. I enjoy Interstate 81. I don't know what I'd do without it. That's a cruise. I don't travel near as much as a lot of people, but I enjoy the Interstate to get somewhere. Say you wanted to fly somewhere. You could just jump on 73, and you'd be in Greensboro in just a little bit. That'd be nice.

I think the simpleness of life is maybe the reason so many German Baptists got into dairy. They're at home, and it's a good way to raise a family. At one time about everybody farmed in some way. I think when it originally started out, they felt like it was a good way to raise a family. But I would be curious today after the way things have been over the last ten years if they would still feel the same way, because if they do, I wonder why they're not farming.

Daniel Layman

Through the Middle of Where My Barn Sits

Daniel and Teresa Layman, German Baptists in their mid-thirties, talked with me inside their home in August 2001. It is an old home they refurbished, along with the old dairy barn that accompanies it. They are some of the most recent farmers to enter the dairy business in the county and this is why their story stands out as different here.

Buried just down the road from the farm is Daniel's great-great-grandfather Daniel Lehman and a photograph of his gravestone appears in this book. The German-born Lehman was originally from the Rhine region. His descendants, who spell their name Layman, have been farming in Franklin County ever since. When I returned to the farm in October 2001, I saw a few small flags planted by the Transportation Department. Teresa showed me a small hole men had dug in their front yard. This was the first breaking of ground for I-73 I had seen and, though very small, so small we laughed at its insignificance, the hole seemed ominous to me, as if it were a small hole in a dike.

Daniel spoke of his entry into farming after a stint as a tractor mechanic. He literally worked his way into dairy overlay a day at a time, making sacrifices to buy land and barns. Daniel, like all German Baptists, does not seem attached to his place, and like his neighborhood relative Allen, accepted stoically that the road will take his farm if it comes through. This would mean selling his land to the government and attempting to find another place to start anew. Though he acknowledges he could probably find plenty of empty dairy facilities, he wonders if he will have the willingness or the physical energy to start again especially after so recently giving his all to start the first time.

This place has not really been in this family for too long. My dad bought it. He was born just up the Maggodee Creek that runs through this place. When this place came up for sale, he bought it in 1936. He and Mom moved here. I was the youngest of the seven children, and I was actually born in a hospital. The rest of them were born right here.

Dad really wasn't a dairy farmer until later on in life. He raised chickens and produce mostly after he bought the place. They raised a lot of what they call "broiler chickens" and fryers. That's probably how he paid for it, by taking the chickens to the market. Back in those days, you could get as much for chicken as you get for them now. That's back in the 1930s.

When he went to dairy, he always milked C Grade, and had chickens too. He just milked a few cows, ran an egg route in Roanoke, and sold C Grade milk. Then, he quit milking. At that time, I had a job in town. I thought one time when I got out of school I wanted to get into the dairy business. I got a job and worked off the farm and I guess it was sixteen years before I actually came back home and got in the dairy business. In 1992 I decided to upgrade things and go into Grade A dairy, and it took a lot of work.

What I have today is just the shell of the old barn. We went inside of the old hay barn and converted all of the facilities, closed it all in, and put in a different well because we had to have more water. We also built silos and manure facilities. There wasn't any of that stuff here, so it's kind of like starting up almost from nothing other than they had the shell of the old barn. We built a new milking parlor. It had concrete floors and all in it before but Dad didn't even have a milk pipeline. Because it was C Grade, he milked in the pails and carried it to the milk tank. He milked some cows by hand.

I started out on a shoestring. I took the milkers and all of the stalls and things out of somebody else's barn who had quit. But I had somebody build the block walls for me, and then I went in and set all the stanchions and had some carpenters to help me with that. I didn't really want to go into debt a great deal because of the uncertainties. I mean, it's tough to make it. We were trying to stay within what the family could do. To buy everything new would've meant more cows beyond what we could've handled, which would've meant hiring more labor and so on.

When you're talking about a farm for sale, it's difficult for a young person with a desire to farm to buy the land, the facilities, the cattle, and all the machinery. It's just so hard to make a profit if you have to take on so much. If you can work with another farmer and buy their cows, get them paid for and buy the machinery and lease his land for a period of time, then he could work with you to buy the land at some later time. You can work your way into it a lot easier than you can just lay out the cash up front and buy your way in. It's almost impossible unless you have outside sources of money you've saved up from somewhere else, or you've sold a farm where an Interstate went through, or sold your land where town took over your farm. It's just difficult for a young person to decide, I want a farm, buy a farm, and make a go of it. It's been difficult for me.

People talk about I-73 bringing jobs. A lot of jobs and textile industries moved out of Henry County, and Franklin County's lost some industry and they'd like to have a road to help promote industry. But I'm not sure which comes first, industry and then a road, or a road and then industry. I don't know if they're even tied together. But one thing I do know is if you go to Route 220 and try to get on the road, you have to wait and wait and wait, and it hasn't always been that way. If they continue to grow at the same rate they have for the last twenty years, for the next twenty, they're going to need something.

And especially if this county continues to go into housing, everybody's going to have to work somewhere besides here, because there's not really that much industry in Franklin County. They'll drive somewhere else to work. They'll live in the country but they'll drive to Lynchburg or to Roanoke, some of your major cities for work. Where it is now thirty minutes to Roanoke, with an Interstate road it might be a twenty-minute drive to Roanoke. The more houses you have, the more congestion you have. Sometimes when roads are built, they help people, and sometimes they hurt people.

The Interstate's going through three dairy farms right here and in my case through the middle of where my barn sits. In the case of the other two, maybe a hay barn might be in one of the routes and the other is kind of off to the side of the property. It goes through my uncle's farm, but he's just rented to another dairy farmer.

I suppose one reason they chose this route is the lake's not that far away. I'm sure they're looking at as much undeveloped land as possible and displacing as few homes and things as they possibly can. Some routes might have had less homes displaced, but maybe for some other geographical reasons they chose the route they have here. So as far as whether it makes sense, I guess it does. I have to trust their judgment. It's been a thing I've not really spent much time thinking about.

I've heard so many people say that, "What's going through my place is going through my place." They originally had a lot of routes. I did go to a meeting. After they chose the route, we went to VDOT [the Virginia Department of Transportation] and looked and it was coming through my place. But what can you do? We don't really take a strong stand about issues like that. It's not that I might not have some feelings and I may not like it, but where am I gonna go to voice my concerns? As a German Baptist, I don't really feel like we should write letters to politicians. We don't vote. If we don't vote, we're already saying we're not a part of the political agenda. We are saying we're going to submit to whatever comes along as long as it's not against what we believe. Now, if laws were made that were against what we believe scripturally, sometimes we may have to stand. The way I feel about it though is if I don't vote and I haven't elected any leaders, I shouldn't be trying to use my influence to get them to vote a certain way based on what would benefit me.

I see a lot of facilities that are sitting empty today. Farmers have decided to quit, and really nobody else ever comes there and milks. Somebody rents their land maybe, and may use a part of their facilities. But I'm not sure it'd be a wise investment to just go and build a new place, especially if you weren't going to use it but ten or twelve years before you could retire anyway.

Even though prices are going up here, in Wisconsin there are a lot of smaller family farms and there's nobody there in that community to buy them. These people are old. They want out and there's really nobody to buy them. Nobody wants to get in. There are farms everywhere, and if you have a lot more farms for sale than you have buyers to buy them—and it's not an area that has a lot of development potential—it's holding the price down.

6   *Membership*

"We're Franklin County people," said Elsie Turner. "I've spent all my life right here, and I'm ninety-three years old." She was a second grade schoolteacher for forty-five years and taught my mother, among thousands of other children raised in the county. Along with teaching, she continued to live and help out on the family dairy farm alongside her brother and his family. All around her home the community is changing and she knows it.

I heard about her breadth of knowledge when I stopped at Boone's Country Store, owned by a German Baptist family. Emily Boone was working the counter that day and sent me to Elsie. "She knows all the history of the county," she told me, "and she knows a lot about farming, too." I went to see her the next day.

As we talked on a pleasant afternoon in June 2001, Elsie served me cake and iced tea. She lives on a farm in a rambling two-story white house. Her brother, William Turner, lives nearby on the same farm. He joined us and we talked mostly about the past, of farms and neighbors and old students, many of whom are now grandparents themselves. This conversation could have easily turned to pure nostalgia, a talk of the good old days, but we went beyond that. Instead, from our conversation emerged a basic definition of what rural life means to farmers and others, which turned into a political lesson for me.

William said, "When the men got out of the farming business, it changed into just neighbors, you see?" I did not see what he meant by "just neighbors" at first. Then he added, "You don't know who your neighbors are anymore because of the change. I used to bring you on this

Siblings Elsie and William Turner on the porch of Ms. Turner's home on their farm near Rocky Mount, Virginia. Photograph by the author.

road and tell you every farm owner and everything, but now I wouldn't be able to tell you one-tenth of it." Then I started to comprehend what he was saying. Farmers are fully neighbors with one another in a way that involves commitment to a place, longevity, and, above all, everyone working toward common goals, helping each other, and knowing others in substantive ways. Following on this, Elsie began placing names on the geography of the place, as though earlier settlers were synonymous with a part of the landscape: "We didn't have people just move in and move out the way they do today. They settled. You had the Ferguson family down here and the Joneses had a dairy. But they're down now to one son. And then the Newels down here. All those boys, six of them . . . there's only one of them on the farm. Thank goodness, one. And then come on up and find the Burroughs, but that family name has completely died out here. And then the Kinseys have a nursery out there. And when we go along that way, the Prices on the other side where the old Taylor store was, well, that is a bed and breakfast place now. The Prices are all away from there. The next farm here turned into a nursery. Used to be a farm, what's left of it."

Elsie and William remember that there were once people who were part of a membership.[1] They were farmers, different from those who merely move in and build a house. While the newcomers bring wealth and their own interests and talents, they do not belong to a place and human communities, and the landscape lacks connections. Common work is lacking in such a scheme, and thus common knowledge.

It is easy for such an emphasis on the local community and agriculture to stoke the fires of provincialism, and for any talk of settlement to revert to a harkening back to "good times" that really never were. William and Elsie, however, sought to identify a sense of commitment to people superseding mere reminiscence. They described, instead, a sense of community that causes people to reach out to others and even to embrace those considered different. This contrasts starkly with the so-called urban neighborhoods where people are linked only because they happen to live near one another. The sense of belonging they once had, lamented Elsie and William, is nothing like the type of settlement Smith Mountain Lake has brought.

"It brought people in we didn't know," William said. That much is obvious, and of course, new settlers are not a bad thing. But then he added a powerful political reality: "When people sold the land down there, well, they didn't make it public, but they had blacks come in [their office] and [they] made an offer to them on their land. Some of them didn't want to take it. So they went to court with it. [Eventually they bought] land down there for $75 an acre, when they had black people on it." Then it became clear to me that William and Elsie, who are white, were contrasting settled people, in this case African American, with those who push their way onto a place despite the wishes of those who lived there before. Developers forced an African American community—a people linked to William and Elsie because they too had worked hard to become landowners and who had farmed the land in that section of the county—to sell their places for a song, for as little as $75 an acre. Today that acreage can go for $100,000 an acre or more. Rather than making a neighborhood, this type of development stemmed directly from profiteering and exploitation, discarding members of a longstanding community as they went.

Then Elsie and William spoke of the German Baptists. To them, the Brethren represent the last remnant of what once was more widespread: a membership dedicated to being neighbors to others and perhaps the last of those in their vicinity trying to keep farms afloat. "They are our people now that are staying with agriculture," Elsie said. "They're the farmers, you might say. They're going into other businesses, but they have more farms than anybody else in operation now in this area. Quite a few of the German Baptists live in this area, several of them have big families and they've stayed on and multiplied until there are a number of our farm neighbors who are members of the German Baptist Church. They're good neighbors, fine people. I had one of them visit me yesterday afternoon a while."

We have already learned in previous chapters how the German Baptists view the task of building a community, raising citizens to be part of it, and how farming fits into this equation. Their commitment has benefited a much broader population than the Brethren community. As William and Elsie describe the community, the German Baptists have helped the entire county, not only through their maintenance of farms, but also through small acts of kindness such as neighborly visits to the elderly. Part of William and Elsie's lament, however, is that this sense of commitment is waning due to forces outside the community. In today's economic climate, whether we like it or not, keeping a farming community together requires much more than being good neighbors or raising children who want to farm.

Maintenance of a single-farm community today requires policies, development plans, real estate deals, and agricultural inventiveness dreamed up by agricultural professionals far from the farm gate. Though the German Baptists refrain from political participation, their lives are nonetheless governed by people who may be their neighbors by proximity but who are in touch with people and their plans much farther away. In this way, these interviews could have included policy makers in Washington, or even the CEO of a large grain company, or even a manager of a California farm that milks five thousand dairy cows a day.

The interviews, however, do not range nearly so far. Rather, we hear from local government administrators, an extension agent, an equipment dealer and auctioneer, and a realtor. I have chosen interviews with people who make their living in part by being in touch with these outside forces while also understanding intimately the people of Franklin County farms. Through their words we learn of influences both local and extralocal, of what agriculture and the broader community look like to people who know and respect German Baptists and other local farmers, but who also make a living by dealing with realities much farther afield.

Richard Huff and Bonnie Johnson

The Small Farms Are Going to Survive

*I met Bonnie Johnson at the community forum where I presented pho-
tographs and excerpts from oral histories from this project in order to
gauge the community's reaction before I proceeded with this publica-
tion. Impressed with her eloquence and passion regarding farm issues
in Franklin County, I asked if we might schedule an interview to talk
about farming, German Baptist faith, and development in the county
from a local government perspective. Bonnie (BJ, below) the assistant
county administrator, agreed to meet me in her office in downtown
Rocky Mount. Richard Huff (RH, below), the county administrator,
joined us and participated in the first half of the interview in the afternoon of July 18, 2002. The two work with, and for, the county Board of
Supervisors helping set county policy on growth and development
among other issues. Both professionals are deeply committed to helping farmers in the community, as they are deeply committed to keeping farmers on their land, though they also believe strongly that the
county needs Interstate 73. In this interview they negotiate the fine
line between both rural values and economic growth. We talked in a
windowless room. After we talked and said our goodbyes, I left the
building and realized a huge thunderstorm had passed over us, dumping an inch or more of rain, without our awareness.*

What is the importance of agriculture in the county?
    RH: I think you'll find that people are very quick to give at least lip
service to agriculture, but quite honestly, what I detect is that people
draw a relationship with the agricultural community because many of
the values that exist in an agrarian society are escaping us. I think that
frightens many of us because the relationship between family values and
hard work and honesty and a full day's work for a decent day's pay, and
all the basics that many of us grew up with, are going away in our society. I think we all want to hang onto those. Second, I think that there's a
growing segment that has seen what has happened to Loudon and Fairfax counties [northern Virginia] of the world that were thriving agricultural communities twenty years ago and today are all but nonexistent.
What they turned into and now represent scares very many of us that
still appreciate why we live in a rural community. And so to the extent
that agriculture represents the antithesis of Fairfax County or the exact

opposite of what growth brings to lots of communities, then anything we can do to prevent that is still pretty important to many of us.

There is also another segment that believes that we need to be able to feed ourselves. They say there'll come a day when self-sufficiency will determine those who make it and those who don't, depending on where we as a society end up and what happens to our nation as a whole and our economy in general. Also, from a political standpoint, there's the whole taxation issue. The agricultural community contributes much more in tax revenue than they could ever hope to demand in services, as opposed to residential growth and its appetite for services, which far outstrips anything it could hope to contribute in tax revenues to the community.

We frequently see folks come in with petitions to move to more intensive land uses, and they use as their rallying point, "Well, it's going to generate x number of dollars for you." But many representatives understand that that is such a fallacy and that we need to guard against that. So, support for agriculture will keep some of the things that we don't want to happen from happening. The longer we can help sustain the whole agricultural community the better off we are. There's also the rural communities that say, "I don't want my kids growing up thinking milk comes from Kroger." That's sort of a catchy phrase these days. But we have to understand the sacrifices that are made for you and me so we can have dinner tonight.

Are those in Franklin County government from farm backgrounds and, if so, does that have a bearing on how the county deals with agriculture?
RH: I think it does have a bearing. I was not raised that way and I find myself from time to time needing to be reminded of the importance of agribusiness to the county's economic development. I was raised in a small town, but it was not a rural town. It was a suburban housing town.

BJ: We must also think of the county's tourism draw adding to our tax base because agriculture preserves open space and the beauty of the county and it brings the tourist dollars in from time to time.

RH: There is still a significant number of people who want to come see what agriculture looks like because they don't know it in today's society.

BJ: There's a movement in the south of France. You can go and stay on one of the farms there, and not in a sweet little chateau or anything, but stay on and learn about the farm. You can spend your vacation that way.

RH: I have to chuckle because when I was thirteen, fourteen, fifteen years old, having grown up in a small city, my father decided to send me to a friend's farm for the summer, which I thought was neat at the time. I later learned, though, that his whole purpose was that he thought my education needed to be a little more well-rounded. So I spent a couple of hundred-degree days on a farm baling hay. I got my dose of pulling the hay bales out of the baler and throwing them back on the wagon. I don't know how much of that's done today, I don't see it out in the fields much anymore, but that's how I began understanding what hard work was. I learned that one real quick. Doing it just for a couple of weeks didn't work real well, but I certainly had an appreciation for hard work and getting up early and that sort of thing.

BJ: I would say that members of the Board of Supervisors have an abiding respect for agriculture and its place in the community. My feeling is they want to hold onto that precious resource and see that most of the open space in the county remains in the hands of farmers. They know that if farming is no longer viable, people can't hold onto the land and this county would be changed forever. It will never be able to recover when the farmers are gone and they know that.

Why is the development in the county seemingly so random?

BJ: The county is probably the only one in the state that I know of that is half-zoned and half-unzoned, so the growth management tools are considerably different depending on the part of the county you're in. And we have a comprehensive plan, which is a guide to development. However, even in A-1 zones, the zones largely meant for rural type uses and agriculture, you can come in with a subdivision.

RH: The comprehensive plan does not prohibit single-family homes on what you and I might think of as small lots, even in A-1 zones. We do not have a zone that protects agriculture only and that would prohibit residential development of any kind, though some counties have gone to that as a strategy to slow it down.

I want to mention tax policy as well. The county offers tax protection to the agricultural community through the exceptions of personal property. We don't tax farm machinery, for instance. That's a significant revenue loss to us, but it's a significant asset to the farmer who's trying to build his business and has to have that equipment, although it may only get used three weeks out of the year. We also have all four tax exemptions available under state statute, so we are offering as many of the tax benefits to the agricultural community as the state code currently allows. The next step might be conservation easements and some of the other kinds of growth-management strategies that are out there for the agricultural community. Another tax policy out there is the tax on estate transfers, the extent to which mother and father want to tie sons' and daughters' hands when the family farm passes on, saying what can be done with land beyond their lifetimes. They may want it preserved, but the flip side is that the kids may be ready to sell it as soon as the estate transfers.

BJ: So the governmental policies that can affect the farmer are land use policies, taxation policies, and the transfer development rights.

RH: There are two land transfer programs in the state. One is now authorized by state statute in Virginia. The other has not yet been successfully shepherded through the General Assembly. These land transfer programs mean that you give up your rights in order that somebody somewhere else can build a more dense development in a designated growth area. But once you give them up, then you've committed your heirs too. Significant decisions!

BJ: So any appreciation that would happen in a piece of land that's had development rights transferred down the road could not accrue to that family or to the heirs. For instance, if they do rezone it at some point in time and do housing, then they couldn't take advantage of it if they'd already signed into that program. Their hands would be tied. That's the problem for these folks.

There are farmers who are interested in aids to conservation because it's hard to make a living on a farm. But if there were ways to help them over the short term that didn't tie the hands of the heirs, they'd be less concerned. Some of them will say, "We don't want anyone telling us what we can do on our piece of land during this period of time," because some conservation easements will tell them, "you can do this, you can't do that." Some say you can't spread your manure, or different things, and so they don't want that sort of thing over their head. So there are some problems with the tools that are offered, and I don't think any of us have come up with a good tool yet.

Why is Franklin County especially hard hit by pressures on agriculture?

BJ: I think the road network has something to do with it.

RH: Our proximity to Roanoke.

BJ: And the existing infrastructure of the little towns, the little urban areas and factories and so forth that have accumulated here. That's made it a little bit of a different community than one that's more rural altogether and sort of tucked away and distant from urban places to work.

RH: About 48 percent of our workforce drives out of the county to work every day. So the business center that Roanoke has become is driving residential development into Franklin. Land is cheaper here, taxes are cheaper, and there's scenic beauty. People don't mind a twenty-five-minute drive if they can get those kinds of things. Quite honestly, our school system is good. I would say it's better than what you'd find in most of the places in Roanoke. They won't agree with that, but I believe that. So if you can have great schools for your kids, a twenty-five-minute commute, lower taxes, a view of the mountains, crystal-clear water, why would you live in Roanoke?

Smith Mountain Lake and its proximity is a piece of all of that too. Here it's easy to get to a shopping area, a medical center, a cultural center. We have the best of both worlds here. We are a well-hidden secret that's about to be discovered. People are discovering it and we're starting to see the effects of that.

BJ: The Census between 1990 and 2000 shows that people are moving into rural areas but with a preference for suburban type of housing. They want the larger tracts of land, larger than suburbs that were created in the previous two decades. When I look around, I say, well, that's right. That's exactly what's happening here.

Where is Franklin County heading demographically?

RH: We've seen our senior population go up, not radically, but by 2 or 3 percentage points, which over just a ten-year period is significant enough to get your attention. It tells us we're becoming more of a retirement community in many ways. Our two strongest population bands are still 25 to 35 and 35 to 45. But we're starting to see the upper end creep up a little bit. What do I see long-term? We'll be a retirement community more and more. We'll continue to be a bedroom community. Bedroom communities eat agricultural land, and that's pretty disappointing. As land values continue to go up here, folks won't be able to stand the pressure anymore financially.

What are farmers, including German Baptists, most concerned about regarding land use?

BJ: The ones that I've talked to are very concerned about environmental compliance, because that puts another cost burden on them which they are not equipped to deal with. It's the Water Quality Act of 1972 that was passed really without anybody's knowledge of what was going on.

What was the purpose of that act?

BJ: To try and get the sewage treatment plants to have programs so that the water that they put out into the streams and creeks would be clean, as clean as they could get it. And it limits the chemical elements they could discharge into the water. Now most of the point sources have been regulated and the regulators have decided to turn their attention to non-point sources and they have come to our county, and all across the state, with a water quality–monitoring program in the creeks and rivers. They consider all the waters, all the streams and creeks and rivers and so on, state waters. And they want to regulate what goes into them so that they have to be fishable and swimmable. If you ingest it and you could get sick from it, it's not swimmable. They're saying this for every little stream and creek in the whole state of Virginia. So what they have done through the Department of Environmental Quality [DEQ] is try and develop these plans with the people along the creeks and streams.

Right now we feel disenfranchised by these efforts that the state is deciding that they want to implement. But once we began to understand what it was all about and that they wanted our farmers who already had milk prices so low to take on debt to implement these policies, we told them, we're interested in water quality, which is reasonable, but agriculture is a legitimate water user. If this is a policy that you want to implement and is a federal policy and a state policy, you pay for it. We do not expect our people or the locality to pay for it. The people of Franklin County, including farmers, should not be charged for paying for this.

But a lot has already been done to meet environmental regulations, right?

BJ: A lot of work has already been done through cost-sharing programs that preceded all of these implementation plans, and that's what we tell them. You do not have a county here full of people who do not care about water quality. But you cannot ignore the historical water use when you make your plans. And then we began to tell them, you make it hard for the farmer to make a living and you will see the farms disappear. We've already seen ads for the farmers to go out West. They say, "Bring your farms here to Idaho," for example.

The environmental lobby will tell you, "You don't believe in the environment, you don't care about it, and here's the way it should be." And we try to explain to them that people are making their living and have been for centuries on the edges of these creeks and they cannot change simply. What they need to do is realize that they cannot legislate everything. People have to have some common sense. And there's not enough money in the world to do what they have in mind doing. And even when they do it, they haven't succeeded because of the feces of wildlife entering the streams, and do they want to get rid of wildlife too? Of course they don't want to get rid of wildlife! The environmentalists say, "The farmers can take care of it, they can do something. The wildlife can't."

The problem that I see in America today is that people really have lost the connection between the farm and the urban environment and those that move into Franklin County are part of the urban culture. They just want a pretty vista and they really don't understand what supports that pretty vista. It doesn't just happen because it's a nice thing.

So with both the federal EPA and the state DEQ, people are afraid of these large agencies, whether the people are German Baptist or not. They're afraid that if they come out and say anything it will somehow come against them. Even without the public outcry, the agencies have realized they cannot afford to implement what sounded so good in 1972. So, they have come up with the idea of secondary standards. This means that you can go in water and splash around and not have the risk of ingesting water, so that the fecal coliform counts can be higher. If they set them at a higher limit, more of our creeks will pass and they can get us off their list. But this has not passed yet; they're only just talking about it, and the environmentalists are not in favor.

We've had to go to these meetings and tell them, "We're sorry, we couldn't bring the farmers with us today because they are out cutting hay," because the rest of those in the room are paid by somebody and they can come and sit down at these meetings in the middle of the day in Richmond. Well, a normal person cannot do that. And we're trying to make them aware of that. You need to be listening to the people's representatives and not making your policy based on lobbying groups. Because if you're just good people and you believe in God like the German Baptists do and you want to live your faith, your voice is not going to be heard.

When I read what the EPA has done to set up these little rules and regulations on water, they had a little committee that got together with only one local representative on it. One locality was represented for the whole United States of America. And they made these water quality rules that they proposed. We wrote against them and everyone in the whole wide world who caught on wrote against them. They had so many responses they could not put them all in. Luckily, Congress told them to go back and do all sorts of new studies, which they're doing now and the secondary idea has grown out of that. So, we're hopeful that there will be a more realistic development of policy. But it's hard to say I'm against water quality—that misses the point. It's a complicated explanation, but I say I'm for water quality that fits the way water is used in my state or in my country. I'm for the usage of water at its best and highest purpose.

The more that we say we are here for the farmers, the more it has helped us. And when we have been able to get one or two of them to go with us and the policy makers hear directly from this person who makes his living farming, they begin to see that it's not just some bureaucrat standing in front of them. It's a real person, and a rural community that goes with that person.

The state of Virginia holds largely an urban interest and unless the people who come into these halls of government have some rural background, they really don't know what they're making decisions on anymore. We had to listen to one lady who was the head of the James River Basin Association tell us about cows and what they did to land one day. We were fortunate to have our county agent, Sue Puffenberger, with us that day who was able to explain the cow and its digestion and to tell the lady that the cow didn't work like the human being does. It really taught me a lesson that these folks get up and they anthropomorphize their statements and it's not accurate. They often work off of assumptions instead of fact.

What is the stance of the Board of Supervisors on I-73?

BJ: There was a gentleman who came to the board meeting just a couple of days ago, a citizen, who asked the Board of Supervisors if they would change their support of I-73 and it was a 6–1 vote to still support I-73. The board feels that we have certain industries here that have to get goods to market, so a varied transportation network is very important to Franklin County and its diversification. We cannot rely on textiles and we cannot rely on furniture to carry us anymore. Those industries have moved off-shore. If we're going to attract industry that is going to give decent-paying jobs to our citizens and if we want to retain our young people and a sense of community here, we need to put into place the infrastructure that we need for economic development. They see the road network as part of that. That is as simple as it gets.

Most people would also tell you that Route 220 is extremely dangerous and that it would be foolhardy to think that you could put sufficient traffic on that road to give us the diversity of infrastructure that we need. It's just not going to happen. And with most traffic management system roads like 220, you have to reduce the speed limit to make it work. So that means that you don't have that alternative available to you that competing localities have at their disposal. Without an Interstate you're going after economic development with one hand tied behind your back.

I think industry will want to be close to a major artery or within a mile or two of I-73, so it could go anywhere in the county so long as you have good access roads to that artery. The county's comprehensive plan, when it's updated the next time, will probably focus a great deal on I-73, and that will give the citizens a good opportunity to let us know how they feel about development around the Interstate. But you've got to be sensible about it. You see, that road will give jobs as it's built, and there are a lot of people who could use a good job like that, and it'll take fifteen years or so to get all of that built. I'm sure the Board of Supervisors love the county and they would not have voted for this if they had not thought it to be in the best interests of everyone in the county. The long-term impact on land is always hard to gauge, but I don't think you would have a big network of development that would happen here.

But what about those who have to sell out because of development?

BJ: What is the person going to do? Isn't it better for that family to be able to do something with that land if they can't make a living on it? I mean, we have to accept the one thing in life we all know: change. What are you going to do with change? Well, the German Baptist people have chosen to control it. But some people would not control it in the same way. But I think change is inevitable.

I don't get blue about the German Baptists as a community at all because I see their community surviving. It's strong, it's survived through centuries and it's adapted in its own way to hold onto its strongest values. It's protected its strongest values. So I don't see it dying. If there was something horrible that happened that pushed them all out, if they can no longer make a living for their children or if something happened that made it so they could no longer hold onto the particular agrarian base that they have, I have every reason to think that they would evolve into another type of economic activity. I believe they would make just as much a go at something else as they have made this a go. They're not afraid of hard work and they're not afraid of using the resources at hand.

If agriculture is going to move into a big business forever and ever amen, and it enters corporate America, then it becomes something altogether different and at that point in time I would imagine it will move off-shore like anything else where the hands that make it have to be inexpensive to make it happen.

But I also think about the farmworkers that we have coming to us from other countries. I think, if they are lucky enough to come to one of the German Baptist farms, it would be wonderful for them to see America through the eyes of the German Baptist people. I think they would really gain a depth of respect for what America is and has stood for. I always think about that in the back of my mind.

Sue Puffenbarger

I Love the People I Work With

Sue Puffenbarger, a young and innovative dairy extension agent for Franklin County, was awarded the title "Agriculture Woman of the Year" for Virginia in 2001. She told me that one of the reasons she might have been selected, though she said she never in her "wildest dreams" expected it, was because she "talks a lot." In other words, she is unafraid to speak her mind, even to men twice her age. She prods people to do things that she believes will help them. For this reason, though she is a woman who grew up in New York, she is well received and everyone refers to her as an expert whose views are essential when learning about Franklin County agriculture. We talked in her office in May 2001 in the old house that serves as the extension office in downtown Rocky Mount.

I grew up in Staten Island, New York, did my bachelor's at Virginia Tech in animal science, and did my master's in dairy science and reproductive physiology. I graduated in '96 and then I went and worked for Michigan State University for a couple of years before I came here. They've got three dairy herds and I coordinated the research program at Kalamazoo, Michigan. Some of my master's work was done here in the county. So when this job came open I snatched it right up.

I came here for the people. I've liked everybody I've worked with. I love southwest Virginia. I was here for seven years. I took a little extra time to do both my degrees and I never in my wildest dreams imagined I'd get back here. Roanoke is close, there's plenty to do if you want to do something, and the people are wonderful, for the most part.

I do a lot of everything. Troubleshooting is a lot of it. I do a lot of help with limited-resource farmers. I do evaluations for them and try and help them get on the right track so that they can either stay in business or make the decision to go out or improve what they're doing.

Their production is generally below the state average. Finances are pretty tight.

We have seventy-four dairy herds in the county right now. They are all Grade A. We lost quite a few herds in the last two years for a number of reasons. Environmental concerns are probably the number one reason. Money is a close second. I think one of the reasons why Franklin stayed such a large dairy county is that it's fairly close to services and at the same time we're kind of hidden. We're not in the public eye.

Farms-going-out-of-business is definitely a national trend. If you look at U.S. statistics the average age of the farmer is fifty-some and there's not a lot of kids that want to go into it. You work seven days a week. The cows have to be milked two times a day. You can get paid more elsewhere and work less. A lot of the herds that have gone out of business, the older fellows are just tired, and they're ready to enjoy life a little bit. And they're getting out because they see what's coming down the pipeline, you know, as far as environmental issues, and milk prices certainly haven't gotten better. Milk prices are the same as they were in the 1970s. Feed price has gone up, the cost of labor, taxes, everything else has gone up and milk prices haven't.

Milk is priced by the hundred weight and right now their check is probably running about $14.50 per hundred weight. Feed is the number one cost in producing milk and it usually accounts for 60 percent of the total. If they have a bad crop year out west, corn is going to be terribly expensive here. Feed cost is first. Labor is probably a close second.

Some families may have it a little bit easier because the land's been in the family for a while. But we have a lot of old equipment around here. We also have a lot of new equipment. The John Deere dealer is right down the road. Cow comfort is the best way to increase milk production, but a lot of the barns in Franklin County are old and they're not set up for cow comfort.

Franklin County farmers are very bottom-line conscious because they have to be with herds this small. If one cow dies, it means something, where if you were in a herd with a thousand cows, well, one cow really isn't much. But here one cow could be a significant part of your herd.

Gross income in the dairy industry is probably one of the highest of all farm businesses, but net is only $15,000 to $20,000 for a family. It's hard for me to say the upper limit of what our farmers net, but $10,000 would probably be the good lower limit, net. Think about if you had four kids and your wife didn't work, and you made only $10,000! And there are quite a few of those in Franklin County.

I have no idea why farmers with such low incomes continue to farm. I ask that question all the time because I wouldn't do it and I tell them that. It's frustrating for me because I know what their financial situation is and I know what needs to be done but how can you recommend something when you know they financially can't do it? A lot of these farmers have to get this environmental stuff done. How are they going to do it? One of the things that frustrates me and this all comes back to the environmental groups that say, "Well, you got all that cost-share money coming your way. Use it." Well, in our area, Franklin County, we're lucky to get 50 percent cost-share. Fifty percent of $100,000 is still $50,000 that the farmer has to come up with. If they're making $20,000 a year, where's it going to come from? And the same thing with loan programs! For example, one of the agencies has a 4 percent loan program. I commend them for that, but again, it's another loan payment. It's just another payment that they can't afford to make.

The EPA has actually written in the law that you're not required to do anything, except if you're milking 200 mature cows, or some number that's confined that equals 300 animal units, which, for example, could be 150 milk cows plus 75 heifers. Those are the only herds that are required by law to do anything. Anybody else, it's a voluntary practice.

Farmers are not by any means anti-environmentalist. In fact, if you were to look at erosion, for example, we've reduced erosion by 40 percent or 60 percent. Ninety percent of our herds have some sort of waste storage pits. So it's really not an issue here in the county. We do have a couple of herds that don't have anything and they're resistant to putting anything in because they feel that the government shouldn't tell them what to do. To them it's not really an environment issue at all, but it's a property rights issue. And again, there are a couple of herds that I can think of that don't have pits because money is a factor. They weren't set up for lagoons. They just don't have the money to put one in. If you get into the German Baptist population, they traditionally don't have a trust of government. If there is money there, for example, there's federal aid to do best management practices, they won't apply for it, even if they're not at that income level where they can afford it themselves.

Probably half of the producers in this county are German Baptist, if not more. I think I have a good relationship with them, but you might have to ask one of them. I was a little worried at first. When I did my master's, I worked with a woman who had worked in the county for one of the semen companies and she knew quite a few of them. So I had already known some of them before I had got here.

When I got here I wasn't quite sure. I'm a New Yorker. I didn't grow up on a dairy farm. I'm a woman. And I don't have any kids. So I wasn't quite sure how I was going to be received, but it wasn't as bad as I thought. In fact, I might just do more work with the German Baptists than I do anybody else. And I can railroad my way into things fairly well. I'm definitely an extrovert. I don't mean to twist their arm by force, but by just being persuasive or persistent I have gotten them to take more of an active part in things. I guess I'm well received, I don't know. I've never really asked.

The German Baptists work together as a community more. They'll go in and buy pieces of equipment together and when crop time comes around they'll help each other out. They have said there are disadvantages to that because you have one piece of equipment and three farms and all the corn's ready at the same time. So I guess there are pros and cons, but they do work together a lot more. As a community they do more things together, which is a big difference. Henry Jamison's barn burned down last year during their Annual Meeting. The whole community got together and rebuilt it. They are just a better community together.

If we don't keep young kids in farming, then we'll keep losing small farms. Thousand-cow dairies are going to be the norm in the future because they tend to be family-owned businesses. We have some of them in the county, but I don't see us totally moving away from small herds because we still have very profitable family-owned small herds that are making progressive management decisions. They're making the most of what they have. They're willing to make changes right now. You have to think out of the box or you won't be in business. So I still see a future in small family farms. Again, the challenge is trying to entice the younger people to stay there. Some families have done it. They've got a registered herd of cows and the kids are just so excited about registered cows and breeding a good cow and that type of thing. So that's what's keeping them.

Here's another problem: Dad'll send Junior off to college to get experience. Junior will come back and want to try all the new stuff he learned when he got some experience working other places while he was away. Well, Dad's not willing to change. Dad's not willing to try any of Junior's new ideas because he's a know-it-all now. Or maybe he's not even willing to give up the reins. I have a farm here where the gentleman's never going to retire, and if he doesn't watch it, the child will not be there because he doesn't have any control. You've got to figure out a way to give up some control. But you've got to trust your children sometime because you're going to die and it's better to do it now when you're still alive and can guide them than to leave and have them thrust into fire without you. I feel for the parents and I feel for the kids.

For the most part, I'd say the farm families are closer. And children provide free labor. All the kids help out, doesn't matter what age you are. It's just a personal bias, but I don't think a five-year-old should be driving a tractor, but it's done.

I think you probably tend to have better quality with a family system because it's a pride thing. Not that company employees don't have pride but there are so many companies that are just not people managers, and it all boils down to being able to manage people. So when you get disenchanted with your job why should you do a good job? It's not my farm. Who cares?

One farmer in the county is at the barn at 6:30 every morning and doesn't get in till 10:00 at night, except for meals. And then I have other farmers who work from seven until three or four because they've got other people to rely on. Actually, it's not that the one from 6:30 till 10:00 doesn't have anybody to rely on, but he just feels that he needs to be there too to do work.

You have to make the time. I will argue that with anybody. Again, it boils down to trust. You have to be able to trust your employees and your family to cover things when you're not there.

A future challenge is going to be getting farmers heard in the state legislature. One of the most frustrating things for me is I respect the German Baptists' decision to not be involved in government issues, but these environmental laws and regulations are going to affect them. And there's got to be some way that we can get their views out in the open and known. I know they can't participate, but there's got to be some way.

I go out and I talk to a lot. And I love my job. I love the people I work with and I don't hesitate to prod them to do things because if it's in their best interest they need to be doing them. I'll be here thirty years unless they fire me, or unless we have no more dairies.

Floyd Anderson

Every Time a Dairy Farm Shuts Down

Floyd Anderson, in his sixties, owns the John Deere tractor place in Rocky Mount and is the owner of an auction company specializing in farm sales. Though he profits from auctioning defunct farms, he would much rather keep the farms in business. Floyd has positioned himself as a farm defender and educator. He speaks to school groups all over the county about the importance of farming and farmers. In his John Deere showroom it is clear that he needs farmers in order to survive, though now his lawnmower sales are outstripping farm equipment profits. We spoke in his office adjoining the showroom, huge combines and corn cutters visible outside the window.

I'm in the auction business, which I've been doing for about thirty years, and that includes selling real estate, personal property, farm equipment, cattle, and so forth. Then my son and I bought the John Deere farm equipment business here in Franklin County. We're just going into our tenth year.

Mainly we serve Franklin County, but we do venture out. We even go plumb to the East Coast. We go into Carolina, West Virginia. But the best customers that we've got are our local customers and they're the ones that we tend to look after the most. The biggest farmers we have are our dairy farmers. We do have a lot of beef cattle farmers here in Franklin County and also tobacco.

I would say the average farmer in Virginia is probably in his sixties. Young people don't have that much interest in farming. We have some farmers who are coming in from other states now, into Virginia, and building a nice herd because they're getting crowded out. They're just pushing them all out. The suburbs are going out of the cities into the country. But we're having the same problem here. Every time a dairy farm shuts down, somebody's buying it and subdividing it.

They're getting older. Nobody wants to take it over. So they're just selling out. And they'll call in somebody to do an auction and sell their equipment, sell their cattle, and a lot of them end up selling their land. When it's gone it's gone. So that's what's happening with your smaller dairies today. No more mom and pop. It's got to be a bigger operation or they're not going to survive.

Other farmers are still looking for a bargain and when an auction comes up people think, maybe I can get a bargain. If you've got a good herd of cattle you can still get a good price for your cows and if you've got good equipment you can still get a decent price for that. But they're going to take a beating because they're getting rid of everything they've got. It's their livelihood. And when it goes on the block that's it!

A lot of the cattle now, especially your dairy cattle, are going to other states. A whole herd a lot of times will end up going to Florida or somewhere like that. If they sell them here they'll have people coming from everywhere like Florida, North Carolina, and South Carolina to buy these cows. They're going all over the country.

A lot of farmers that have quit farming are trying to lease out their farm or their equipment. And some of them are letting somebody else do the farming as far as making the grain and the hay and they're doing nothing but milking the cows. It's working that way. I have a salesman who works for me who's done that. He rented his farm as far as the cattle and stuff and milking, and he's doing the farming, making the hay. I had some calls this week—people looking for farms to rent where they can rent a dairy to start milking.

These latest people are from outside of the county. In fact, the last one I talked to was up in Harrisonburg, Pennsylvania. He'd been down and looked at one farm here in Franklin County and he just called me and asked me if I knew of another one that might be available. So there are people that are still looking to do dairying but they are few and far between.

A dairy farmer has got to be a master of everything. He's got to mix feeds. He's got to take care of his hay. He's got to test his milk. He's got to be a weatherman. He's got to know when to cut his hay and when not to. He's got to know how to take care of his corn. He's got to be a veterinarian. He's got to know how to take care of these animals. He's got to be a master technician because this equipment today is nothing like it was twenty-five years ago. It takes somebody who has got to have skill and knowledge to work on this equipment and that's where we come in, thank God. When they need somebody like that they can call us.

Your equipment—combines, tractors, or machinery—has got computers that'll tell you what's wrong with that tractor or what's wrong with that piece of equipment. John Deere's got satellites in the sky that they can program into and it'll tell them how much yield they're getting off of a certain acre of land out here in the field. If they're getting twenty bushels of wheat here and thirty over here, they know. They can program into this satellite and get all that information. It tells them how much more fertilizer they need to put per acre on this tract of land versus this one over here. It's amazing what goes on with computers today.

I was just in Albuquerque, New Mexico, on Wednesday at a John Deere show. Everything's bigger, more expensive. You've always heard the story about the tractor that had no steering wheel and no seat. That was for the farmer that lost his rear end and don't know which way to turn. Now they're making that tractor. They're making it with no seat and no steering wheel. I was sitting there right in the auditorium with probably three thousand people and one of the big John Deere officials was giving a talk. All of a sudden here comes what looks like a green and yellow terrapin, but it's a John Deere. Drives right up into the coliseum, goes up and circles some other equipment, comes back, and stops right beside the speaker. The engine turns off. No driver—simply done by a satellite up in the sky and a man with a remote control sitting in an office. They're already using them in California. They hook a sprayer behind them. They'll program them to spray these orchards. The person never has to get out there and get in that environment of spray that could damage his lungs. That tractor goes out and does it, and comes back. And he sits in an office or in his living room of his house on a control set. You'll see that in the next ten years real strong. It's coming fast.

John Deere's developing technology simply because there are less people interested in farming. If a dairy farmer has got two men hired and one quits then he's got to do more. This kind of equipment will help somebody like that. There's not going to be a tractor can do everything out there by itself. They can do a lot of work with technology like that but they're not going to do it all. You've still got a lot of hands-on work that has to be done. Somebody's got to put those milkers on those cows every morning and every night when they go to milk. Somebody has got to plant these crops. A tractor cannot go out there by itself and do all of that. Somebody has got to help it.

Farming's really been the main source of living in this area. It bothers me when I pick up our local paper and their biggest concern is the largest industry in the county is shutting its doors. Lane Furniture or J P Stevens went out and we lost five hundred jobs. The main industry of Franklin County is still farming and I wish they would get that into their heads. They need to be training people to farm. They're buying land for what they call industrial parks, but we don't have industry coming in. Industry is going out, but yet they buy more land for the industrial park. Think about the farmer. He's been here all his life and his parents and their parents before them and they're still here. That's the biggest industry we've got in Franklin County.

More than anybody else, the German Baptists in Franklin County still run the little mom and pop dairies. They are great farmers. They are one of a kind. They raise their families to work. A lot of them raise their families to farm. A lot of them are getting out of farming, but the ones who are still in it do a great job and I have a great deal of respect for them. You can go on their farm and see where they keep their farm cleaner than most other farmers do. They are very, very organized at what they do. They are so close knit and I think that's very unusual to see.

You don't see as many of them sell. The Brethren mostly leave their farm to the kids and the kids will keep it and keep farming. I think they've got a system. Maybe the youngest boy gets the whole farm. The older boys go out and buy a farm. They'll get help from the parents.

I've done auctions for a lot of the German Baptists as far as home sites, personal property, and things of that nature, maybe a little farm equipment, but I've never sold out one of their farms. Don't see many of them go out—once in a while, but not many. Of course, we've got some of the German Baptists here in this county who are selling out and going out West, one went to Kansas and two went to Wisconsin. They can buy a bigger farm for less money. So they're taking advantage of that.

In the Far West, like New Mexico and California, most of that land is a desert, but what they are doing is going into these deserts where they don't have a problem with manure. They're setting up five thousand-cow dairies, milking cows, taking the manure out, and spreading it on the desert. They don't have the problem with the neighbors complaining because the nearest neighbor might be fifty miles away. Now they've got dairies going up in the deserts of Idaho. Potato country out there, Idaho is, but they go out to the desert land and put up dairies and buy their feed. And yes, we're going to get their milk.

Our milk prices here are based on the Wisconsin market. I don't think that's fair because they've got larger dairies than what we've got and that's what hurts us. They export a lot of milk to Virginia. I think we should be able to use our milk here first and then if we need more milk get it from someone else, but that's not the way it happens.

I'm sure Virginia could produce enough milk for Virginia. Just pay the farmers a little more for what they do, you'd have more farmers farming. You wouldn't have that many going out of business. Let them have a little more money for what they do. They deserve it. Then they could buy more equipment!

There's always going to be farming in Franklin County. It might not be as big as it is now, because these people coming from up North like this part of the country because of our cheaper taxes, and people are moving in here from all parts of the country just to get the tax break. Plus we've got beautiful mountains. We've got good clean air. We want to keep it that way. The only thing that bothers me is these people will come in from up North and then once they get here they want to change everything to the way it was there. I don't like that. If they don't like it the way it is when they get here, they ought to go back. If they want the same thing they had let them go back to where they were. Leave Franklin

County like it is. I don't think Franklin ought to have change for them. They need to change if they want to live in Franklin County.

Interstate 73 will have a big effect on the county. There will be a chance of getting more industry if you've got a road like that, but it's going to mess up a lot of farmland, and when you start doing that, you're cutting out the farmer. But I don't think I'll see I-73 built in my lifetime. Maybe I'm wrong. I know a lot of people want it, especially down in the lake area. It'll mean better access for them to the lake, to Roanoke, and to North Carolina. But I just can't see where it's going to help the farmer.

I know we've got to have limitations on what we can spray or other things like that, and I know we've got to protect our water. I'll be the first one to admit that. Maybe the farmers do pollute the creeks a little bit, but I read also where runoff from a golf course is worse for water in the streams than what comes from a dairy farm. And there's more golf courses going in now than anything I know of. In fact the last big dairy farm that was sold here in the county was sold so a golf course could be put there and it's right down there close to that lake. Water going off of it runs right into the lake. What's around Smith Mountain Lake? Golf courses! So what's that doing to the water in Smith Mountain Lake? I don't think that green stuff you see in there is all manure from the dairy farm.

Billy Kingery

I Don't See How in the World You Can

Billy Kingery, an ex-dairy farmer, is perhaps the county's most success-ful rural land and farm salesman. He is also related to me by marriage. My Uncle Walter, mentioned in the Introduction to this book, is also his uncle. The two of them were partners in Kinvale Farm for a genera-tion. Billy and his family still live on a hill overlooking the family farm. Just before our interview he received word that his house was in the direct path of Interstate 73 and that he would lose his home should it be built there. We spoke in the conference room at his realty com-pany and were interrupted by urgent phone calls about a house closing perhaps five times over the course of the hour and a half we had together. Judging by the frantic pace of that time and his positive energy, it is easy to see why Billy has succeeded in his new line of work. Obviously land sales are brisk.

My great-grandfather started with a smaller parcel and then my grandfather and my grandmother bought a couple of outlying parcels and added to it. Then my dad and my uncle bought two adjoining farms and there were about 366 total acres once it was all put together. I was a third generation. My dad retired after I finished college, and so I went into partnership with my Uncle Walter and I was with Uncle Walter twenty-three years until 1997. When Walter retired, I decided that I was going to pursue something else because I felt that in order to support my family in the way I wanted to, I needed to have some more income. Walter had told me all about his target date, so I had gotten my real estate license before we stopped. I also got my auctioneer's license and I was doing some of that on the side. So when the date came, I was prepared and it wasn't something new for me. It was quite a transition, but it's been a good one.

Farming was good. When I came back from college, we did really well for quite a number of years. But milk prices tend to stay the same. They were going up gradually but the cost of machinery was going out of sight. For example, when I came out of school in '74 we bought a 90 horsepower John Deere tractor brand-new and a corn cutter together for $13,000. But when Walter and I sold out 23 years later that same equipment had inflated to $160,000. But the price of milk had only gone from maybe $12 to $16 over that period of time.

The challenge is being able to make a living and keep your equipment up to date, and it's expensive. You start spending $70,000 or $80,000 for a tractor, and you've really got to be using that tractor a lot to justify that cost. That's a huge expense compared to your product. For instance, we never raised any wheat, but 50 years ago it was $1.50 a bushel. It was $2.00 in 2000. So you can see there's no comparison between the cost of production and what you make. You can buy corn during harvest for $2 a bushel, $2.25. Back in the 1930s it was $1.80. If we have dry years the price of those commodities will go up, but they still have never caught up with production costs.

Cash flow just wasn't there, so to keep up with cash flow you either had to increase production with numbers or with better management. We tried to do the management thing, and we did well. We had a good herd of cows. But if we had chosen to increase numbers, we would have had to spend hundreds of thousands of dollars to add on new facilities and equipment. But then you're talking about more people, then it gets away from the reason you're farming. You start managing people instead of managing the farming operation, and that's not what I really enjoy doing. In order to really make a good living at it you'd have to milk three, four, five hundred cows and then you're talking about managing ten or twelve people. And that takes all the fun out of the rural lifestyle. I wasn't willing to do that.

Dick Angle, who used to do a lot of welding for us at Angle Welding Shop, a three-generation country shop that started out as a blacksmith shop, told me when I was a teenager something I haven't forgotten. Tractors and things like that were getting bigger and bigger. When we brought stuff over there to get it repaired, he would say, "Your granddad did this with horses and hay. Y'all got these tractors and it's kind of funny." He said, "The worst thing that's happened to the farmer"—and this was probably in the mid-1970s—"was when they made a tractor bigger than 50 horsepower and they made a plow bigger than two bottoms." Now these guys out West can farm ten thousand acres in the time it used to take them to farm five hundred and then they dumped all these commodities on the market and that's keeping the prices down. There's just too much production and there are no controls on it. It's unlimited and some people think that the government should try to control it and they do to some extent, but their intent is to have a cheap food policy for the USA. That's not to help the farmers. Another thing is we're not exporting as much as we were because we have been overseas and we've taught every other country how to produce and now they're competing with us. So we don't sell to them. That's keeping our prices down and that was a snowball effect.

Farming is a great life but you've got to have money to live on and it's just not there anymore. At least it wasn't for me. There wasn't enough to support my family. Of course, my family may require a little more than some, but they deserve to have a decent lifestyle.

Now some other folks may tell you different, but I just couldn't see how to keep up with inflation. If it increases two and three percent a year you've got to increase your production enough to have at least two, to three, to four percent every year. And then you look at your other cost of production, your fertilizers and so forth, the price of gas now has more than doubled. This year it was out of sight for the farmers to grow corn. It probably cost $100 an acre to put in a corn crop. By the time you put your chemicals, your liquid nitrogen, and if you figured anything at all for your labor and equipment, you're probably looking at $80 to $120 an acre just to plant a crop of corn, and you sometimes don't even make that back.

I probably shouldn't say this, but probably a lot of small farms are bankrupt and don't know it till they get ready to retire. In the real estate business I've worked with some farms over the years that, like most farms, borrow to put their crop in. And then they don't pay back this year what they borrowed last year. Then the next year it kind of snowballs and then, when it's all said and done, you realize that you've been depleting your equity for the last ten years. And it's a sad thing really.

There's a lot of folks that have done quite well and they've managed to save and put money in the bank as they came on. But today for a child or a son or daughter to follow in his father's footsteps, they're going to have to almost give them the land. You can't go out and buy the land. I don't see how in the world you can!

That's the thing I tell guys that I have worked with who have talked about selling their land. I say, okay, we can offer it as one big piece. That's the way I would like to sell it for you because I'm not one who likes to go out and subdivide a lot of land and break up these nice farms. But, they're asking me for advice and I have to give the best advice that I can and I want to make them the most money. So I say, we can subdivide this into some larger tracts, fifty-plus acres or twenty-five. And you go over it with them on the surveys. And we give them an estimate. It's clear they can make a lot more money subdividing it than they can selling it as a farm. And they can't even sell it for a farm anymore hardly, and if they do, the person who's buying it is a hobby farmer. Without a lot of young folks going into it, most of your farmers are not expanding their acreage like they used to in large tracts.

Most of those buying hobby farms are coming in having made money elsewhere and they need a tax break. So they come in and buy a farm, they buy a tractor. That's every man's dream in the world: to be able to get out and putter around on a farm. And I see a lot of that. They want some horses; want to run a few cows. So they'll go out and buy a 100- to 150-acre farm and they'll piddle around for a few years and then they say, Maybe this is not what I thought it would be. Then the next thing you know it's back on the market again or you're subdividing it into smaller parcels.

Until farming gets to be profitable again, the only way to stay in farming is to grow larger. But I did not encourage my son to go back into the home farm. He liked farming. He worked with me up over through the years. He'll be twenty-three in October. And so he chose a career in civil engineering and he has one more year of college. He's always liked the farm, but he knows that there's not enough money there to support a family. The kids today like to travel. I like to travel. I like to spend time with my family. In order to be able to do those things you've got to make money, and in farming it's just not there.

The demand for housing has pushed the price of farmland up in Franklin County. We're a bedroom community to Roanoke and even Greensboro, North Carolina. I have worked with an airline pilot who flew out of Greensboro. He bought property in Franklin County and it was not a problem. They didn't mind the hour drive. They didn't go out but two or three times a month and they were gone for several days at a time.

There were a couple of German Baptists that thought it was growing too much around this area. They wanted to get back into the rural lifestyle. When one around Wirtz sold out, he wanted to get as much as he could for his land. So we ended up cutting that property up and it averaged better than $4,000 an acre the way we did it. Of course he was really pleased because he could go up to Wisconsin and buy farmland for a lot less than that. So he's put together a pretty nice farm up there. Selling out here allowed him the opportunity to go somewhere else and buy lesser-dollar land and keep going.

Another German Baptist farmer close-by sold. We sold that farm in its entirety for golf course development and got top dollar for it. And he went out to Kansas and bought land for $500 an acre. So he bought close to three thousand acres. And that's what I tell folks if they fuss about the pressures of growth and development around them, particularly with hauling manure and their neighbors complaining about the smell. If your land is that valuable and your facilities are old and need remodeling and updating, maybe your best option is to sell that high-dollar land and go out to another county where the land is not as expensive and build brand-new. But after you get several family members involved and people pass away, well, the family ends up having to do something with it anyway.

I'm still active in the young farmer groups and they're always kidding me about selling all this high-dollar land. Well, I can't help what the land's bringing. Hopefully a lot of them have already appreciated that you get them top dollar for their land when it sells. Of course with I-73 coming through, I've sold enough land that that will "comp" out. So if it goes through, hopefully the comps will make their farm bring top dollar per acre, so they can at least get out of it what they should if they have to sell their farms.

I-73 displaces fewer people and businesses by going through rural areas, no question about that. I think they took the route that displaced fewer churches, fewer homes and cemeteries, environmental areas, and things like that. The way it's routed, there are a lot of farms right next

Farm with a view of Cahas Knob for sale. The site is within a few miles of the original Brethren settlement in Franklin County. Photograph by the author.

to the Interstate. Of course, when it separates the farm into two parts sometimes it's troublesome to get from one side to the other or to your cattle. I think they have to make a culvert that you or your cattle can go under to get to the other side of your farm, so you don't have to travel that far to get to the other side.

Land buyers coming to Franklin County are from all over. They're from Roanoke who want to get out and have a little piece of America. They're from New York, New Jersey. They're coming out of the south, Florida, Georgia, Alabama, Maryland. A lot of them are moving from the larger cities. They're tired of the fast pace and they see Franklin County as a real laid back area to live in and bring their children to. They don't want their children to be in areas where there are a lot of crime, drugs, and so forth. And I'm not saying we don't have some of that here, but we don't have as much of it.

The lake's where the economic growth and development is really strong now. Land at Smith Mountain Lake is going for $10,000, or $20,000, or $30,000 an acre up there. Waterfront lots are $100,000 plus an acre, and it costs more than $300,000 plus for a home. People's eyes are wide open, their mouths hang open, when they see all these mountains surrounding the views. Everybody wants a view, and we've got some beautiful views here in Franklin County. So they want to capture those and the peaceful rural lifestyle and their own little piece of peace and tranquility somewhere out here. And then there are others who are not that concerned about the peace and tranquility as much as they are just moving to a rural area and they want to be in a subdivision where there are other children and activities going on down the street. So there's a mixture.

Even though that part of the county's growing, we've had a problem with the textile industry leaving. We lost quite a few jobs there. A lot of those folks picked up with Wal-Mart. They hire a lot of people and they're open twenty-four hours a day there. They've got three shifts going and our textile people seem to have found jobs because our unemployment rate is pretty good even though we lost probably several hundred jobs. Many of those folks are going to the adult ed center now trying to get their GED, getting retrained for different careers. To get jobs, some of them I'm sure will have to go to Roanoke or Martinsville because that's where the jobs are. But Martinsville has probably been hit worse than we have. The furniture industry is especially hard hit, including Lane Furniture here in Rocky Mount. But the Board of Supervisors announced last week that they've been negotiating with another business to come into Franklin County. So if they can bring another five hundred-employee business we'll be good shape.

Probably the next thirty years we'll see more and more dairies go out. We'll see more and more subdivision of these farms, unless something happens and milk prices go up. But that could change. But also there's a lot of land that's not being farmed at all. I'm around the county all the time. There's a lot of land just lying vacant, setting idle. People, families, have died off and the siblings are living out in other areas. They pay their taxes and never come back and see it. Farmers are just too good at what they do. They know how to get the most out of every acre. They know how to get the most out of every cow. They're the best and most efficient producers in the world. That's part of the problem.

I'm probably working more hours now than I did when I was farming, but I like to work. I work Saturdays and Sundays, and I worked Saturdays and Sundays when I farmed. If I feel people are up and ready to negotiate I need to be there. So it's like going out in the middle of the night and helping a mama cow have a calf. Just a lot cleaner!

In farming you can work and work and work and still not gain—I mean, you're just spinning your wheels. But I tell farmers that I talk to, "You know, it may be gloom and doom, but look at the price of your land. I try to encourage them. I say, "Look, you can always sell your land. You always have got that in your back pocket. Just don't lose it by continuing to spend it away. Then when you sell your land you've got to use your equity to pay your debt off."

I think that my farm background has made me a better realtor because I feel like I'm compassionate with people. I want to treat them like I wanted to be treated and I see a lot of folks that don't have that background that just want to close the deal and get the money and go on. But, I'm not like that. I don't want to mess anybody up. We're going to lose some of that as we get more and more folks off the farm 'cause they're going to be working with people that are highly stressed and that's just the way it works out. And there's religion, but a lot of people have gotten away from that too. So that's going to change our culture probably more than the farm part.

The German Baptist have family farms with their own internal labor force and they don't require as much in general. They raise a lot of their food. They make their own clothes. And as long as they stay small and there are not too many sons that want to continue that same operation they can do okay. But if three or four of the sons want to stay in that operation, then they're going to have to expand also in order to maintain and buy the equipment.

You're seeing a lot of the German Baptist children not wanting to farm. I think if you talk to some of the families you're going to see that they're not happy there. They want to do something else. They're great craftsmen. They have a lot of good talents that can be utilized in other areas: plumbing and carpentry. But then again, on the other hand, there are some families that almost drill in their children farming's what they've got to do and then I think they're never happy there.

A lot of those guys that used to farm are now in the building business or the logging business. A lot of them are not staying on the farm because they just don't like it. They see their other friends and so forth driving nice pickup trucks and they want that, too. So they're going to look for the better-paying jobs.

Franklin County is a great place to live. I mean, the pressure stuff that I was talking about, we don't see it like they do in Atlanta, Georgia, or Charlotte, North Carolina. The huge traffic jams, and taking an hour to get to work, and road rage. We just don't have that. Our biggest road rage is driving up 40 past Wal-Mart. Three stoplights!

The German Baptist fit well with our life here. I deal with them all the time, probably more now than I did when I was farming. All my neighbors were German Baptists, but now I'm always sending mill jobs to them and cabinet jobs and plumbing and wiring. I always give a list to people that asks, "Do you know anybody that does this?" So just because they're leaving the farm doesn't mean they can't go into these other fields and do quite well. A lot of them are doing quite well. Now they're glad they left the farm. They're still independent and they don't have the forces of nature to worry about as you do in farming. They can set their price and they can get the price. And they are conscientious. They do good work and people call them back. And as long as they do that there'll be work for everybody.

7 *Hope*

From the fallow ground of farming's decline emerge a few sprigs of hope for community-based agriculture. Though farms have gone out of business, new German Baptist farm families now grow pick-your-own-strawberries, sell their own produce at the Rocky Mount Farmers Market, and plant orchards in hopes of direct sales to consumers. Though farm futures seem bleak, an exciting small-scale creamery has opened, bottling and selling its own milk in grocery stores all over Franklin County and beyond. Where farm financing seemed too risky, a German Baptist man nearing retirement has taken in a young non-German Baptist family as an equal partner. On a farm where a family had been out of the dairy business for nearly fifteen years, a new beginning materializes.

As we have seen, German Baptists caution that their hope does not lie in agriculture itself, but in God and the community of believers who struggle to remain separate from the world. They try to resist the rapaciousness of consumption-based economics and the pressures it exerts upon farms and upon all things local, but in the same way they are non-resistant to physical persecution. They do not fight against change. Rather, they are deliberate about its adoption and consider decisions with utmost seriousness. Yet, often when it comes to agriculture, they eventually upgrade, not to lead a technology but just to stay in business.

The German Baptists' challenge is to live within the world's system while not being swallowed up by its attitudes. Thus, while many hope that agriculture can be a refuge for their families, few are sentimental about being attached to just one place. To grow too fond of a farm would risk succumbing to a form of idolatry equal to any other worldly attachment. To stress family farming as the goal of their lifestyle would be to miss the reason for separation in the first place. So, to resist participation in the world requires a delicate balance of nonconformity and knowing when it is time to pick up and leave.

Leaving, as we have seen, is a theme that runs throughout German Baptist history, from the German Brethren who fled to Wittgenstein to members of the Franklin County community who have moved to Kansas or Wisconsin to start new farms. Yet those who remain in Franklin County's farm community are not all ready to pick up and leave farming. The stories, that the Brethren and their neighbors inspire, offer some assurance that possibilities remain for agriculture and for the concept of membership in a community after all.

Donnie Montgomery, Brandon Montgomery, and Jamie Montgomery

It's Just Not Like Any Other Business

Donnie Montgomery, forty-eight at the time of this interview, and his two sons Brandon and Jamie, in their early twenties, are German Baptist dairy farmers who, along with David Bower, bottle and sell their own dairies' milk at Homestead Creamery in Burnt Chimney, Virginia. The creamery sits on the road to Smith Mountain Lake and the rapidly growing community of Lakewood. Both sons wanted to join their father on their farm. Seeing this as a financial impossibility, the family researched selling directly to consumers as a way of making more money from their milk so all three could work together. So far in their new venture they have succeeded. We spoke in their small office with a window that looks into a room of white surfaces and stainless steel vats—the bottling room at the creamery. From where we sat I could see three employees in white lab coats and hair coverings busily making cottage cheese and butter. In the same building, in the space next to us, is a store displaying a variety of sizes of glass-bottled milk, plain and chocolate, and other dairy products, including ice cream, all crowned with a large aerial photograph of their farm. Customers stop by to buy an ice cream cone and often leave with gallons of milk. There are many other sales outlets in convenience stores and groceries as well. People born in Franklin County and newcomers alike talk about the quality of the milk, a rich taste unavailable anywhere else. Many also understand

that each purchase helps two Franklin County dairy farms, the Mont-
gomerys' and the Bowers', stay in business.

Jamie (youngest son): This is Homestead Creamery. We started this
in hopes of carrying on the tradition of family farming. This is where we
process our milk and sell it retail directly to the customers.

Donnie (father): My grandfather actually acquired the land for our
farm in the early 1900s. He built the house in 1913. Then he bought two
or three other tracts of land and put it all together over a period of years.
At that time farming was more diverse. They made butter and had
chickens. At one time they were raising tomatoes. There was a cannery
close by. They always milked several cows. At one time when Dad was
still at home—he was one of the younger children—they were milking
about twenty cows by hand. I think it was in the early 1950s when we
started shipping Grade A milk. Then in about 1971 I graduated from
high school. I started farming with him after that. I was born in 1953,
and I remember the milk cans we used. I also remember when we
bought a tank in the early 1960s.

Both the boys were interested in farming, but they weren't interested in milking a lot of cows. We were milking between ninety and a
hundred. For all three of us to stay on the farm we figured we might
have to milk more than that and that our facilities would need a lot of
work. But this would have cost us a lot. So our interest in keeping them
on the farm was what prompted us to think about the creamery. After
they were both interested in being on the farm we started talking about
it and with the development that's been going on in the county and
farms being crowded out or sold out, we just thought this might be
another option to help keep the farm.

Brandon (eldest son): Part of the problem with farms going out is
that the children aren't really interested in it. They don't see any profit
in it, or any way to make it work. They're not interested in carrying it
on so there's nobody to take it over. So they sell out. That's what's happened to some of them.

Donnie: And there's a lot of hard work involved. When they start
thinking about how much hard work it is they don't feel like they're
getting paid enough to farm. They can do better in other jobs, make
more money.

Brandon: This is seven-day-a-week work. They can work somewhere else for five days and get off on Saturday and Sunday and make
better wages.

Jamie: Dairy farming is what I've always done. I've never really worked anywhere else. I like the variety of the job. It's not monotonous. You get to work outside. I like working with the cows. It's actually the part of the job that I like most. It's all a better environment. I don't know that there was one certain point where I said this is what I want to do. I've just grown up with it.

Brandon: I didn't decide right out of high school that I was going to farm. As soon as I graduated when I was seventeen, I went out West and worked on the wheat farms. I've always enjoyed equipment. I've always enjoyed working in the shop. I haven't enjoyed cow work as much as Jamie does. So it works out well. I enjoy the fieldwork and the shop work and he enjoys the cow work and neither one of us minds doing the other's job if need be. So I came back to the farm.

Our neighbor owns a milk hauling company. So I drove some for him on weekends and on days when he needed a sub driver and I enjoyed going to the milk plants. I didn't want to drive a truck all my life. So then I got married and I saw that the farmer is home all the time. It's not like you're at home exactly, but you're right there in case they need something and especially when I got baptized and realized I was getting out in the world among all the other people. It's not as easy to be the Christian you ought to be out in the world as I think it is on the farm. Then you can get out there each day and you do your own thing. You've got deadlines, but they're just things you know you have to get done. So you get them done.

But when I came to the farm we decided that we were going to have to do something. We had people come in and tell us we need to sell out and move to a bigger location and milk five hundred to six hundred cows. A lot of people were afraid for us. But we didn't want to move out of the area. So we decided we were going to have to spend money and diversify somehow in order for all three of us to farm. I think it's always been a dream of Dad's to process his own milk. We talked about it a couple of years ago—we saw an article in the paper and we said that would be nice—but we didn't pursue it anymore then.

Donnie: Dad and I were on the farm ten years ago and we were doing okay. I saw some articles about processing milk then. I thought it sounded like a good idea. I knew it would be a lot of work.

Then in 1999, Brandon and Dave Bower did some research and went and looked at a few places. And then in February 2000 we met with a salesman from Pladot [a small-scale milk processing manufacturer from Israel] along with two or three other farmers. He showed us what he had and from that point it evolved into what it is today. So Burnt Chimney ended up being a prime location to have a little store.

Jamie: One of the biggest reasons it's in a prime location is because it's on the road to Smith Mountain Lake. You get tons of people heading for the lake and in the summertime we've had a lot of people in here from New York and up North and they hear about us and stop in on the way. So when we started we thought that was going to be our biggest market. But since we opened, the local people just around here have really supported us and I think one reason is because Franklin County is still small, so they know who we are and they know about our farms and they know the milk comes from our farms. To some people, it may not be that the milk's worth that much more money to buy, but it's the fact they know where it comes from and are supporting people in the community.

Donnie: I know the Franklin County people have always supported local business real well. But I hear it from the people from New York and around talking about stopping in the store. I've been in the store a few times when they come in and they were used to going to a cream-ery in New York or New Jersey. And this was something they hadn't been able to find since they moved down here. And there just haven't been any creameries in this area for a while.

Brandon: We draw in a lot of the people who used to go to the creamery in Roanoke and I know that they used to go get ice cream cones there. They used to get orange-pineapple and they can come here and do that and that's a big thing to them. We get a vanload of senior cit-izens from churches that come by here. They all used to go over there in Roanoke together to get a cone. It brings back memories.

I had a lot of people tell me when we started that you can go ahead and throw the tractor keys away because it's going to take up all your time. So we knew that, but we also figured that if we as the owners were involved and we could come in and get it started and manage it for a while it would be a whole lot better for the company. We especially want to keep our main focus and that's not to make all the money, but to enjoy our work, to make the farm more profitable, and to enjoy meet-ing the consumer. They get milk straight from the farm and you can see the faces of the people that drink it. But there's no way that one man can run both the farm and the processing plant.

Jamie: I'm not used to dealing with the public and that's one of the biggest changes I had to make. When I'm home on the farm it's most of the time just us three and you don't deal with the outside too much. And I think that's the reason you see the Amish and the Mennonites

Homestead Creamery milk bottles in a dairy cooler beneath an aerial photograph of the Montgomery dairy farm in Franklin County, Virginia. Photograph by the author.

and a lot of German Baptists on farms because I feel like it is a better lifestyle for our churches as opposed to working outside.

Brandon: I think for somebody who wants to farm it's more than just a calling. A lot of businesses are driven by profit and the need to make more money, but farming is something you've got to enjoy because it's so much work and there's so little return sometimes. It's just not like any other business.

Jamie: Our message to customers depends on the class of people we are communicating with. For the people of Franklin County, we put on our trucks, "Fresh from our Family Farms." I think Franklin County has a deep respect for farming because it's a farming community. A lot of people come in here to say things like, my grandfather used to farm, or I grew up on a farm. They can relate to what we're doing.

When we get people from Roanoke, a lot of them have never been to a farm. They were raised in a big city somewhere. They don't really understand, but they're interested in the farm because they can come here and get this view of it, plus I can show them a picture of the farm and tell them about it and it amazes them. We've got a window right here. They can see everything we do and they're welcome to go on the farm and see what happens there.

I guess that's really all we have as far as advertising goes. We want the people to understand that our dairy milk doesn't come from just any farm. Other milk plants can get thirty truckloads of milk a day and there might be six to eight to ten different farms in each truckload. This creamery has just two farms and they're right here. You're welcome to look at either one of them. We keep both of them clean. So they can be assured it's the freshest, cleanest product that they can buy.

Donnie: Another thing is we're putting it in glass bottles and most people agree with you that it tastes better out of glass than it does out of plastic or paper.

Jamie: You don't have that plastic or cardboard taste in the milk.

Donnie: Plus the glass is a better insulator. You have a lot of spoiled milk because it's not kept cold. It tastes a lot better when it's cold.

Jamie: And the skim milk, most skim milk that you buy, has all the solids taken out of it, the protein. But all that we do is skim the cream off of it. It still has the protein, the solids, in it. That gives it more texture and it tastes better.

Brandon: A lot of people say skim milk is blue but ours isn't blue and that's the reason. I think in today's economy people don't mind paying more for what they consider a better product and with ours they're getting something local and they're getting something that is fresher and they know where it comes from. They know where the farms are and that's worth a lot to some people. I mean, you're not going to get the whole population drinking our milk. So we're after a niche market.

Jamie: We're not going for the cheaper market because there's no way we can compete. But the people who are going to buy our milk are going to buy it regardless of the price difference, and the people that ain't, ain't. That's the way I look at it.

Donnie: The creamery started up when the economy was doing well. Now, the economy is going down. For instance, Lane Furniture in Rocky Mount is shutting down. That's 550 people out of a job, most of whom live in Franklin County and have worked hard all their life, not to make a lot of money but just to have a job. I was talking with my grandfather about how we really feel sorry for the Lane people because they're honest-to-goodness hardworking people that are not making big money. They've worked there for thirty and forty years. But these big

Homestead Creamery milk bottles ready for filling. Photograph by the author.

furniture companies and everything are closing down and going to Mexico. I really think it will make Franklin County take a look. Are we an agriculture community? Look how many businesses in Franklin County are supported by farming!

Jamie: I think the creamery helps the community. I think it's drawn the focus back on farming. Not just our farms, but any farm. When they drive by, I think they're going to think of this place and they're going to think about milk a little more. They're going to think about farms a little more.

David Bower

Most People You Talked to Said,
"Naw, Ain't No Way"

David Bower, a German Baptist farmer in his early twenties, is a partner with the Montgomerys in Homestead Creamery. David also owns and operates a successful landscaping business with numerous employees. Though he earns good money landscaping, his dream is to return to the farm full-time where he can work with his wife and other family members. We spoke in David's small landscaping office on the farm as employees came and went. Because David has so many responsibilities off the farm, their farm is one of the few in the German Baptist community that has hired Latino workers, who were doing the milking in the barn nearby.

David is savvy about self-employment. Here he describes his realization that something had to change about dairy marketing to make his farm profitable. David talks about the challenges of public work and of his preference for work on the farm. His goal is to make a small farm pay for itself and he articulates the measures it will take to do so, all based on a local marketing strategy.

About 1995, I started to realize that either the farm was going to have to become more profitable or I was going to have to sell it. But I didn't really want to sell it, because it's been in our family for generations. Back in 1991, I had started a landscape business just to make money, and that kept growing and growing, so in '95 I was doing both. I was still with Dad on the farm. But in '96, he told me something was going to have to be changed. He was at the point where he said, either you buy it, or it's going to auction.

So in 1997, we started working on buying it. I bought him out of the business end of the farm, cattle, and equipment. At first milk prices were good. It was making money, and with the low debt load, you could make a pretty good living. Then in the late 1990s, milk really started dipping, and the markets were real unsure. But when the markets really got low, the landscape was doing good, and it allowed me a little time to work it out.

I started digging into it. Everybody you talked to said, "Naw, ain't no way for a small farm to make it unless you do a little something different to subsidize it." What we said is we want to create our own markets. We don't have to worry about somebody else's market. In the agriculture business, you take what you get. Nobody worries about it, and farmers cannot become united. They argue amongst themselves.

When Virgil Goode was first elected to Congress, he was telling us, I can't help y'all until y'all unite. You're one citizen, but when tobacco farmers united, they got somewhere. Any rights group will unite, and they'll get somewhere. But farmers won't unite and a lot of times they're hard-headed to work with. The reason they're hard-headed is because they've been taken advantage of so long in the marketplace. They get numb to people telling them these theories about how they're going to help them make them more money. Usually it ends up costing them.

So that's when we decided we were going to try to build our own milk facility and just do it small. We worked with the Pladot company and Richard Jamison [see his interview earlier]. We talked them into letting him be a dealer. He helped us put together a plan so that we could go to the banks. Then we just started going full force, and what really drove it was the low milk prices. We were like, man, we got to do something.

In the landscape company, you deal with hundreds of customers a year, ten customers a day, if not more some days, and trying to make that many people happy is sometimes impossible. But being on the farm, you just deal with a few customers. You spend time with your family, with your children, your wife. As a general rule, we hire somebody if the boy was raised on a dairy farm or in an agriculture environment and his parents made him work, whatever religion they were.

I think it's the best blessing you can give a child, because when we see that in him, we'll hire the guy and pay him twice, because they're good, hard workers, and they're on time. When they're taught young like that people are just amazing. Anybody that tells you that they've come from an agriculture background in their family when they were young, they are better workers, just about every time. And so I'd like to be there to teach my children the same way I was taught and give them that choice. We do believe it's been proven throughout generations and generations that the family is where the teaching begins. And if all you are thinking about is money and dollars, you'll never spend any time with your family. Then your family's not going to really mean anything to you and you're not going to mean anything to your family. You don't have to be fishing with them. You don't have to be on major vacations with them. It's just that quality time every day on a daily basis. We believe that that's the best way, and it doesn't matter if you're on the farm, it's just the farm's the ideal way to do it. In our faith, you'll always find that if they could make good money a lot of them would be on the farm.

We'd like to see this company make a good profit, but most of all we want to see our dairy farms succeed. It's been interesting to do, but eventually, I'd like to see people running the creamery and me more on the farm. The bad thing is you add a lot of stress, and the stress was just overwhelming when we first started. That's why I'm trying to get out from under it. There are not enough people you can hire really. The major stress is not necessarily getting the market, but getting the product made right, perfect, delivered right, everything fresh to them like we want it.

Young German Baptist farmers David Bower (left) and Brandon Mont-gomery joined together with several other partners to start Homestead Creamery. One of their employees makes cheese in the background. Photograph by the author.

It's been just overwhelming, but it's getting better. If we can make this place pay for itself and give us a good steady market so we can sit down at the farm and budget and plan and we can plan our growth, we'll be all right.

We're closed in. There's absolutely no way I can buy any farming ground to grow bigger. The lake and Rocky Mount's coming from both sides, and so we don't really have a way to grow at our facilities. So our goal is to get into a niche market where we can try to have a better product and get a little more for it and not have to grow.

There are people who appreciate the smaller farms with the family life. Maybe that doesn't mean anything, but they care about preserving what they've got rather than just destroying earth. The smaller farmer's got the green grass growing. People don't want to see mud banks and cows all crapping in the creeks everywhere and stuff like that. They like to see the cows grazing out on the grass. I think they like to see that close to where they live. That's one reason I feel like they're supporting us here. A lot of people care about issues such as genetic corn. They don't want anything to do with that, so we quit planting genetic corn.

The hormones are another issue. People don't want us to fool with that, so we're trying to offer the most natural product that you can buy in the store. The anthrax scare, the chemical scare that's got people worried about what's in their food. But if you know the people that from beginning to end are handling your food products, and it's a small deal, you got more of a guarantee that it's clean and better, especially if it's a family farm, a good, smart family farm.

You can't have big ideas though. You can't be thinking you're going to go to a thousand cows. But if you keep everything small, do it yourself, you can make money there. Be efficient in every way. Be smart. It'd be hard to put a small farm down because you can survive on virtually nothing.

Another reason families are hard to put down in farming is the women enjoy working with the books and some enjoy the cattle and the calves. And so when the woman looks after something like that, usually a woman's a good manager. You see a lot of marriages as a team working together in farming. There's probably about the same balance in our church as it would be in others, but I think if the woman's out there working with the cows and the calves, really taking an interest in those animals, you'll see a lot of tender care there that helps.

You can't hold onto just what your granddad taught you, 'cause that's gone in the past. You got to look at the new ways. You've got to be willing to accept change. If you don't, change will get you, because the change will be auction. But that's what happens to a lot of farms. The fathers are not willing to make the changes. But if you're willing to make changes, you can be successful in family farming.

The government's trying to get out of farming, but they're in it just enough that they mess it up. The problem is when the government does something, it's for both the big and the small. There's nothing really that the small farmer can get that the big one can't get, and it probably wouldn't be fair if they did. So sometimes, I wonder if it wouldn't be better just to let the farms, especially if it's going to go up and down anyway, go on their own and let the market drop.

I can tell you one thing for sure: if you have a thousand-cow dairy and you start losing, you lose a lot more. If you go to losing $100 a cow, a small family farm can change some ways—they're going to be stronger than the big boys. You're going to have bankruptcies, and I know that. So when the market starts fluctuating, I think the small, solid-managed family farm is going to be able to hold on.

Terry and Rebecca Austin

We Make All Our Major Decisions Together

As we have seen earlier, Terry and Rebecca Austin work in partnership with the Bowmans, a German Baptist couple old enough to be their parents. The Austins have two daughters and live in an attractive two-story country house adjacent to the farm where Terry works. The arrangement is unique. Not only is it unique for two unrelated families to go into the dairy business together, but it is also rare that a German Baptist farmer would join with a nonmember on a farm. It seems to work well for all concerned, though even after a long talk I was still uncertain what might happen when Terry's partner retires. Their relationship is akin to that of father and son, but there is no talk of inheritance. This is strictly a fifty-fifty partnership. As land prices continues to escalate, however, the question loomed, How can we raise farmers if they cannot afford to buy the land and there is no inheritance? At least on this one farm there is a future for now.

Terry: I guess my interest in farming started when I was young was just to make money. It really wasn't a passion. It just started out as a teenage job when I was twelve years old and then it grew into a way of life. I've been on the farm for twenty-seven years. Dairy farming was the only thing I really knew and I was good at it. So I just decided to continue with that path. Then when I'd been married a few years it came to a point that we decided, well, what are we going to do here? We're either going to have to get in farming or get out of farming because you can't work for somebody else and live the way we wanted to live. Hired labor just doesn't pay that well. So I approached Howard [Bowman] and told him either I was getting in or I was getting out.

We made out an arrangement where I bought half the cattle and equipment and he keeps the land. He still owns the land and I own half the cattle and equipment and the farming operation. And it's worked out excessively well because with him being German Baptist he goes to the Annual Conferences and the stuff that they go to and in summertime when I want to go to the beach he's not wanting to go to the beach the same time I'm wanting to go. So it's worked out really well for our partnership. It was a good deal for both of us because he couldn't have kept on doing it without me—with three daughters who weren't interested—and I couldn't have started without him. I own 50 percent—not 49, not 51—50 percent. We make all our major decisions together.

Usually in the mornings when we milk is when we talk about things. We both get up in the mornings. Well, every other week I start and the next week I get to sleep in late. I get to sleep to 5:30 that week. And then the next week I get up about 4:10. Try to be at the farm at 4:30. So we have a time there that we can talk about things that we need to talk about or what's going on or what we're doing for the day.

We milk about eighty cows. Eighty is the maximum that our facilities will handle, and if we put more cows in there we're going to get less production per cow. If we get to milking any more than that, we sell cows 'cause that's all I'm going to do. We don't have any hired help. What we don't do, don't get done. My wife and the kids help and that's all we have.

I feel like I am probably the son Howard didn't have and he was probably the father that I was looking for. I had a father at home but he wasn't necessarily the role model that I wanted to follow. And I did spend time and I lived with Howard for a few months when my mom and dad were having problems. It's always been more like family than an employee/employer relationship.

When you're passing on land to the next generation, it doesn't make any difference what the land is worth. It has to be what you can afford to pay for it. The land might be worth $5,000 an acre, but if you can't afford to pay but $1,500 because that's all you can get out of it from farming, then that's all you can afford. You can't pay $5,000 an acre in farming, because you'll never come out. So you have to lose the attitude of "I have a farm that's worth a million dollars" and get the attitude that if I want to pass it on to the next generation, I have to be able to accept what they can pay. And there are some that are willing to do that.

There's a lot of dairy farms sitting empty. There's one right here in sight. This man had two sons and they weren't interested in the farm and he got to a certain age and he decided if his boys ain't interested in it there's no point in me doing this. He's got his harvesters and the whole facility sitting there. A nice operation. I think he was set up for seventy cows, but nobody can afford to go in there and start and milk seventy cows there and pay the rent on the setup. He's had a couple of people look at it but no one's ever taken it. It's been sitting for two years.

The people-selling-out doesn't concern me as much as no one coming back. You always have the turning generations and people that are going to quit and that doesn't bother me because farming is not for everyone. You get tired and you get burned out or you just want to slow down. But I think there's a genuine concern that no one's coming back. And I understand why they're not coming back.

With the German Baptists, dairy is definitely a way of life. It's a family business. A lot of times you have the wife and kids all out there doing chores and I think that it's good. It's good for a German Baptist family if they can involve their whole family, to be able to stay at home.

Rebecca: Farming allows the German Baptist people to deal with the feed salesmen, the people from the milk co-op, and in this area they understand because they do deal with so many German Baptist people. They're not like someone in a county that does not have a lot of German Baptist people who wouldn't understand their way of doing things. For example, any kind of businessman around here is going to know not to call a German Baptist person on Sunday or probably not even to ask them questions. They don't have to face dealing with those kind of things.

Terry: Actually, we consider the German Baptist lifestyle a real plus. Being in business with a German Baptist man, we don't work on Sunday. We do our chores on Sunday, but that gives me a day off too. I don't have to worry about whether he's going to want to cut silage today, because even on our busiest times Sunday is a day off. You don't work on Sunday other than what you need to do. It gives me a break too.

I would see it more as a tradition than a calling. I think there's a whole lot more tradition involved in farming than there is a divine urge that you need to do this. You do it because your dad did it and you want to keep the family farm. And part of it is just owning the land too. Everybody wants to keep the home place, and even if you don't farm it you'd still like to have the home place.

Some of the best times that I've had with my children have been at the barn when they come help milk. I think maybe a lot of fathers don't have one-on-one time, and dairying gives you a real intimate time with your children or whoever you're milking with to have discussion on what's important to you. I think that's been a particularly good time for me since my girls have gotten older, since they've gotten thirteen or fourteen years old. We've talked about a wide variety of things at the barn. That's something that I missed when they were little. We had one graduate this year and I can see where I wish I had taken more times to go to the ballgames and events and I just couldn't because the farm was demanding. It demands a lot of your time.

Rebecca: I think a farm kid grows up with an understanding that the farm has to come first. The hay has to be baled. Cows have to be fed. Things have to be done and it gives them an understanding of the importance of why. I heard one of my kids say to somebody one time—

probably it was about Terry not being at an event—and she said, "Well, aren't you glad somebody's willing to grow your food?"

Terry: There is a tremendous amount of pressure on German Baptist sons of farmers because no one wants to disappoint their parents. There is a tremendous amount of pressure to farm but it seems like a lot of them are standing up and saying they don't want to. And a lot of it is because they've seen how hard their dad has had to work and some of it is because their dad has made them work so hard with very little money. They say, "This is not for me. I'm not willing to do this." And I admire the ones who want to stay and I admire the ones who say they need to do something else. I don't think you should do it just to please someone else because there's more to life than just trying to please your mom and dad. The main problem with that would be resentment. If they realize later that they didn't want to farm then they feel like they were pressured to farm and though they didn't really want to, they spent their whole life doing this and now they're fifty years old and they haven't done anything they wanted to do. That's a tough situation.

I think our farm is more of a business than a father-and-son operation would be because when you have the father there he still is dominant over the son even if the son is doing a lot of the work and making a lot of decisions and stuff. The father really believes he can instill into the son the need to do the work. With our farm, when I bought in it was fifty-fifty and something was said about seniority and I said, "Hey, there ain't no seniority here. You started the same time I did as far as I'm concerned." It's not just a family affair here. It is a business because you're in it to make a living. If you can't make a living you're going to have to do something else.

Bill and Karen Webb

The Difference between Corporate Farming and Family Farming

Bill and Karen Webb, both forty years old at the time of the interview in 2002, left the dairy business nearly fourteen years before when his father was injured and was forced to sell. Since that time Bill has worked and saved to return to the business. He has held a variety of jobs since leaving farming, including driving a truck for the county, but his heart has always remained in dairying. The Webbs are not German Baptists, but are farm neighbors to many of them. In 2001, Bill and

Karen rented a farm from an elderly neighbor and began making arrangements to get into dairying with a small investment. Rather than putting up the hundreds of thousands most farmers say it would take, Bill and Karen plan on borrowing just $30,000 to start a grass-based grazing system with fifteen cows. They live in an old historic home already paid for and raise most of their own food, so their expenses are low. As we talked, Karen prepared a meal from their home-canned meat and fresh garden produce. When the meal was done Karen and their teenage daughter dressed in their softball uniforms to head to Martinsville for a night game. Bill and I stayed behind with their teenage son and ate our meal. Though both Bill's father and his son were recalcitrant about the whole idea of returning to dairy, gradually both the older and younger generations began to warm to the idea. Oriel, the son, recently read about a small cheese-making operation on a farm and exclaimed, "That's what we should do." Then, Bill and Karen knew that their son was on board. The father has been helping ready the barn for milking. A family farm has started anew.

Bill: Dad told me, "If you want to buy it, I'll sell it to you but I can't really help you because I've got four other children. It wouldn't be fair to give you the farm and them nothing." That's all he had. So we talked about it. I was twenty-eight years old and I said, "You know, I hate to be in debt." Six hundred thousand was what he was wanting. I just couldn't think there would ever be a time I could pay that off. So we just decided to sell out then. We had an auction in 1988, and that was a sad day. It was a choice we had to make. I had to live with it because I had no other way of going about it. And we don't regret it. There's things that you regret but at the time I think it was the best thing to happen for us.

We called the auction service, probably the leading auction company in the state of Virginia, and they took care of pretty much everything. They came in, got cow records together, got everything set up, ordered gravel to put in the field there for a driveway if it rained. And we got everything situated. We didn't milk that morning. We milked late the night before and waited until after the auction. When they came out of the show they went right in the barn and got milked. The cow's udder gets bigger holding that much more milk. It's just a show sale thing. You delay the night milking and then you delay the morning milking a few hours or so.

It was a cold, rainy day, and it was a dreary day for me, for all of us. We didn't want it to happen but it was inevitable. We had to make that decision. But, it give my dad a chance to retire. With him being in the shape he was in, we knew what was going to happen. He was going to keep on and keep on until he hurt himself bad with a tractor or something because his reflexes and movements weren't quite as fluid as they once were. And the sale went good. I mean, everything bought good.

They put up a tent. Truckloads of sawdust were dumped in on the grass, knee deep in saw dust. The church sold food. They set up in the front yard over under the big maple tree there. It was a rainy, messy day. We had a lot of people. Dad had been there thirty years, and of course you gain a lot of neighbors. And a son-in-law and some uncles from his family came, just to support us more than anything.

Karen: It's like a social thing, just like if somebody dies everybody goes to the funeral home and you go to pay your respects. But it's also a time to go and see people who you normally don't get to see, especially some of the older people in the community. You go in, you hug and kiss and say, "Hey, how you doing?" and then you don't see them again until either the next funeral or the next wedding. It's sad because it's a way of life, but then in a way it's almost a relief at the same time, especially if the bidding's going well. It's a big relief. They know they're helping you. If nobody bids then you wouldn't sell.

Bill: It's a hard time. It was hard for me and Dad both, because you're looking at all the cattle that you've built up over thirty years, all the equipment that you've used and nobody else has ever sat in the seat of it but you, and you know now it's going somewhere else beyond your control. And we had a closed group of cattle. We never brought in a whole lot of cattle from other places. We had one called Tulip and she was a heifer and she could open gates. She would open gates in the middle of the day, get out, and walk in the yard and eat the tops of the tulips. My mom laughed. She said, "Well, she walked right by mine and didn't even bother them." And then the next day she opened the gate and got out and ate all my mom's. So that was her name, Tulip.

Karen: But you know, even to this day, we've been out of it how long? Fourteen, thirteen years, and you still remember them. Twenty-Nine was blind in one eye, and she was the hatefulest cow I've ever known. She would get up where she shouldn't be and Bill would get mad at her and be trying to get her out and then it would make me mad. It would go round and round. Then I believe it was Sixty-One. As a heifer, she hated me too. I'd walk in the barn and she would go to shaking. She would try to kick me. She wouldn't even see me, she could sense me walking in that barn and you'd see her start shaking. She hated my guts. I could not wash her, nothing.

Bill: Cows are like people. I mean, you remember certain ones.

Karen: Eighty-Six. I loved that cow. You could lay all over her. She was one of the last cows in the barn and she always knew her spot. I could rub her all over and she just didn't care. There were quite a few that had special personalities.

Bill: I listened to the sale and helped. We had a couple of young boys who would come by after school and help milk and we kept cows flowing to the barn, after each cow was sold, the boys were milking them, running them through. So I helped keep cows flowing into the barn because they were going in a different way than they normally would. And I just kind of milled around and talked and watched the cow sale, answered questions that the auctioneer would have about a cow.

Karen: But really if you stop and think back and look at it, it's almost like going to a wedding. You can't wait, but the day finally gets there, and then two weeks later you're like, "Where did it go?"

Bill: The day of the sale was pretty long. I got up that morning about 5:30 a.m. like any other morning, went to the barn, wasn't nothing I could do, so I took off to town and got two bags of biscuits for the sale guys and us to have some.

I had never thought of doing anything but farming. That was from childhood on. It's all I ever knew and it's all I ever wanted to do. Everything that I took in high school was geared toward agriculture. About everything I ever picked up to read was geared toward agriculture.

A fellow told us once and it kind of always stayed in my mind, you run a million-dollar operation on a welfare check. That's about the way it was. You had the money coming in but your end part is about like getting a welfare check. You got to really love what you're doing to want to do it.

Karen: I came in one evening and he was sitting in there on the bed just like he'd lost his best friend and I said, "What's wrong?" and he said, "I've got something I need to talk to you about." And I said, "What, did you get fired or did you quit?" He said, "No, it's worse than that." I said, "Well when are you going to pack your bags?" He said, "No, it's worse than that." I said, "Well, what is it?" He said, "What do you think about me going back into farming?"

And, I think I surprised him. I said, "We'll see if we can stay away from this and stay away from that and we can do it, let's give it a try." And then we had everybody, especially people who's been in farming or around farming, coming up to us and saying, "Are y'all crazy? Y'all know what y'all getting into?!" But you run a cycle in life and we'd come to that point, we were ready to make that sacrifice. Our kids are pretty well raised.

We're going about it together, and we've enjoyed it. It's been hot, hard work down there getting this barn prepped to get it started again. We've almost killed each other at times but we've had fun and we've enjoyed it.

I think when we were younger we kept thinking, "Got to have more, got to be bigger, got to have more of this, more of that," and I think we're mature enough now that we realize we don't have to have the newest, the best, and all that. We've got a goal set in mind and we've done the research on it with a county extension agent and so I think it's reasonable. We're not going to get rich on it by no means.

Bill: Most family farms to me are family members who run and operate the everyday business. They're hands-on. They don't live a hundred miles away and call in and ask the farmers what's going on and if everything's alright. Most of them know what they've got to do. They know they're going to be there next year. They're going to be there twenty years from now, or their grandchildren're going to be there twenty years from now. So they're gonna take care of what's there. It's making them a living and that's the bottom line. So they're not going to abuse it.

I think you would find more binding hearts in the farming community than you will in any other community in this area. Since we've started this farm plan I've had numerous friends and people in the dairy industry and farming that's offered help. They say, "Let me know, whenever you need something, when you're going to be building fences, whatever you need, let me know, I'll be glad to come by and help."

Karen: In farming you don't have that, "Well, I'm going to be better than you" thing. It's, "I want to do good myself but can I help you? What can I do to help you, neighbor, what can I do for you, neighbor?" Because they want to see you succeed too.

Bill: I'll tell you how I feel about it. I'll tell you a situation that I was in two weeks ago, at an auction sale. Not near here, in Vinton. I went to a little auction sale, they had a few pieces of farm machine. A friend was there and he was bidding on some gates and I wouldn't bid against him because I wanted him to get them. It didn't matter that I could have used the gates, but why run them up on him? I would have probably bid, but he's young and he's getting into farming too. He's trying to accumulate some stuff. We were standing side by side and nobody else bidding. There were about ten gates piled up there, and they weren't like new, but they were usable. He got them for fifteen dollars, opening bid. Nobody else there seemed like they were going to bid on them, so I just let him have them.

Karen: A good friend of Bill's has bought land up here. We've got some bulldozer work to do and he's like, "Well, when you get ready to bulldozer work come over and get the bulldozer." Bill asked, "How much will I owe you?" "Oh, don't worry about it. Just get it when you need it and bring it back." Back when Bill was cutting corn, family and friends would take time off from work to help. It would take them a whole week and they would be cutting and I can remember making some stuff at the trailer and taking it down to Shirley's because she cooked for them all and at lunchtime they all came in. That was the thing, if they were going to cut corn on your farm then you cooked them a meal. And I can remember doing that. They took actual time or vacation time from their work to come do that.

Bill: Never asked for a penny.

Karen: No pay, not asking for anything. They actually enjoyed it. It was like a party. It was like a working vacation. It's like people who go to dude ranches, it was almost like that in a way, except they didn't have to pay to do it and they actually got fed to come and do it. They actually looked forward to it every year. "When's the corn going to be ready?" They worked hard, I mean, they were tired when they left and the work would beat them to death but they'd laugh. You'd hear them out in the field hooting and laughing.

But if you enjoy it, it's a good life. I miss it, but back then I was too young to really realize what I miss now. And I guess maybe when he talked about going back into farming that's the reason I said, "Yeah, it sounds good to me." I think everybody's life nowadays is so crazy and just wide open and farming can be that way, too. But there's something about farming when you get around the animals and around the earth and you learn to quit going so fast. You still go, but you learn to breathe as you go. It calms you. Something about working with the cows, working with the land, calms you. It just helps to chill you out.

Bill: Ain't no more quieter time than six o'clock in the morning milking. There's nothing going on. Nobody's running in and out, in the wintertime especially.

The day we sold out we started thinking about getting back in.

Karen: That's what I was going to say. He's talked about it ever since he sold out. But I will say here just a while back he was tired and he made the comment, "I sure am glad I'm not having to milk right now, I'm glad we did sell." But that's what we've talked about, going back into milking. But we're going to be going back into it a totally different way.

Bill: We couldn't afford to go back into it borrowing the money to buy or rent a farm, plus $300,000 worth of equipment and $300,000 in cattle and machinery, milking machinery, and pay interest on it. There was no way. I don't think there are too many people around who could start up with nothing. And I talked around to a few of the older farmers around the area, hoping to get my foot in the door there, take over theirs when they got ready. None of them at the time were quite interested. Most of them were just wanting to shut their dairies down. They didn't want anybody else doing it when they were living right beside it. And I guess that was because they'd still have their hearts into it, and would want to get out there.

We have plotted and I have pondered and I have watched and looked, a quarter of a mile down the road here sits a farm that for twenty years nobody was doing nothing with, dairy-wise. There've been a few beef cattle and a few crops there, but now there's a new thing going up—of course it's nothing new, it's just new to this area, New Zealand have done it for years—called rotational grazing and it's catching on.

I talked to the extension agent Sue Puffenbarger one day [see her interview in this volume]. Sue and I sat down there and put in all the numbers and I said, "Well, it'll work, it'll work! I can make a living doing it. I'll still have to have some supplemental income with a few cows, but in time I could do it without borrowing hundreds of thousands of dollars." So then I thought, "I've got to find a place to do it."

So this place had been open. The gentleman that owns it is eighty-seven. I talked to him, and he said, "You crazy!" He used to dairy, he knew the old way of dairying, raising crops, and, he said, you can't do it, can't afford to do it. So I told him a little about seasonal grazing and using grass as your crop and we talked a little bit and I said, "I'll come back and talk with you later. You think about it."

I went back and talked to him a little bit and I showed him a few papers and leaflets and he said, "Me and the wife talked about it," and he said, "you know this farm is dying. For the last few years there's been no cattle on it, the tenant that was farming doesn't keep it clean. I decided that if you can do it and you will clean it up and make it look like a farm again, I'll work with you." I got a ten-year lease. So we started painting the dairy barn, getting everything looking pretty decent, and he come down and he said, "You going to make my taxes go up!"

Karen: If I have my afternoon off, like on a Thursday, if I want to go help him milk, I can. People have asked, "What are you getting into? How are you going to go on vacation?" This is what I've been telling everybody: "If all you've got to live for is those two weeks out of the year, then we ain't living right." I told Bill, "If that's what you want to do, do it."

Bill: With a family farm, you basically report to yourself and not to anyone else. But I've seen it over the years that different neighbors who've had troubles or problems had neighbors be there for them. One had his barn burn down one night and about thirty-five of the farmers drove his cows by road over to another farm to be milked until he could rebuild. I don't think if Lane Furniture in Rocky Mount burned down that Cooper Wood would be over there helping them rebuild it. I don't think you'd see that in industry, same with corporate farming. But you do see neighbors helping neighbors a lot in family farming. Night and day . . . the difference in corporate farming and family farming is like night and day.

Epilogue: They Go Quietly

From the time of their arrival in Franklin County in the mid-1700s to today, the German Baptist Brethren have tried to remain a quiet people who avoid self-aggrandizement, never speak out on political issues or engage in lawsuits, always keep to themselves, and accept ridicule and even persecution without protest. While avoiding the world, the Brethren have become most noticed by their work, not what they say. This makes their words about their faith and farming both rare and significant. The Brethren narrative, grouped together in this book with historical research and interviews with their neighbors, provides a glimpse into not only Brethren faith, but also a look at a community of farmers who have deliberately clung to a rural lifestyle of simplicity and earnestness. Because of their world-avoidance, they have remained in farming longer and for reasons more explicit than most communities in the Southeast. Even as they remain apart, many people benefit in tangible and intangible ways from their commitments.

One striking benefit is that the German Baptists have helped build and define Franklin County economically, changing positively that part of the world even while shunning other parts of it. Nowhere is this influence stronger than in the dairy industry, which has been the predominant economic force in the county—at least until second home development overtook it. They helped build all this not by lobbying or pulling strings, but by working diligently, cooperating with one another, and persevering even when the politics and economics of U.S. farming have pushed many out of business. Of course, they are not

One of Rob Rutrough's cows anticipates her afternoon meal and milking. She also knew there was someone different in the milking parlor. Photograph by the author.

without their critics, but many people outside the faith deeply appreciate their contributions and draw from their example.

If their story reaches other communities, the Old German Baptist Brethren could help many discuss the future of agriculture where they live. For example, German Baptists' emphasis on community membership as an essential part of farming helps us think about the importance of people who nurture farm values and continue to pass down knowledge accumulated over generations. Many have already told us that the alternative to community-based agriculture could become a science experiment gone wrong—and it is too often a polluting industry with little concern for consumers or even its employees. As a strong alternative to this corporate model, the German Baptists' example teaches that people must be the focus rather than farm techniques or the goods produced. At the same time, German Baptists avoid romantic attachments to land and environmentalism as reasons for what they do. They would never choose to be grouped among the "back-to-the-landers." Rather, when asked about why they farm, they talk about the occupation as a means to raise their children to be good community members and as a way to live faithfully. Farming as an occupation is a way to remain true to both family and faith, but is not an end in itself.

The Brethren usually describe the conflict in modern agriculture as different from a natural approach versus a corporate chemical approach, as proponents of organic farming have done, but rather as a human-scale approach versus one that has discarded the meaning of people. German Baptists espouse community-based agriculture because to them it is a way for people to live rightly. Its opposite is an industrial agriculture that is focused on maximum output and minimal restraints.

Perhaps the best way to describe community-based farming is to return to the young family from the Introduction of this book. When the farmer, bankrupt and depressed, left for New York and left behind his family and his work, much more than one farm business was lost. In fact, this farmer's downfall is part of an entire rural societal fabric that is fraying. Perhaps the young farmer believed he was completely alone and this perhaps more than the loss of a business is the greatest tragedy. Some light appeared in an otherwise bleak situation, however, when the young woman's family and community in Franklin County arrived to help run his farm. They demonstrated that in fact there were still family ties to this one farm. The Brethren wielding hammers and paintbrushes repaired those ties as best they could. Their help could not sustain the young man, but they could at least help pick up the pieces of the broken farm he left behind. These are examples of Brethren faith intertwined with farming, where people disregard personal gain or convenience in order to help another, a value opposite of that exhibited by corporate greed, or even an impact statement related to an Interstate. Community-based values cause people to see places one person at a time but also as part of a group and interconnected with others.

A relatively small group of religious outsiders—about five hundred and fifty members in Franklin County—has altered not only the landscape there but the very feel of the place. By remaining skeptical of mainstream society's values, and rejecting consumerism in many cases, they have provided an alternative to rampant materialism. They show that constantly following new trends and buying the newest goods is not all that life holds. They have reminded people that neighborliness is still important. In such ways their quiet nonconformity is a strong witness and their actions influence many, even those who may never think of joining the group.

The key to understanding German Baptists is to learn about their doctrine of nonconformity. To understand their nonconformity one has to understand nonresistance. Nonresistance means the Brethren refuse to fight for a worldly cause, even one that directly affects them, because their allegiance is to a higher calling not of the material world. This has nothing to do with weakness or passivity, however. As their endurance of persecution throughout their history and their belief that martyrdom is an ever-present possibility show, the German Baptist faith requires courage. They seek to live their difference every day regardless of animosity. By standing apart from the world in their "uniforms," they constantly remind themselves of their commitment to the Ancient Order and their potential for suffering again at the hands of a fickle state. On the other hand, they say their lives are deceptively easy now as luxury can tempt one to become complacent. Experiencing ease today is no guarantee of having it tomorrow. All this affluence and comfort that Americans experience could turn on them quickly. German Baptists believe this condition requires their constant vigilance, but not their active intervention. They must wait upon God rather than take matters into their own hands. Nonresistance, while nonviolent, requires spiritual action amounting to holding to faith and strong convictions while never resorting to physical or even legal resistance.

German Baptists believe standing for one's faith in the face of persecution without fighting back precludes protesting material changes in the world, including losing one's land and farm. Nonresistant preparedness means knowing the world can provide only fleeting comfort and assurance. Thus the Brethren accept changes in economics, politics, and even real estate development in their own backyards because these issues will pass away and are only temporary discomforts. Brethren people expect adversity because Christ promised suffering to his believers and thus it is unavoidable. As they believe God promised they would be cared for despite suffering, the Brethren turn the other cheek during conflict. Rather than seeking to change the world, they emphasize that God will provide for them in the world as it is, not as people might want it to be. Depending on brothers and sisters is their means of living day by day. Farming is secondary, but works well with their emphasis on remaining watchful while close to home with their children.

Because of their lack of emphasis on worldly security, when I turned to the Brethren for help in interpreting the sometimes tragic effects of industrial agriculture, at times I found little solace. As a community awaiting Christ's return to change a world full of sinfulness, they do not see the world getting over its problems by its own willpower. Farming will change as the rest of the world changes, but what is important is to remain faithful. As they interpret the world, change only comes through God's will, and not through the work of people. Worrying about a breakthrough is a futile exercise. Indeed, when I drove by the parking lot of the Wal-Mart in Rocky Mount and saw the parking lot full, I knew what the Brethren meant. Local farms seem almost an anachronism in that setting, but at the same time, an essential counterforce. I never appreciated them more. This is not to say they would not shop there. The point is they are in the world, including the world that created Wal-Mart, but they are not of it.

Despite the total separation from politics, Old German Baptist Brethren do provide an example of remaining outside of society's march toward consumerism, affluence, and violence, all of which seem to be connected at some level. They demonstrate that by steadfast commitment, love can work against the powers of darkness in the world. They teach that by living in close touch with community and family and remaining steadfast in their emphasis on simplicity, nonconformity is a powerfully creative force capable of influencing others.

A healthy community-based agriculture can only be sustained today with community support and not just by the hard work of individual families. The Brethren model of caring for one another is crucial for understanding how farms can be saved. Some of the Brethren have watched as government policies ostensibly designed for farm aid have gutted family farms and aided mega-farms that have replaced them. Some of the smaller farmers say that maybe no support at all is better than this. The "Wal-Martization" of food, leading to anonymous marketing at the lowest prices and distribution through international channels, will always work against local communities. Only by putting people in touch with each other and creating a tangible sense of mutual dependency intertwined with a connection to the earth beneath us—the way the Brethren believe a community should work—can we build a healthy farm system. To be successful, however, community-based farming also requires community-based consumption. Even some of the Brethren say this will also require policy makers waking up and supporting these values legislatively.

As a small number of Franklin County farmers enter small-scale production for local markets, including a local creamery, and as some young people explore with their elders local financing for farms, perhaps we are witnessing a type of community revitalization of farming from the ground up. Interestingly, these developments have occurred without government help, except for advice from a sympathetic agricultural extension agent. Through local marketing perhaps consumer awareness will grow and by consumers' involvement in agriculture make producers more aware of issues of health, including additives in food, the treatment of agricultural labor, and land and water use. As people build relationships with food as the catalyst, community-based agriculture can grow. Most likely it will, even as the forces for increasing concentration in production continue mounting their resources as well.

When people are able to farm in a community setting they are more likely to farm responsibly than if their farms are factories removed from where they live, or when farmworkers hired by the dozens do all the work but are marginalized from local communities.[1]

Community-based agriculture does not advocate getting government out of farming—not even the German Baptists have argued that. Rather, community-based agriculture needs programs to benefit the many rather than the few. Agribusiness ceaselessly lobbies for unlimited payments to farmers regardless of the farm's size. If we look at agricultural policy from a community perspective, starting from the point where people live and going from there, the whole equation shifts from an emphasis on sheer production to one of connection. When policy makers forget people in communities, when they think of farms and think only of profit margins and total output, we all lose on many levels. National farm programs must always target the small, local, and well-placed farms in communities or not exist at all.

In community-based agriculture there is room for new farms and new families to enter the business. Largely, these people must be their own source of change. Solutions to farming problems cannot be left up to the experts in some far-off place. Yet neither can single individuals or families alone solve their problems. Consumers and farmers must depend on each other and, as the Brethren teach through their example, we are all responsible for cleaning up the mess we are in. It will take a community of support for a single farm to make it. And this kind of cohesion is key to building healthy people and communities. How we raise our food is crucial to the fabric of rural life and, given that how we make our money and provide our food is also related to how we raise our children, these factors influence our entire national character.

Two years after the interviews in this book, I had a conversation by phone with German Baptist member Teresa Layman, who is the wife of Daniel Layman. We talked about the status of farming in the county and I heard about the status of their farm in the proposed pathway of Interstate 73. Teresa explained that since 2002 milk prices rose and then fell again, an old pattern that dozens of people confirmed in my interviews. Nothing price-wise has changed substantially for dairy farmers it seems, though not much is drastically worse. Some farmers during the two years have gone out of business due to indebtedness, but a few other young farmers had been making a go of farming at the same time. As people have already said in this book, farms are holding on just as much because of values as commercial viability. Homestead Creamery continues to enjoy widespread community support, though Brandon Montgomery and David Bower are no longer directly managing the business. They have returned to their farms and are away from the public, where both wanted to be.

Since the interviews occurred, the Virginia Department of Transportation (VDOT) announced that the route for Interstate 73—through the German Baptist farms discussed in this book—has been approved. Daniel and Teresa Layman's farm is one of those in its path. They needed a new barn and were waiting to hear if they should build it based on the final decision regarding the highway. When they read about this major decision, Daniel called VDOT, not to complain but to see how the decision might affect him immediately. He was given word that while the project is approved, there is no funding for it and that he should go ahead with the barn. He has recently completed the structure and his cows are loafing in it today.

In 2004, a new group began fighting the proposed routing of the Interstate through Brethren farming country, though none of the group were themselves German Baptist and, not surprisingly for the readers of this book, they could find no Brethren member to speak on their behalf. They called themselves Virginians for Appropriate Roads and, appropriately in my opinion, questioned whether it would be a good idea to pave over farmland when there is already a four-lane highway some five miles away that could be upgraded. Their fight to save the farms centered around the fact that the Brethren arrived over two centuries ago and had been in continual residence as farmers ever since. After some study, an independent contractor determined that the area was not significantly intact to count as a historical area, in part because of the presence of some newer homes. As far as I could tell from the study, few if any German Baptists were asked what they thought, and, if they were asked, had no words included in the final study. Again, none of this is surprising if one understands the Brethren.

What people in agencies such as the Virginia Department of Transportation must understand if they are to go forward with their plans is that the Old German Baptist Brethren will not advocate on behalf of themselves regarding this or any other nonfaith issue. German Baptists will not fight to save their farms. If they have to move, they will do so without complaint. They have moved before and, in fact, have always been somewhat in exile as they see it. They take literally the scripture that tells them this world is not their home.

This book has traced Brethren history from the Rhineland to Holland to America and finally to Franklin County. That the German Baptists are in Franklin County today is the county's good fortune. At times during the Revolutionary War and Civil War they might have moved, but they clung to their farms and maintained their persecuted community then. Centuries later, as development pressures began to take hold around Roanoke and Smith Mountain Lake, German Baptist farmers have continued to hold to their farms, not because of attachments to land but to family and church. If the Interstate takes their land in the years to come, Brethren farmers will simply accept this and move on, perhaps to the other side of Franklin County if they can afford farms, or perhaps all the way to Wisconsin or somewhere else. If they do so, some may feel some pangs of homesickness. Some may not want to go. But they can and they will go. There is nothing about being German Baptist Brethren that has anything to do with land tenure.

This book has told a story of one unique place, so unique perhaps in its beauty and its character that its own popularity will make it impossible for people to farm there. Unless, of course, the state and the county decide that farms are worth preserving. Despite what the Virginia Department of Transportation concluded about the lack of historical significance of this place, there is a profound story mixed with soil there, a story of faith and farming that reaches back to Germany and Holland and that made this county what it is. That story will have more chapters and most likely will be mixed with soil somewhere. Whether that soil will be in Franklin County, Virginia, depends on many issues that we will most likely not hear the Brethren speak about in public. It is more likely, I believe, that one day people will realize that the Brethren have again gone to a new location, just as they found one in Wittgenstein three hundred years ago and Franklin County shortly thereafter. There will be no agricultural impact statements or studies that point to the loss. The Old German Baptist Brethren will go quietly.

NOTES

Introduction

1. John S. Salmon and Emily J. Salmon, *Franklin County Virginia, 1786–1986: A Bicentennial History* (Rocky Mount, Va.: Franklin County Bicentennial Commission, 1993), 188.

2. An example of such Germanic construction, crafts, and clothing can be viewed at the Blue Ridge Institute at Ferrum College, Ferrum, Virginia.

3. Roger E. Sappington explains that in 1785 all Brethren spoke the German language as their native language. Over the next fifty years, they were "forced to learn English because that was the prevailing language of American society," although throughout these years German remained their first language. As late as 1841, the Annual Meeting heard the question: "Whether it is proper for teachers to speak both German and English in meetings, when there are only a few English members, the majority of the church being German?" They ruled that "not too much time ought to be taken up in English" (Roger E. Sappington, ed., *The Brethren in the New Nation: A Source Book on the Development of the Church of the Brethren, 1785–1865* [Elgin, Ill.: The Brethren Press, 1976], 245). Hymns were still being sung in German as late as 1881, when the Old German Baptist Brethren officially formed (Donald B. Kraybill and Carl F. Bowman, *On the Backroad to Heaven: Old Order Hutterites, Mennonites, Amish, and Brethren* [Baltimore: Johns Hopkins University Press, 2001], 143).

4. Donald F. Durnbaugh, *Fruit of the Vine: A History of the Brethren, 1708–1995* (Elgin, Ill.: The Brethren Press, 1997), 163–64.

5. Donald F. Durnbaugh writes, "The Brethren way was to gain adherents by living their faith, not by overt evangelism. Their neighbors saw their sincerity and piety and were sometimes impressed enough to join them" (Donald F. Durnbaugh, "Early History," in *Church of the Brethren: Yesterday and Today*, ed. Donald F. Durnbaugh [Elgin, Ill.: The Brethren Press, 1986], 14).

6. Salmon and Salmon, *Franklin County Virginia, 1786–1986*, 189.

7. Carl F. Bowman, *Brethren Society: The Cultural Transformation of a "Peculiar People"* (Baltimore: Johns Hopkins University Press, 1995), 97.

8. For an account of this development, see Salmon and Salmon, *Franklin County Virginia, 1786–1986*, 371–73.

9. *1900 County Level Census Data*, http://fisher.lib.virginia.edu/cgi-local/censusbin/census/cen.pl.

10. See Chapter 17, "Agriculture and Farm Life," in Salmon and Salmon, *Franklin County Virginia, 1786–1986*, 361–76.

11. See William Cronon, *Nature's Metropolis: Chicago and the Great West* (New York: W. W. Norton, 1991).

12. See Cindy Hamamovitch, *Fruits of Their Labor* (Chapel Hill: University of North Carolina Press, 1997).

13. See T. Keister Greer, *The Great Moonshine Conspiracy Trial of 1935* (Rocky Mount, Va.: History House Press, 2003).

14. In 1860, Franklin County produced 158,337 pounds of butter and 846 pounds of cheese. By 1910, this had increased to a yearly production of 781,302 pounds of butter and 2,104,538 gallons of milk (Salmon and Salmon, *Franklin County Virginia, 1786–1986*, 374).

15. Ibid., 319–20.

16. Ibid., 374.

17. *1940 State Level Census Data,* http://fisher.lib.virginia.edu/cgi-local/censusbin/census/cen.pl.

18. *1959 Census of Agriculture,* U.S. Department of Commerce, Bureau of the Census, November 1961.

19. Ibid.

20. Ibid.

21. *1969 Census of Agriculture,* U.S. Department of Commerce, Bureau of the Census, June 1972.

22. *1978 Census of Agriculture,* U.S. Department of Commerce, Bureau of the Census, May 1981.

23. *1959 Census of Agriculture; 1969 Census of Agriculture.*

24. For more on this, see Wendell Berry, *The Unsettling of America: Culture and Agriculture* (San Francisco: Sierra Club Books, 1977); Jim Hightower, *Hard Tomatoes, Hard Times: The Original Hightower Report, unexpurgated, of the Agribusiness Accountability Project on the failure of America's land grant complex and selected additional views of the problems and prospects of American agriculture in the late seventies* (Cambridge, Mass.: Schenkman Publishing Company, 1978); Ingolf Vogeler, *The Myth of the Family Farm: Agribusiness Dominance of U.S. Agriculture* (Boulder, Colo.: Westview Press, 1981); and Marty Strange, *Family Farming: A New Economic Vision* (Lincoln: University of Nebraska Press, 1988).

25. The first of these "Tractorcades" was held in 1978, when over three thousand farmers descended on the capital in protest over the 1977 Farm Bill. The following year, 1979, over nine hundred tractors again filled the streets of Washington, D.C. Such protests continued into the 1980s.

26. For more on this specialization, see Kenneth W. Bailey, *Marketing and Pricing of Milk and Dairy Products in the United States* (Ames: Iowa State University Press, 1997), particularly 4–6, 142–43, and 247–63.

27. See Sara D. Short, *Structure, Management, and Performance Characteristics of Specialized Dairy Farm Businesses in the United States* (Washington, D.C.: U.S. Department of Agriculture, Resource Economics Division, 2000).

28. In a recent *Franklin County Real Estate* brochure (2001), 4.95 acres, to be subdivided into "4 beautiful building sites," was advertised for $35,000. A "nice building lot" of 1.52 acres was selling for $19,950, and one of 1.27 acres for $18,950. In the *Smith Mountain Lake, Virginia: Visitor and Newcomer Guide, 2001,* Ilma Mowery, a Franklin County resident and real estate agent, says, "The

first lot I bought—three-and-a-half acres with 220 feet of shoreline—cost $8,950. That was in 1972. . . . This year, lot prices are selling for an average of $200,000 to $300,000" (Norma Lugar, "Smith Mountain Lake: A Lake Without Limits," in *Smith Mountain Lake, Virginia: Visitor and Newcomer Guide, 2001* [Roanoke, Va.: Leisure Publishing Company, 2001], 63).

29. *1987 County Census: Franklin County, Virginia*; interviews.

30. Franklin County is the second largest dairy county in Virginia, with only Rockbridge County ahead of it. Augusta County ranks third (*Franklin County, Virginia: The Best of Both Worlds* [Roanoke, Va.: Leisure Publishing Company, 2000], 38).

31. E-mail to Charles D. Thompson Jr. from G. M. (Jerry) Jones, March 8, 2002.

32. For example, see the writings of rural sociologist William Heffernan and G. M. (Jerry) Jones, dairy specialist at Virginia Tech.

33. John Wagner, "Bill Could Preserve Dairy Farms," *The News & Observer* (Raleigh), July 26, 2001, 1A, 14A.

Chapter 1. The Ancient Order

1. By 1708, the Germanic territories had been in economic and religious upheaval for more than two centuries. The German Palatinate or Rhine Valley had suffered through such conflicts as the Peasants' War (1524–25), the Thirty Years' War (1618–48), and the War of the Grand Alliance (1688–97). In 1708, the War of the Spanish Succession (1701–14) was only half over. During and between these conflicts, soldiers marched across, looted, and burned much of the Palatinate. Hundreds of thousands of people died; perhaps three hundred thousand perished in the Thirty Years' War alone. Millions more perished from plagues and starvation directly resulting from the wars' aftermath.

2. See the excellent overview of these conditions in Donald F. Durnbaugh, *European Origins of the Brethren: A Source Book on the Beginnings of the Church of the Brethren in the Early Eighteenth Century* (Elgin, Ill.: The Brethren Press, 1958), 19–31.

3. Bowman, *Brethren Society*, 3–4.

4. For a more thorough discussion of these values, see ibid., 26–50.

5. Durnbaugh, *European Origins of the Brethren*, 21.

6. Carl F. Bowman in *Brethren Society* explains that the Brethren were "heavily influenced by South German and Swiss Anabaptists, especially Mennonites, with whom they had very close contact. . . . The Brethren had so much in common with Mennonites, in fact, that outsiders (and perhaps some insiders) had a hard time distinguishing the two. Relations in the early years were particularly close." Bowman lists those Anabaptist principles adopted by the Brethren as follows: "(1) commitment to an unadulterated biblically based doctrine; (2) fidelity to the New Testament ordinances of believer's baptism, the Lord's Supper, and feetwashing; (3) restriction of the Lord's Supper to those united within the fellowship; (4) rejection of all use of force and violence (nonresistance); (5) refusal to swear oaths of allegiance or truthfulness; (6) the view that the church is a gathered community of believers living in close fellowship with one another; (7) the loving use of mutual correction and church discipline (including excommunication and the ban) to

promote Christian living; and (8) commitment to religious liberty—freedom of conscience to practice one's faith without state interference" (5).

7. Quoted in Durnbaugh, *European Origins of the Brethren*, 408.

8. An account by Sander Mack (Alexander Mack Jr.) reported, "After they had all emerged from the water . . . , they were immediately clothed inwardly with great joyfulness" (quoted in Durnbaugh, *Fruit of the Vine*, 29).

9. Bowman, *Brethren Society*, 6.

10. Durnbaugh, *Fruit of the Vine*, 45–50.

11. Although the title of Alexander Mack's book was *Rules and Ordinances of the House of God*, it was less a system of laws for the Brethren to follow than it was an interpretation of the faith held by the Brethren. Donald F. Durnbaugh writes, "Because the Brethren were in reaction to what they considered to be an overly creedalized and dogmatic state church, they opposed any effort to spell out their beliefs in a systematic and complete fashion" (*Fruits of the Vine*, 45).

12. Durnbaugh, *Fruit of the Vine*, 23–24.

13. Donald F. Durnbaugh explains: "One probable reason for his [Count Albrecht's] tolerance was a desire to attract hard-working settlers to his thinly populated and poverty-stricken territory. Harshly ravaged by both friend and foe in the Thirty Years' War, the territory was badly depopulated" (*European Origins of the Brethren*, 109).

14. Ibid.

15. See Thieleman J. van Braght, *The Bloody Theater: or, Martyrs Mirror of the Defenseless Christians who Baptized only upon Confession of Faith, and who Suffered and Died for the Testimony of Jesus, their Savior, from the Time of Christ to the year A.D. 1660*, translated from the original Dutch language from the 1660 edition by Joseph F. Sohm (Scottdale, Pa.: Mennonite Publishing House, 1951).

16. Durnbaugh, *European Origins of the Brethren*, 120.

17. Earl C. Kaylor Jr., *Out of the Wilderness: 1780–1980: The Brethren in Two Centuries of Life in Central Pennsylvania* (New York: Cornwall Books, 1981), 30.

18. Durnbaugh, *Fruits of the Vine*, 54–61.

19. It is not fully clear why the Brethren chose to leave Schwarzenau, since Count Albrecht continued his policy of religious toleration until his death in 1723, three years after the Brethren left. Carl F. Bowman claims that it was for economic reasons, and that the Brethren were enticed by glowing reports from earlier Mennonite and Brethren settlers in Pennsylvania (*Brethren Society*, 6). Yet this does not seem to offer a complete explanation, as the Brethren did not migrate to the American colony for another nine years, in 1729. Donald F. Durnbaugh offers what is, perhaps, a more compelling reason. While also acknowledging economic considerations, Durnbaugh explains that in 1719, Count Albrecht was forced to give up part of his sovereignty to his younger brother, who had no sympathy for religious outsiders. Indeed, early in 1720 (before the Schwarzenau Brethren left), the brother complained to the Imperial Court about the damage to forests and thus game that the religious settlers were causing in Wittgenstein. Had the Brethren remained in Schwarzenau a further three years until Count Albrecht's death, they certainly would have been no longer welcome. Durnbaugh writes: "It could well be that the Brethren saw the handwriting on the wall, when this count [the brother] attained complete rule" (*Fruit of the Vine*, 63).

20. Durnbaugh, *Fruits of the Vine*, 63–67.

21. Kaylor, *Out of the Wilderness*, 32.

22. Erik Bruun and Jay Crosby, eds., *Our Nation's Archive: The History of the United States in Documents* (New York: Black Dog and Leventhal, 1999), 60–61.

23. Frank Benjamin Hurt, *The Heritage of the German Pioneers in Franklin County, Virginia* (Rocky Mount, Va.: Franklin County Historical Society, 1982), 3–5.

24. Donald F. Durnbaugh, *The Brethren in Colonial America* (Elgin, Ill.: The Brethren Press, 1974), 33.

25. Ibid., 52.

26. Kaylor, *Out of the Wilderness*, 33–34.

27. See Chapter 4, "On the Frontier," in Durnbaugh's *The Brethren in Colonial America*, 141–69.

28. Durnbaugh, *Fruits of the Vine*, 81.

29. Hurt, *Heritage of the German Pioneers*, 4.

30. Durnbaugh, *Fruits of the Vine*, 76.

31. Ibid., 77.

32. Ibid., 81.

33. S. Loren Bowman, *Power and Polity Among the Brethren: A Study of Church Governance* (Elgin, Ill.: The Brethren Press, 1987), 43.

34. Bowman, *Brethren Society*, 11.

35. Ibid., 13.

36. Ibid., 15.

37. See Francis Jennings, *The Ambiguous Iroquois Empire: The Covenant Chain Confederation of Indian Tribes with English Colonies from Its Beginnings to the Lancaster Treaty of 1744* (New York: W. W. Norton, 1984).

38. Parker Rouse Jr., *The Great Wagon Road: From Philadelphia to the South* (New York: McGraw-Hill Book Company, 1973), ix.

39. Ibid., 37.

40. Salmon and Salmon, *Franklin County, Virginia 1786–1986*, 29.

41. Kaylor, *Out of the Wilderness*, 49.

42. Klaus Wust, *Saint Adventurers on the Virginia Frontier: Southern Outposts of Ephrata* (Edinburgh, Va.: Shenandoah History Publishers, 1977), 33.

43. Ibid., 35.

44. Kaylor, *Out of the Wilderness*, 44–45.

45. Ibid., 49–50.

46. Wust, *Saint Adventurers*, 37.

47. Ibid., 34.

48. For more on the French and Indian War, see Fred Anderson, *Crucible of War: The Seven Years' War and the Fate of Empire in British North America, 1754–1766* (New York: Alfred A. Knopf, 2000). For the evolution of the emerging American national identity, see Clinton Rossiter, *The First American Revolution: The American Colonies on the Eve of Independence* (New York: Harcourt Brace & Company, 1990).

49. Mark Noll, *The Old Religion in a New World: The History of North American Christianity* (Grand Rapids, Mich.: William B. Eerdmans Publishing Company, 2002), 176.

50. Daniel Wunderlich Nead, *Pennsylvania Germans in the Settlement of Maryland* (Lancaster, Pa.: Press of the New Era Publishing Company, 1914), 33, quoted in Rouse Jr., *Great Wilderness Road*, 22.

51. Benjamin Franklin, *The Autobiography of Benjamin Franklin* (Boston: Houghton Mifflin Company, 1923), 190–91. Although Franklin identifies Wohlfahrt as "one of the Dunker founders," he was not, in fact, a member of the Brethren but was a leader in Beissel's Ephrata group. Nevertheless, Franklin's words convey his sense of the Brethren and other Anabaptist groups, and Wohlfahrt's reply to Franklin has since been adopted by the Brethren as an accurate portrayal of their beliefs.

52. Sappington, *The Brethren in Virginia*, 61–63.

53. Durnbaugh, *The Brethren in Colonial America*, 356.

54. Donald F. Durnbaugh, "Revolutionary War, American (1775–83)," in *The Brethren Encyclopedia*, ed. Donald F. Durnbaugh, 3 vols. (Philadelphia: The Brethren Encyclopedia, Inc., 1984), vol. 2, 1105–6.

55. Ibid.

56. Ibid., 1106; Durnbaugh, *Fruit of the Vine*, 148–63.

57. Richard Ruda, "An Oasis of Peace and Contemplation," *New York Times*, October 19, 2001, E42.

58. Bittinger, L. F., *The Germans in Colonial Times*, (Philadelphia: J. B. Lippincott Co., 1901), 230.

59. William Duke, *Observations on the Present State of Religion in Maryland* (Baltimore, 1795), 33–34, quoted in Durnbaugh, *Fruit of the Vine*, 162–63.

Chapter 2. The Carolina Road

1. Salmon and Salmon, *Franklin County, Virginia, 1786–1986*, 24–29.

2. Interview, Roddy Moore. See examples of this at the Blue Ridge Institute, Ferrum College, Ferrum, Virginia.

3. Adelaide L. Fries, *The Road to Salem* (Chapel Hill: University of North Carolina Press, 1944), 42.

4. Salmon and Salmon, *Franklin County, Virginia, 1786–1986*, 189.

5. Ibid.

6. Interview, Roddy Moore, director, Blue Ridge Institute at Ferrum College, Ferrum, Virginia; Salmon and Salmon, *Franklin County History, 1786–1986*, 20–21.

7. Durnbaugh, *Fruit of the Vine*, 193.

8. Sappington, *The Brethren in Virginia*, 5–34; Salmon and Salmon, *Franklin County History, 1786–1986*, 191.

9. Durnbaugh, *Fruit of the Vine*, 148–53.

10. Salmon and Salmon, *Franklin County, Virginia, 1786–1986*, 75.

11. Ibid., 69.

12. Willis A. Hess, Ray B. Hess, and David Benedict, eds., *Minutes of the Annual Meetings of the Old German Baptist Brethren from 1778 to 1955* (Winona Lake, Ind.: BMH Printing, 1981), 8.

13. Ibid., 24–25.

14. Ibid., 9.

15. Salmon and Salmon, *Franklin County, Virginia, 1786–1986*, 113.

16. Ibid., 114–19.

17. Mavis F. Boone, *History of the Antioch Church of the Brethren* (Boones Mill, Va.: Antioch Church of the Brethren, 1980), 5.

18. Donald Durnbaugh, ed., *Church of the Brethren: Yesterday and Today* (Elgin, Ill.: The Brethren Press, 1986), 18.

19. Sappington, *The Brethren in Virginia*, 66–67.

20. Letter from T. B. Greer to General J. A. Early, Rocky Mount, Virginia, April 25, 1861, reprinted in *Civil War Letters from Franklin County Residents, 1861–1864* (Rocky Mount, Va.: Franklin County History Society, no date).

21. Salmon and Salmon, quoted from Legislative Petitions, Franklin County, December 14, 1799, in *Franklin County, Virginia, 1786–1986*, 194–95.

22. Sappington, *The Brethren in Virginia*, 70.

23. Ibid., 71–72.

24. Hess, Hess, and Benedict, *Minutes of Annual Meetings*, 301.

25. See Boone, *History of the Antioch Church of the Brethren.*

26. Durnbaugh, *Fruit of the Vine*, 291f.

27. Ibid., 291–92.

28. Marcus Miller, *Roots by the River: The History, Doctrine, and Practice of the Old German Baptist Brethren in Miami County, Ohio* (Covington, Ohio: Hammer Graphics Inc., 1973), 56.

29. Ibid., 57; Durnbaugh, *Fruit of the Vine*, 297f.

30. Today the Old German Baptist Brethren, still around 550 strong nationally, continue to believe that this world is separated from God and for that reason neither their clothing nor church structures should resemble those of the world. Their Doctrinal Treatise states their beliefs as follows:

> The fact that the Church was established by Christ as a necessity in order for man to meet the approval of God, is in itself proof that the world with all its sufficiency was inadequate to meet the spiritual needs of man. This necessity is sufficient proof that the Church has a mission which sets her apart as separate and distinct from the world. . . . The extent of this separation is not determined by keeping a certain distance from the world, or in being different just to be different, but is determined by the distance the world is from the ways of God. The conformity of the Church to Christ prevents her conformity to the world. (The Vindicator Committee, *Doctrinal Treatise* [Englewood, Ohio: The Vindicator, 1954])

Nonconformity is the key to Brethren theology. Basing their beliefs on scriptures such as Romans 12:2, "Be not conformed to this world, but be ye transformed by the renewing of your mind, that ye may prove what is that good, and acceptable, and perfect will of God," their Doctrinal Treatise says "children of God" are a "peculiar people." This peculiarity means, according to German Baptist theology, exhibiting a conspicuous difference from the world in dress, in church practices, and, even as the world modernizes around them, in lifestyle.

31. Hess, Hess, and Benedict, *Minutes of the Annual Meetings*, 472–73.

32. Miller, *Roots by the River*, 59.

33. Bowman, *Brethren Society*, 126f.

34. See also Durnbaugh, *Fruit of the Vine*, 300.

35. Miller, *Roots by the River*, 59.

36. Durnbaugh, *Fruit of the Vine*, 313–14.

37. According to their own literature, the elders conduct worship in the following manner:

Commonly there are [seven] . . . or more ministers in attendance who take their places back of the ministers' table, in the order of their official rank . . . When the time for the appointed service arrives the presiding elder or minister who sits at the head, says to the other ministers, "Brethren, there is liberty for one of you to offer a hymn to be sung to begin the services." One of the ministers will then take the liberty and announce the number of the hymn in the hymn-book, and will read two or four lines of the hymn which will then be sung by the congregation, then the next two or four lines will be read and sung, and so on till a part or all of the hymn is sung.

After the hymn has been sung, the presiding ministers will give liberty for one of the ministers to read a portion of the Scripture that he may select from the Old Testament. Following this, liberty will be given for a minister to arise, line another hymn which will be sung in the same manner as the first [or in-gathering] hymn, and exhort briefly upon the importance of prayer and worship and invite all present to bow the knee with him in a season of prayer. One of the ministers will then lead the congregation in earnest, vocal prayer at the close of which another brother always concludes repeating the Lord's prayer. After the prayer the presiding minister will give liberty for some brother to name a chapter of the New Testament to be read. This being done the chapter named is read usually by one of the deacons. Then one of the ministers will take the liberty given, arise and address the assembly upon some Scriptural theme based either upon a text of the chapter just read or some other part of the Bible.

When he has finished his discourse, if there is time, he may be followed by one or more other speakers, with additional remarks. The presiding minister then directs some brother to close the services in the regular manner as the opening service, by singing, exhortation and prayer. Instrumental music is not tolerated. After the closing the presiding minister announces the next regular meeting, and any other appointments necessary, thanks the people for their attendance, and interest, invites them to come again and dismisses "in the fear of the Lord" (John M. Kimmel, *Chronicles of the Brethren* [Byrne, Ind.: The Economy Printing Concern, 1972], 264–65).

38. Interview, January 24, 1993, with the author.

Chapter 6. Membership

1. I am indebted to Wendell Berry for the concept of membership. To learn more, see, for example, Wendell Berry, *The Wild Birds: Six Stories from the Port William Membership* (San Francisco: North Point Press, 1986).

Epilogue

1. See Charles D. Thompson Jr. and Melinda Wiggins, eds., *The Human Cost of Food: Farmworkers' Lives, Labor, and Advocacy* (Austin: University of Texas Press, 2002).

Index

Page numbers in italics refer to photographs.

adversity and perseverance,
101–3; Barnhardt, Mark and,
122–28; Bier, Jerry Anne and,
118–22; Jamison, Richard and,
128–34; Layman, Allen and,
134–39; Layman, Bruce and,
103–11; Layman, Daniel and,
139–42; Montgomery, Melvin
and, 111–18
African Americans, 96, 145
agriculture, xx–xxii, 35, 57; in
Franklin County today,
xxxi–xxxvi; Richard Huff on,
147–49. *See also* adversity and
perseverance
Albrecht, Heinrich, 7, 208n13,
208n19
Allen, 8
altar calls, 29–30
America, 8–11, 47
Amish, 57, 107
Anabaptists, 4, 6–7, 14, 15, 16,
207n6

Ancient Order, xix, 30–31, 32;
German origins of, 3–8; journey
to America, 8–11.
See also Old German Baptist
Brethren
Anderson, Floyd, 160–65
Anderson Farm Equipment, 66
Angle, Dale, *40*
Angle, Dick, *167*
Angle Implement, 66
Angle Welding, *167*
Annual Meetings, 11, 23, 24, 26,
29–30, 58, 79
Antioch Church, 28, 32–34, *37*
auctions, 161–62, 190–91
Austin, Rebecca, 51–55, 186–89
Austin, Terry, 186–89
automobiles, xix–xx, 67

baptism, 5–6, 7
Barnhardt, Mark, 122–28, *126*
Barny Bay, xxxii, 122–28
Becker, Peter, 8, 11

Beckleheimer, John, 26
Berleberg, Germany, 7
Bethlehem Church, 28
Bible, 45, 47, 56, 57, 58, 59–60, 62, 134, 212n37. *See also* New Testament
Bier, Jerry Anne, 118–22
Biessel, Conrad, 11
Blue Ridge Institute and Farm Museum, 51, 53, 205n2
Board of Supervisors, 114, 117, 147, 149, 154–55, 171
Boon, John, 26
Boone, Billy, 61–71, 64; on farming, 63–67; on finances, 67–70; introduction to interview, 61–62; on separation from world, 62–63; on technology, 68–69
Boone, Emily, 143
Boone's Country Store, 143
Boones Mill, Virginia, 21
Bower, David, 175, 177–78, 181–85, *184*, 203
Bowman, Carl F., 207n6, 208n19
Bowman, Dean, 101–2
Bowman, Howard, 52, 186–87
Bowman, John, 52
Bowman, Martha, 101–2
Brethren, 3–8; change and, 35–36; first settlement of, 19–20; journey to America, 8–11; migration of, 11–13; modernization and, 28–29; religious thought of, 6–7; Revolutionary War and, 13–17; slavery and, 23–24; war and, 21–22, 25–28. *See also* Old German Baptist Brethren
Brubaker, Galen, xxiii
building trades, xxxiv, 40, 59, 116
Burnt Chimney, Virginia, 178

butter, xxii, xxiv, 64, 175, 176, 206n14
Butz, Earl, xxvi

cabinetmaking, 59
Carolina Road, 21, 22
carpentry, xxxiv, 40, 59, *115*, 116
Catholicism, 3
CCC (Civilian Conservation Corps), 57
Charles II, King, 8
children, 34; in interviews, 46, 63, 69–70, 116, 130–32, 159–60, 164, 188–89
Christ, 6, 47, 60, 200, 211n30
Church of the Brethren, xix, xxi, 32–34, 57
citizens, raising: Austin, Rebecca and, 51–55; Boone, Billy and, 61–71; Jamison, Joel and, 51–61; Jamison, Loyd and, 43–51
Citizens Concerned About 1–73, 118–22
Civil War, 25–28, 57
Clemmons, North Carolina, 39–41
clothing, xix–xx, 26, 28, *33*, 34, 56–57
Common Sense, 16
communication, 55
community, xxvi, xxxiii, 198. *See also* citizens, raising; neighbors
community-based agriculture, 72, 199, 201–2; Cook, James and, 89–94; Jamison, Henry and, 72–81; Rutrough, Robert and, 81–89; Ward, Irwin and, 94–100
computers, 54–55
conduct, xix
Confederacy, 25–26

conscientious objectors, 26–28, 34, 57, 62–63
Continental Army, 15
Continental Congress, 15
Cook, James, 89–94
cost share, 158
Cox, David, 125, *126*

dairy industry, 157–58; Barnhardt on, 127; Boone on, 64–65; in Franklin County today, xxxi–xxxvi; grades of milk, xxiii–xxiv; rise of, xxii–xxvi. *See also* Old German Baptist Brethren
debt. *See* finances
Department of Environmental Quality, 152, 153
development, 35, 87–88, 149–50, 155–56
Doctrinal Treatise, 211n30
dress, xix–xx, 26, 28, *33*, 34, 56–57
Dunkard Massacre, 12
Dunkards, 6, 12
Durnbaugh, Donald F., 205n5, 208n11, 208n13

Early, Jubal, 26
education and schools, 29, 65
eggs, xxii
Eisenhower, Dwight, 70
English, 11–17, 20
environmental issues, 87–88, 113–14, 127, 151–54, 158
EPA (Environmental Protection Agency), 113, 127, 153, 158
Ephrata Cloister, 11, 16
equipment, 162–63, 166
erosion, 158
evangelicalism, 10–11

Exchange Milling Company, 103, 104–5, *108*

factories, 59
farming: adversity and perseverance, 101–3; as a business, 52–53. *See also* agriculture; community-based agriculture; dairy industry
finances: in interviews, 67–68, 74, 84–85, 129, 137–38, 157–58, 166–69
Flora, Jacob, Jr., 30
Flora, Joseph, 26
Floyd County, Virginia, 21, 130
Fralin, Henry, 129–30
France, 11–13
Franklin, Benjamin, 13–14, 210n51
Franklin County, Virginia: agriculture of, xx–xxii; Brethren today, 40–41; census of (1786), 22; farming today, xxxi–xxxvi; Huff and Johnson on, 148–51; production of, 206n14; settlement of, 17; slavery and, 24
Franklin County Brethren, 23–24
Franklin County Extension Service, xxiii
Franklin Welding, 59, 61
Fraternity District, 39–40
fruit farming, xx, xxii

Galax, Virginia, 130
Gates, Bill, 67
German language, 205n3
Germantown, Pennsylvania, 8, 9–10
Germantown, Virginia, 24–25
Germantown Brick Church, 25, 28

Germany, 3–8, 207n1
God, 15, 63, 69
golden rule of life, 45
Goode, Virgil, 182
Gospel Visitor's, 30
government, 5, 97–98, 202
government subsidies, xxxiv, 65,
    105
Grade A milk, xxiii–xxiv
Grade C milk, xxii–xxiv
Great Britain, 11–17, 20
Great Wagon Road, 17
Great Wilderness Road,
    xxxv–xxxvi
Greer, T. B., 26

Hairston, Robert, 22
Harrisonburg, Virginia, 130
head coverings, *33*, 34
Hellenthal, Anthony, 12
Highway 220, 118–19, *120*,
    154–55
hobby farms, xxix, 112, 168
Homestead Creamery, 175–81,
    179, *181*, 203
homesteads, *xviii*, 22
hope, 174–75; Bower, David and,
    181–85; Montgomery, Brandon
    and, 175–81; Montgomery,
    Donnie and, 175–81; Mont-
    gomery, Jamie and, 175–81;
    Webb, Bill and, 189–96; Webb,
    Karen and, 189–96
hormones, 185
Huff, Richard, 147–56; on agricul-
    ture, 147–49; on Franklin
    County, 148–51

Ikenberry, Elizabeth, 32
Ikenberry, Henry, 26
Ikenberry, Peter, 26

Ikenberry, Samuel, 32
Industrial Revolution, xix, 64
inflation, 167
integrity, 67, 68
internet access, 54–55
Interstate 73, 35, 41, 53, 70,
    116–17, 118–22, *120*, 138,
    141–42, 154–55, 165, 169–70
Interstate 81, 79
interviews: Anderson, Floyd,
    160–65; Austin, Rebecca,
    51–55, 186–89; Austin, Terry,
    186–89; Barnhardt, Mark,
    122–28; Bier, Jerry Anne,
    118–22; Boone, Billy, 61–72;
    Bower, David, 181–85; Cook,
    James, 89–94; Huff, Richard,
    147–56; Jamison, Henry, 72–81;
    Jamison, Joel, 51–61; Jamison,
    Loyd, 43–51; Jamison, Richard,
    128–34; Johnson, Bonnie,
    147–56; Kingery, Billy, 165–73;
    Layman, Allen, 134–39; Lay-
    man, Bruce, 103–11; Layman,
    Daniel, 139–42; Montgomery,
    Brandon, 175–81; Montgomery,
    Donnie, 175–81; Montgomery,
    Jamie, 175–81; Montgomery,
    Melvin, 111–18; Puffenbarger,
    Sue, 156–60; Rutrough, Robert,
    81–89; Ward, Irwin, 94–100;
    Webb, Bill, 189–96; Webb,
    Karen, 189–96

Jackson, Stonewall, 27
Jamison, Henry, xxxiii, 72–81, *75*;
    on church, 79, 80; on commu-
    nication, 74–75; on dairy indus-
    try, 75; early life of, 73–74;
    family of, 74–77; introduction
    to interview, 72–73; on role of

farmers, 81; on sharing labor, 78, 79–80
Jamison, Joel, xix, 5, 55–61, *58*
Jamison, Loyd, xx, 43–51; on challenges of modern life, 47–48; on dairy industry, 49–50; introduction to interview, 43–45; on separation from world, 45–46; on small farming, 48–51
Jamison, Richard, 128–34, 183
John Deere, 160–63
Johnson, Bonnie, 147–56; on agriculture, 147–49; on development, 155–56; on environmental issues, 151–54; on Franklin County, 148–51; on German Baptists, 155–56; on I-73, 154–55
Jones, Jerry, xxxii

Kingery, Billy, 165–73
Kingery, Jacob, 26
Kinsey, Jacob, 26
Kinvale Farm, xxvii–xxxi, 165
Kline, John, 25, 26
Krefeld Brethren, 8, 10–11

lagoons, 158
Lake Norman, 90, 91
Lancaster Treaty of 1744, 11–12
land values, 93, 98–100, 104, 116–18, 136, 145, 169–71, 187, 207n28
Lane Furniture, 171, 180
language, 205n3
Latinos, 92, 124–25
Layman, Allen, *xxxv*, 134–39, *136*
Layman, Bruce, 103–11; on children, 111; on farming, 106–9; on finances, 104–6, 108–9; introduction to interview, 103

Layman, Daniel, 139–42, 203
Layman, Dena, *4*, 134
Layman, Frank, xxii–xxiii
Layman, Mary, xxiii
Layman, Teresa, 139, 202–3
Lehman, Daniel, 6, 24
liquor, 24
Lutheranism, 3

Mack, Alexander, 5, 10, 208n11; as leader, 11
Mack, Alexander, Jr., 7, 11
Mack, Anna, 10
Mandy Brothers Transfer Company, xxiii
maps, *38*
Martin, John, 12
Matthew, Book of, 45
Mecklenburg County, North Carolina, 90
membership, 143–46; Anderson, Floyd and, 160–65; Huff, Richard and, 147–56; Johnson, Bonnie and, 147–56; Kingery, Billy, 165–73; Puffenbarger, Sue and, 156–60
men, 33–34
Mennonites, 5–6, 23, 57, 107, 207n6
Miami Valley, Ohio, 29
Midwest, 105
military service: exemption from, 26–28, 34, 57, 62–63
milk prices, xxx, 14, 105, 106, 109, 124, 133–34, 152, 157, 166, 171, 182–83, 202–3
Miller, Jacob, xvii, xviii–xix, 19–20, 20, 22, 25, 26
ministers, 29, 62
modernization, xix, 28–29, 50

money, 65–66, 79. *See also*
    finances
Montcalm, Louis-Joseph de, 13
Montgomery, Brandon, 175–81,
    184, 203
Montgomery, Donnie, 175–81
Montgomery, Jamie, 175–81
Montgomery, Melvin, 111–18; on
    finances, 112–13; on German
    Baptists, 114–16
Montgomery County, Virginia,
    130
Moravian church, 11
mountains, xxi
Mountain View District Meeting
    House, 35–36
Mount Pleasant, 24–25. *See also*
    Rocky Mount, Virginia
Mowery, Ilma, 207n28

Naas, John, 9
Naff, Isaac, 26
Native Americans, 11–13
Nave, Jacob, 26
Neff, Jacob, 12–13
neighbors, 46, 72, 143–46
New Testament, 4, 5, 207n6,
    212n37
Noah, 60
nonconformity, 62, 200, 211n30
nonswearing, 62
Norman, Lake, 90, 91

oaths of allegiance, 5, 15, 62
Ohio Brethren, 29
Old German Baptist Brethren: as
    dairy farmers, xxvi–xxvii,
    xxxii–xxxiii; distinctiveness of,
    xix–xx; Doctrinal Treatise,
    211n30; German origins of,
    3–8; Pigg River District, 39–41;

separation from Church of the
    Brethren, 56–57; they go qui-
    etly, 197–204; worship of,
    212n37. *See also* Ancient
    Order; Brethren
Old Order. *See* Ancient Order
origins: of Old German Baptist
    Brethren, 3–8

Paine, Thomas, 16
Penn, William, 8–9, 14
Pennsylvania Brethren, 11
persecution, 47
Peters, Michael, 26
Peters, Stephen, 26
Piedmont, xxi
Pietists, 6–7
Pigg River District Meeting
    House, 32–34, 35–36, 39–41
plural ministry, 62
politics, xx, 5, 15, 63, 201
post offices, 24–25
pride, 46, 67
Progressives, 30–31. *See also*
    Church of the Brethren
prosperity, 47–48
Protestantism, 3
public speaking, xx
Puffenbarger, Sue, 73, 154,
    156–60
Pulaski County, Virginia, 21

Quakers, 8, 23, 107

radio, 45–46
railroads, 28
real estate prices, xxvi–xxvii, 93,
    116–18. *See also* land values
redemptioners, 9, 10
Reformed, 3
revivals, 28, 29–30, 56

Revolutionary War, 13–17, 21–22, 57
Roanoke, Virginia, 78–79
robot milking systems, 133–34
Rocky Mount, Virginia, 24
Route 419, 79
Rutrough, Ezra, 34
Rutrough, Robert, 81–89; on children, 84; creative means to enter farming, 82–85; on environmental issues, 87–88; on farming, 83–84; on finances, 84–85; introduction to interview, 81–82; way of life, 88–89

Sangmeister, Ezekiel, 12
Sappington, Roger E., 205n3
Sauer, Christopher, I, 9
Sauer, Jacob, II, 14–15
Schwarzenau, Mack, 3–4
sea travel, 9
Serge Milking Equipment, 129
slavery, xxi, 23–24
Smith, William, xviii–xix, 20, 25
Smith Mountain Dam, 104
Smith Mountain Lake, 35, 40, 53, 69, 91, 117, 170–71
Solingen, Lower Rhine, 8
Standing Committee of Elders, 25
Die Stillen in Lande, 5
subsistence farming, 21
Sunday School, 29
swearing, 62

teaching, 46
technology, xix, 174–75
television, 45–46, 114–15
Thirty Years' War, 207n1
Thompson, Charles D., Jr., xxvii–xxxi
tobacco, xxi–xxii

Tractorcades, 206n25
travel, 60–61
"truck" farming, xxii
Die Tunken, 6
Turner, Elsie, 143–46, *144*
Turner, William, 143–46, *144*

United States, 8–11, 47
urbanization, 78–79

vegetable farming, xxii
Virginia Agricultural Census (1900), xxi–xxii
Virginia Department of Transportation, 121, 142, 203–4
Virginia General Assembly, 24, 26–27
Virginians for Appropriate Roads, 203
Virginia Valley, 20–21
voting, 63

Wal-Mart, 171, 201
Ward, Irwin, 94–100
War of 1812, 27
Washington, Booker T., 24
Washington, George, 12, 13
waste storage pits, 158
Water Quality Act of 1972, 151–52
Webb, Bill, 189–96
Webb, Karen, 189–96
Welfare, Michael, 14
Wine, John, 26
Wisenburg, Virginia, 24–25
Wittgenstein, Rhineland, 7
Wohlfahrt, Michael, 14, 210n51
women, 33–34, 58–59, 94, 185
worldliness, 45–46
World War II, 57

Yankees, 116–17

CHARLES D. THOMPSON JR. is Curriculum and
Education Director at the Center for Documentary
Studies and adjunct professor of Religion and Cultural
Anthropology at Duke University. Thompson is an
oral historian, filmmaker, documentary photographer,
and writer who hails from the mountains of Virginia.
His books include *Maya Identities and the Violence
of Place: Borders Bleed*, *The Human Cost of Food:
Farmworkers Lives, Labor, and Advocacy*, and *Indigenous Diasporas and Dislocations*. Presently he lives
with his wife and son in Chapel Hill, North Carolina.